A Country of Shepherds

Stories of a Changing Mediterranean Landscape

Kathleen Ann Myers

Translations by Grady C. Wray

OpenBook
Publishers

https://www.openbookpublishers.com

©2024 Kathleen Ann Myers

Digital material and resources associated with this volume are available at
https://doi.org/10.11647/OBP.0387#resources

ISBN Paperback: 9 978-1-80511-206-8
ISBN Hardback: 978-1-80511-207-5
ISBN Digital (PDF): 978-1-80511-208-2
ISBN Digital ebook (EPUB): 978-1-80511-209-9
ISBN XML: 978-1-80511-210-5
ISBN HTML: 978-1-80511-211-2
DOI: 10.11647/OBP.0387

Cover image: photograph by Costagliola (purchased from Deposit Photos, ID: 266971314)
Cover design: Licia Weber and Jeevanjot Kaur Nagpal

For Mark and Anna

Table of Contents

About the Author

Kathleen Ann Myers is Professor of Spanish and History at Indiana University-Bloomington. She received her doctorate in Hispanic Studies from Brown University. Kathleen has published widely on a variety of topics, including books about women writers in colonial Mexico (Liverpool 1993, Indiana University Press 1999, Oxford 2003) and the Spanish conquest and colonization of the Americas (Texas University Press 2007). Her recent studies include books on cultural geographies and coloniality in contemporary Mexico (University of Arizona Press 2015, University of Toronto 2024).

This research has been generously funded by a variety of organizations, including Indiana University, the National Endowment for the Humanities, the Fulbright Scholar Program, the Spanish Ministry for Education and Culture, the *Centro de Estudios de Ciencias Sociales* (Mexico), the American Philosophical Association, the Huntington Library, and the *Consejo Superior de Investigaciones Científicas* of Spain (CSIC).

Preface

For centuries, pastoralism has occupied a key place in cultural narratives about the Iberian Peninsula, and the traditional locales and travel ways of shepherding hold deep significance for the collective imagination of many Spaniards today. Drawing on a vast array of scholarship, popular culture, and interviews with shepherds and their advocates, *A Country of Shepherds: Stories of a Changing Mediterranean Landscape* suggests that shepherding, and pastoralism in general, is being reconfigured and even remarketed to a new generation. Such internationally renowned events as the annual Festival of Transhumance (established 1997), during which sheep are driven through the streets of downtown Madrid along ancient rights of way, and UNESCO's proclamation of transhumance in Spain as Intangible Cultural Heritage (2023), are integral to this phenomenon. Emerging cultural geographies and narratives of pastoralism shape local, regional, national, and European economic and environmental initiatives as shepherds, bureaucrats, and the public frame their own roles in the development of new national and environmental projects. Indeed, more is at stake than simply cultural identity. Due to the growing threat of global warming, southern Spain in particular is at risk for increasing desertification if modern intensive agricultural practices cannot adapt.

Over the course of decades of traveling, working, and at times living in Spain, I watched this transformation in both the practice of and narrative about pastoralism, but by 2015 I wanted to understand it more deeply. As I started interviewing shepherds, I learned that the success (and even the survival) of these traditions also depends on the support of many governmental and grassroots initiatives and organizations, as well as the general public. As an outsider to this world of pastoralism, I share here both these interviews and my process of coming to understand our own roles in supporting these ancient but very relevant ways of managing ecosystems and cultural landscapes.

Based on a series of about sixty interviews I carried out, the six case studies at the core of *A Country of Shepherds* document the lives of a handful of shepherds, farmers, and families, along with their advocates, in Andalusia, Spain. Through them, we see the landscapes, life practices, and challenges of pastoralism (both transhumance and extensive grazing) as well as the vital significance of their work as a globally interconnected system. They give a face and voice to a complex national and international conversation about sustainability, food systems, and cultural traditions. By sharing this living archive of interviews and my own process of discovery along the way, *A Country of Shepherds* documents this ancient system and its transformation in the twenty-first century — and suggests ways we all, as global citizens, can help.

Acknowledgements

This project has been generously funded by the Spanish Ministry of Culture, Education, and Sports and Indiana University's Presidential Arts and Humanities Program, the Office of the Vice-Provost for Research, and the College of Arts and Humanities Institute. I owe an enormous debt of gratitude to these institutions as well as to a host of individuals without whom this project would have been impossible. With patience, and often humor, people in Spain shared their knowledge and practices, gently guiding a curious but ignorant outsider in the hopes that their story might be told more widely to effect change. My deepest thanks go to my teachers on the ground and their families, who are the focus of five of my case studies: Juan Vázquez Morán, Pepe Millán, Fortunato Guerrero Lara, Marta Moya Espinosa, and Ernestine Lüdeke. They took time they barely had to share their practices and experience with me. In addition, many advocates for traditional grazing and sustainability provided valuable insight into the broader movements and organizations. My special thanks go to Jesús Garzón Heydt, María del Carmen García, Paco Casero, José Ramón Guzmán Alvarez, Ana Belén Robles Cruz, and Paco Ruiz. Yolanda Mena Guerrero is in a league of her own as she helped me interpret the results of my interviews and suggested ways to showcase pastoralism today.

Many friends and colleagues on my side of the *charco* (pond) further supported this project with encouragement, letters of recommendation, and even lodging over the years it unfolded. My sincere thanks to Consuelo López-Morillas, Cathy Larson, Rob and Karen Green-Stone, Charles Ganelin, Steven Wagschal, Manuel Díaz-Campos, Melissa Dinverno, and Alejandro Mejías-López. Five graduates of Indiana University worked with me as valuable cultural interpreters, researchers, transcribers, and translators for this volume; I have been extremely fortunate to have worked with each of them—the teacher learning more than she could have ever hoped for from former students. Indeed, the expertise and support of Damián V. Solano Escolano, María del Mar Torreblanca, Lara Elizabeth Hamburger, and Grady C. Wray, and Pablo García Loaeza ensured this book would come to fruition. In particular, María del Mar joyfully dedicated weeks at a time to team up with me for forays into the field, making sure that these stories would be told for Andalusia. The shaping of this volume also took a team to complete with Mark Feddersen providing astute editorial suggestions, and Giada Mirelli, Nathan Douglas, and Licia Weber offering their keen eyes and expertise in preparing the final text and images. Finally, my unending gratitude goes to my husband, Mark, and my daughter, Anna, for their willingness to take a leap of faith, go live in Seville, and embrace the joys of living there while I carried out interviews. Our time in Seville was made forever memorable by our dear neighbor-friends, Rocío, Chema, and Violeta.

I dedicate this book to the memory of my twin sister, Jeanne, and my parents, Mary and Richard Myers. It was Jeanne's adventurous spirit — and my parents' belief in independence — that helped us land, as eighteen-year-olds, in Seville for the first time. To this dedication I add my siblings, Patty, Chuck, Bill, and Tom, who buoyed me with jokes and sibling power over the years this project unfolded.

Translator's Note

The translation of oral language into a written text presents challenges. At times, speakers express emotions that are hard to capture on the written page. Colloquial expressions contain many nuances that require a thorough contextualization and comprehension of the content. Fortunately, Kathleen Ann Myers's narration well contextualizes each participant of *A Country of Shepherds*, and, to my benefit, her more direct guidance in personal correspondence helped me understand and emphasize the character, tone, and register of the interviewees. Additionally, Damián V. Solano Escolano and Diego Valdecantos Monteagudo bettered my understanding of elusive colloquial and idiomatic expressions that I hope added a subtle richness to the texts. One of the most delicate areas of translation was the general description of a shepherd as "*el tonto del pueblo.*" The term certainly emerges in the interviews as an offensive one that carries traumatic undertones and overtones ranging from mental incapacity to a lack of higher education. Some informants, in fact, did use "lowest of the low" to describe how some people still refer to shepherds. Even though I considered terms such as "village fool," "village dummy," "hillbilly," "dumb shepherd," "ignorant," and "uncultured," in the end, I opted for the more broadly used "village idiot," although it may not precisely contain all the derisive nuances that the insult infers.

As Myers and I discussed approaches to the translations of the interviews, we agreed to leave certain terms in Spanish throughout both her narration and the interviews to enliven the text and add elements of local color. Many of the Spanish terms are defined throughout the narration or in the "Pastoralism: A Contextual Background and Terminology" section and allude to specific practices, places, and professions in the Spanish context. For example, it is difficult to find acceptable equivalents for "*ganadería*" and "*ganadero.*" The term *ganadería* generically refers to the various aspects of livestock farming. Typically, *ganadero* translates as "rancher," "cattleman," or "livestock worker." In the context of *A Country of Shepherds*, however, the term is more connected to people who care for, raise, and/or own sheep and goats. It can denote a shepherd or a goatherd, but it can also imply an owner of livestock, in a more entrepreneurial sense.

Among other terms that we decided to keep in Spanish throughout are *monte, finca,* and *dehesa.* The word *monte* is commonly used to refer to undeveloped public lands, more-or-less forested, often at a higher elevation, but not necessarily in a mountainous landscape. As a concept, *monte* also conveys notions akin to "backwoods," "wilderness," and "countryside." *Finca* can have various definitions that include "ranch," "farm," "plantation," "estate," or "property," but seldom do these English terms conjure up the particular image of a place where sheep and goats are raised in Spain. Therefore, the Spanish flair of *finca* highlights a cultural difference that I believe is appropriate. *Dehesa,* similarly, evades simple translation, describing a particular type of Andalusian farm that mixes extensive grazing with cleared forests of cork and olive trees. Overall, I hope that the inclusion of these and other Spanish terms help to situate the text more specifically and aid in invigorating the descriptions of these multicolored voices who help us understand the past, present, and future of pastoralism in Spain.

Grady C. Wray

List of Illustrations

All photographs by Kathleen Ann Myers (unless otherwise noted)

Fig. 0.1 Scenes from the Festival of Transhumance, Madrid (2017).

Introduction

Pastoralism in Spain

Every fall, Spanish shepherds herd thousands of sheep along ancient droving rights of way that pass directly through the busy Puerta del Sol in downtown Madrid, the urban heart of the city and symbolic center of Spain (marked as kilometer "0" for national highways). First granted as a system of royal rights of way throughout the Iberian Peninsula in the thirteenth century, many of these droving routes, known as *vías pecuarias*, have fallen into disuse. Routes have often been paved over as urban development has spread through the country. Today in Madrid, the celebration of this ancient practice of transhumance, the seasonal migration of sheep and shepherds from summer to winter pastures and back again, occurs only on one Sunday a year.

The practice dates back about 7,000 years in the Iberian Peninsula, and, in 1994, environmental activist Jesús Garzón Heydt helped bring the ancient practice of transhumance and these droving rights of way to national and international attention by establishing this one-day Festival of Transhumance in Madrid. More than twenty years later, I attend the popular festival and meet Jesús Garzón. To find him, I must wind my way through thousands of tourists and a host of international reporters who witness the lively scene. This day, over 2,000 sheep are herded by shepherds who whistle to highly trained dogs and carry the traditional walking stick, the *cayado*. Along the way, I see an exuberant group in striking black and white costumes with red accents dancing the traditional *jota*. Further down the Gran Vía, a handful of women from León wear woolen green foot-liners in their raised wooden shoes, made for the damp weather in the fields. Here, in the oldest

 https://doi.org/10.11647/OBP.0387.00

part of Madrid, the president of the ancient shepherd guild from the Middle Ages, La Mesta, pays the symbolic fifty antique Iberian coins (*maravedís al millar*) to the mayor in exchange for the continued use of the rights of way.

When I finally see Jesús Garzón, he stands nearly a head taller than most of those around him and easily engages them all. For our interview, Jesús — known to everyone as Suso — suggests we move further along past the Puerta de Alcalá. He chooses a bench next to a carved stone marking the royal droving right of way at the entrance to Madrid's central park, *El Retiro*. As founder of Spain's largest cultural and activist organization dedicated to pastoralism (*Asociación Trashumancia y Naturaleza*), he strives to bring environmental, cultural, and political groups together at both the national and pan-European levels but also helps with concrete logistics and legal challenges faced by individual transhumant shepherds. Cultural outreach, Suso explains, is also key to the mission of making transhumance sustainable. People need to know that it helps the environment as a *"máquina de sembranza"* (seed-sowing machine) and an *"ecosistema andante"* (mobile ecosystem) by sowing biodiverse seeds, cleaning underbrush, and fertilizing land. The public can play an important role with their votes and consumer power. Public visibility facilitates policy changes.

The festival has become so successful in its public-facing mission, Suso reveals, that this year a few government officials have tried to coopt it for their own political agendas, going so far as to even change the festival date. Later, when I interview two brothers who herd their flock through the streets, I learn that the change in the festival date, and the requirement to transport their sheep out of Madrid by truck instead of by foot, means they will arrive to Córdoba ahead of the fall rains, and water will be scarce. Nevertheless, Suso insists that this Sunday is still a time to celebrate the progress of putting transhumance back on the map — both literally and culturally. Spain is the only country in the world that conserves 125,000 kilometers of droving rights of way. In a recent interview with the BBC, Suso underscores his basic view: "The planet is facing a situation of real social and economic catastrophe, but pastoralism is going to survive" (Walker 2021).

Fig. 0.2 Jesús Garzón Heydt (right) with festival participants, Madrid (2017).

Transhumance is an ancient solution to the challenge of maintaining sustainable grazing practices. It is central to the traditional practices of animal husbandry, known as pastoralism, and more specifically as extensive grazing, a system that distributes grazing and water across a given landscape. In Andalusia, it is practiced on both public lands and private pastures, including the *dehesas*, which are large multifunctional farms that mix extensive grazing with cleared forests of cork and olive trees. The movement of livestock from summer to winter pastures along extensive droving routes not only benefits the pastures and aids with water retention; it also promotes biodiversity through the fertilization and dispersion of seeds, as well as with cleaning underbrush and overgrowth. Thus, pastoralism is one of the most sustainable food production systems, and transhumance was the primary form of animal migration for millennia. (Definitions and further information about specialized terms within Pastoralism can be found below in "Contextual Background and Terminology.")

Even as the traditional practice wanes, public awareness of the need to protect and preserve the official droving roads and transhumance itself has proved invaluable. Although very few individuals in Spain are still directly involved with these practices, even the average person has likely heard of or enjoys the recreational use of the *vías pecuarias*, or else appreciates the traditional foods created by shepherds that have been popularized in the national cuisine. Many Spaniards also know something about the ecological benefits of transhumance. While most of the population is now urban, rural family roots still tie individuals to their towns (*pueblos*) that their grandparents or great grandparents inhabited, and many return in the summers or for holidays. These visits maintain and strengthen a connection with the land, the animals, and this traditional livelihood. And there still is a major romantic appeal: the outfits, the food, the music, the walking!

During the last twenty years, new policies protecting the traditional ways have been introduced, and related cultural production has exploded. Spanish society has embraced the ancient practice of transhumance and shepherding in general as foundational to Spanish national heritage. Museums and festivals devoted to shepherding practices, like Madrid's Festival of Transhumance, have sprung up everywhere. Best-selling novels, traditional music, news stories, new rural museums, and documentary films about traditional practices underscore how socio-cultural memory, place, and practice are deeply intertwined. This decades-long boom of cultural production has contributed to a more widespread visibility of Spanish pastoralism.

When I first began research for *A Country of Shepherds* in 2015, I surveyed the extent of these cultural activities in Spain and found that there are more than twenty-three museums and interpretative centers fully or partially related to transhumance. Nearly forty festivals occur either annually or biannually. Hundreds of videos, from feature-length documentaries to shorter informational clips, are easily accessible on the web. More than twenty associations related to transhumance and extensive grazing practices have been formed, some with a significant web presence. In June 2016 alone, more than fifty magazine and newspaper articles were published about the movement. And, while the traditional oversized wool pullovers and giant leather leg protectors may not be used by most shepherds now, this traditional dress retains an important place in Spanish cultural memory. In February, during Carnival, young children choose costumes, and inevitably there are a few traditional shepherds in the mix. The children "play shepherd" for a day, donning the trademark wide-brimmed hats, leather accessories, and wooden shoes (see Fig. 7.1).

The cultural resurgence of interest in pastoralism and transhumance has also attracted widespread interest across Europe and the U.S. Popular journals and media events held in France, England, Germany, and the U.S. have brought this tradition to international audiences. In the U.S., for example, such magazines as *The Atlantic* and *Bloomberg* and other leading media outlets, such as *The New York Times* and the BBC, have published articles and produced programs on transhumance. This parallels a more widespread Western interest in grazing practices and the popularization of materials about it, such as James Rebank's *New York Times*-Bestseller *The Shepherd's Life: Modern Dispatches from an Ancient Landscape* (2015). The revitalized pastoral narrative, combined with environmental programs and government initiatives, has amplified a new awareness of traditional grazing practices. Andalusia's Shepherd School (*Escuela de Pastores*), for example, received the European Union Award for best use of funds for rural development (2015). In 2023, UNESCO added Spain to its list of representative countries in which transhumance is Immaterial Cultural Heritage of Humanity, stating:

> An ancestral practice, transhumance stems from a deep knowledge about the environment and entails social practices and rituals related to the care, breeding and training of animals and the management of natural resources. An entire socio-economic system has been developed around transhumance, from gastronomy to local handicrafts and festivities marking the beginning and end of a season. Families have been enacting and transmitting transhumance through observation and practice for many generations. Communities living along transhumance routes also play an important role in its transmission, such as by celebrating herd crossings and organising festivals. The practice is also transmitted through workshops organised by local communities, associations and networks of herders and farmers, as well as through universities and research institutes. Transhumance thus contributes to social inclusion, strengthening cultural identity and ties between families, communities and territories while counteracting the effects of rural depopulation. (https://ich.unesco.org/en/RL/transhumance-the-seasonal-droving-of-livestock-01964)

Pastoral Practices and Shepherds' Narratives

Indeed, this cultural interest in an ancient way of life is how I first came to the topic. As a college student studying history in Spain in the late 1970s, I was fascinated by shepherds herding sheep and goats, sharing roads and hiking trails with me as I traveled around the Iberian Peninsula. But it was not until twenty years later in the 1990s, after becoming a scholar of how life stories reveal cultural practices from early modern times, that I first stopped to talk with a shepherd. As we hiked along a trail in the Northern Picos de Europa, he seemed to appear out of nowhere. He spoke poetically about the mountains and how they seem to hide behind clouds and mist, seeing fit to show themselves only on rare occasions as they did on this hot cloudless day. He also spoke of the trials of solitary life in a field living in his traditional shepherd's hut, suffering from a fever with no one to take care of him, much less his sheep.

Many years later, I came back to his story with a desire to learn more. While doing archival research in Seville in 2015, I had seen shepherds moving flocks through semi-arid land on the outskirts of town in the intense early spring sun. I watched frequent television programs and read nearly weekly articles that focused on transhumance. I listened to a few friends talking about their transhumance vacations in Northern Spain. What had been a distant, rural attraction for me as a student-tourist had now become part of a popular cultural scene forty years later. As I mused about these stories and the growing cultural interest in them, a friend offered to introduce me to a shepherd she knew from the Sierra Norte, about an hour from Seville.

Juan Vázquez Morán practiced transhumance along the *vías pecuarias* for decades, but he recently left the practice to work in extensive grazing, which continues traditional ecological and seasonal use of lands and water but does not necessarily involve migration of livestock for long periods of time to other areas. Juan spoke of growing up as a shepherd and loving his work but also of facing endless challenges that society and governmental policies add to an already difficult vocation. "They ask for this form, that form, and more forms on top of that. You've got to get a guidebook before you start doing transhumance, or they don't let you do it." What is more, over time, the droving routes leaving from Constantina became impassable, overgrown with underbrush and spiny bushes from lack of use. He reports: "The routes are all going away because livestock doesn't come through here anymore to eat any of the brush; you just don't see any animals come through to clear anything." In another interview, long-time transhumant shepherd Fortunato Guerrero Lara added to Juan's list of challenges. Markets for sustainable wool, meat, and milk have weakened with modernization, globalization, and climate change. And all too often, regional, national, or EU regulations and bureaucracy challenge the ability of people who work with livestock to make ends meet. Few young people want to become shepherds because of the long hours and hardships involved. These are realities that simply supplying cell phones and GPS to shepherds cannot mitigate. Not only are transhumance and pastoralism themselves in transition, but so are a host of other factors: rural depopulation, consumers who abandon local products for supermarkets, new EU methods of calculating pasture lands and funding, conflicts in regional restrictions on marketing local products, and access to public pastures.

Yet as Juan and Fortunato weigh the current challenges and look toward the future, they, like the founder of Madrid's Festival of Transhumance, both see educating society as the key to changing these patterns. They even suggest that a foreigner — from a country infamous for exterminating many ancient practices and peoples — might give the story a fresh, more urgent perspective. As I began interviewing more widely, this message was repeated frequently. María del Carmen García, a veterinarian who travels often with Jesús Garzón to photograph shepherds on long treks across Spain, comments: "We're lacking a global view, someone who can share our heritage beyond what's typical folklore." An alumnus of the *Escuela de Pastores* who has also trained in France, Paqui Ruiz observes how working from an outsider's perspective is key to transforming things from within. Ana Belén Robles Cruz, a researcher at *Consejo Superior de Investigaciones Científicas* (CSIC), believes outsiders can help "raise public awareness" by breaking the stereotype of shepherds as "the ones who always make the sacrifice" or "the village idiot." She argues: "You have to put them in the spotlight." Whether shepherd, activist, or scholar, all urged me as an outsider to get the word out, especially about Andalusia. Far fewer stories and campaigns have focused on Andalusia, yet it is at higher risk than many other parts of the peninsula for dramatic climate change. Every person I interviewed delivered the same message: a resurgence in pastoralism as a sustainable food system can help mitigate climate change and rural depopulation, but, to achieve this, consumers need to be better educated and support the true value of shepherds' products, while governments need to greatly reduce subsidized industrial farming.

As I interviewed shepherds and their advocates, it became clear that they are also trying to reverse a trend set in motion between 1970 and 1990, when Spain witnessed the decline of Franco's dictatorial policies and saw the rise of an experimental young democracy. During this transition, Spain's borders opened increasingly to global capitalism, bringing a flood of tourism and, with it, new models of consumption. Over the decades the supermarket model of more prepared foods and cheaper prices has edged out neighborhood markets and hurt the small-scale production economy. People who work with livestock and shepherds say they now depend less on neighbors and more on tourists and elite consumers in the cities: those willing to spend more to know where their food comes from and how it was produced. Two themes recur in nearly every interview I conduct, whether with a shepherd, farmer-owner, or advocate: the need for government regulation to help local sustainable farms and *dehesa*s thrive instead of hindering the marketing of their goods and the need to educate consumers about the "added value" of these products.

Talking with shepherds, I began to realize that another story — not just about the waning practice of transhumance — needed to be told. Larger issues, such as rural depopulation, and broader agricultural and land management practices provide a fuller picture of pastoralism today. While transhumance is the most ecologically sustainable model, broader perspectives show how low-impact grazing practices can help agriculture and pastoralism establish more resilient models. Beginning to correct my own misconceptions about shepherding, I decided to collect contemporary narratives about the practice from the point of view of both practitioners and advocates and to place them in dialogue with the trajectory of historical practices and narratives about pastoralism. The interviews flesh out four general gaps in our knowledge: they provide a fuller portrait of Andalusia (a region often overlooked in pastoralism); of the extensive networks required for pastoralism today (family, collective organizations (*plataformas*), government, scholars, consumers); of the changing role of landowners in this picture; and of the trend toward shepherds becoming entrepreneurs working for themselves instead of either for or along with farm owners. This more complete picture allows us to glimpse both the power of tradition and the call to innovation and resiliency. The future of rural life in an environment that has benefitted from millennia of sustainable grazing practices now hangs in the balance.

Historical Practices and Cultural Narratives

For centuries, shepherding and the movement of flocks has held great historical, economic, and cultural importance in the Iberian Peninsula. As early as 1273, King Alfonso X appointed the first association, La Mesta, to try to regulate it, and over the centuries shepherding evolved into a complex legal, economic, social, and cultural practice. Precious Merino wool became a staple for an emerging market economy in fifteenth-century Iberia. By the late medieval times, the figure of the shepherd had also become central to the formation of emerging socio-cultural identities. Shepherding was the main economic activity in early modern Iberia as the low population density of the peninsula, the skirmishes between Christian and Muslim-ruled regions, and the semi-arid environment in parts of the south made raising livestock more profitable than establishing permanent agriculture. Later, with the expulsion of Muslims, Jews, and other "racially impure" others, cultural narratives turned to pastoralism as a symbol of a collective identity for Christian Iberia in a time of racial anxiety about religious and ethnic difference.[1] This process continued to evolve throughout the nineteenth century as pastoralism became conflated with the idea of national culture, reflecting a certain nostalgia.

---

1   Javier Irigoyen-García notes in *The Spanish Arcadia: Sheep Herding, Pastoral Discourse, and Ethnicity in Early Modern Spain* (2013) that the popular Renaissance pastoral romance is paradigmatic of this new way of how the elite imagined an ideal collective identity for early modern Castile. It is no coincidence that this genre emerged with the birth of more cities, producing a longing to return to nature as a lost paradise.

Fig. 0.3 Bartolomé Esteban Murillo, *Adoration of the Shepherds* (ca. 1650), Prado Museum, Madrid, photograph by Abraham (2010), Wikimedia, public domain, https://commons.wikimedia.org/wiki/File:Shepherd_adoration.jpg; Bartolomé Esteban Murillo, *The Good Shepherd* (ca. 1675), Städel Museum, Frankfurt am Main, public domain, https://sammlung.staedelmuseum.de/en/work/the-good-shepherd

While twentieth-century processes of modernization like the transportation of livestock by train and by trucks and the mass production of cheeses and meats drastically reduced the practice of transhumance, the symbolic importance of the shepherd persisted. Often following an early modern pattern recorded by Miguel de Cervantes in *Don Quijote* (1605; 1615), the image of the shepherd vacillated between idealization and marginalization. During the Spanish Civil War and the first decades of Franco's dictatorship, for example, the "humble shepherd" was re-appropriated in cultural production to essentially turn back the clock on modernization and pan-European processes. Later, as the state discourse of Francoism promulgated developmentalism and promoted modernization, this trend reversed again. The push to modernization then accelerated the abandonment of rural areas and pastoral traditions, which fueled the stereotype, in Ana Belén Robles Cruz's words, of the "shepherd as the village idiot."

Even in the first years of Spain's rapid transition to democracy (ca. 1975–82), pastoralism and the movement of flocks along traditional routes continued to be viewed as anachronistic and an impediment to the modernization of waterways, highways, and urbanization, yet this attitude would soon change. As the new democracy matured into the late twentieth century, the past was "repackaged" for the 1992 Quincentennial. New socio-political movements looked again to autonomous regional traditions in the face of globalization and entrance into the European markets. The year marked a symbolic turning point for Spain as it emerged on the international scene as host of the Olympics (Barcelona), the World's Fair (Seville), and the Cultural Capital of the European Union (Madrid). New debates, political actions, and cultural narratives about Spain's pastoral past and present emerged. A movement emerged and began to revitalize ancient shepherding practices and narratives about pastoralism, identifying them as integral to national culture.

At the turn of the twenty-first century, this transformation gained increasing influence over policy making and environmental activism. The raising of traditional Iberian livestock began to be celebrated for its contribution to the preservation of rural landscapes, biodiversity, and ways of life, to the point that the Spanish state now welcomes shepherds into national parks as a strategy for conserving the Iberian wolf, vultures, and other endangered "natural enemies" of sheep that were all once ruthlessly targeted by the Franco regime for extermination. Regional governments also began to fund programs to train a new generation of shepherds and recognize new justifications for grazing sheep and goats, such as fire prevention. National policies established new protectionary laws for rights of way. Supporters in non-government sectors also joined a larger movement fighting for the survival of sustainable, small-scale agriculture and greater regional autonomy.

Yet even as local, national, and international interest grows, the challenges continue. Many shepherds I interviewed are retiring without replacements. Recent EU regulations about the movement and sale of animals restrict the viability of the practice by making it more costly to compete with large-scale production. Consumer tastes continue to shift, with the consumption of more pork and beef instead of lamb, and more cheeses manufactured and marketed by industrial agricultural interests. In addition, the use of wool has declined as preferences for synthetic "high-performance" fabrics increase. Even as the population generally understands the deep cultural and environmental benefits of traditional practices, there is still the gap just like the one Cervantes depicted in

Don Quijote between the idealized and real shepherd. Shepherds are no longer portrayed as symbols of Christian humility but rather as defenders of a valuable cultural geography integral to the national Spanish patrimony.

Nevertheless, these same guardians of tradition and sustainable practices are often still the targets of social prejudice, as we will hear in many of the cases studied below. Indeed, the gap between urban and rural remains. Until recently, city dwellers, who love visiting pueblos and enjoy a countryside dotted with shepherds and their flocks, often balk at interacting with locals or at the thought of making a life for themselves and their families in a small pueblo. For their part, the rural residents often complain of the lack of respect they get from visitors, which aggravates their own frustration of dealing with limited social services and economic opportunities. Small-town residents also experience resistance from their own neighbors to changing gender roles in shepherding. The country-city divide accelerates the loss of traditional shepherding practices and exacerbates the already widespread depopulation throughout Spain.

Still, some positive changes are observed by my informants. They often remark on the promise of a new generation of *neo-rurales*, young people leaving the city to live and work in the countryside, who are exploring new ways to work within traditional vocations like pastoralism. One shepherd we will hear from below (and who prefers to simply be called Daniel) expresses "the need to get out of the city, the fast-paced rhythm of today's society, and everything that has to do with urban life." He decided to try out shepherding, a profession his uncle had to abandon years ago, because "it motivates me to live out his dream." One of the shepherds we will hear from remarks that he enjoys the psychological challenge of working with animals and the environment and of acquiring the in-depth knowledge necessary to carry out his work. It allows him to "honor the values of people who live freely, far removed from the 'usual' expectations."

This is where my project and experience as an outsider interviewing practitioners and advocates of pastoralism comes in. As people sought to explain to a foreigner what they did and why, I began to piece together a more complex picture of a dynamic, resilient practice that may help suggest a way forward.

Life Stories and Pastoralism: Method and Scope

The centerpiece of *A Country of Shepherds* are the oral histories that provide a glimpse of how the people working in pastoralism articulate the meaning of their work as shepherds, farm owners, and advocates. Although this project draws on extensive scholarship about pastoralism in Spanish Iberia, my focus is the living archive created by dozens of informants who reveal their deep connections with the ongoing practice, regulation, and celebration of both traditional and innovative practices in Western Andalusia.[2]

To date, no study has closely examined the shepherds' life stories within the context of pastoralism in Andalusia and its broader relevance to the more critical role of extensive grazing. While transhumance has been a topic of historical and anthropological study since Julius Klein's foundational study of the practice (1920/1981), more recent scholarly production has tended to explore the important ecological impact of transhumance and its intersection with society (Gómez-Sal, 2004; Manzano Baena 2010; Garzón Heydt 2004). Just a handful of articles study pastoralism and cultural narratives (Alenza García 2013; Acuña Delgado 2012; Cruz Sánchez 2013; and Rodríguez Pascual 2001). Most recent work, such as that by such scholars as Yolanda Mena Guerrero and her collaborators, focuses more broadly on specific practices and benefits within pastoralism to raise awareness about it through public education (2015), national patrimony (2010), and rural development (2007). Elisa Otero-Rozas studies the notion of traditional ecological knowledge that is integral to pastoralism in Spain (2019). Although *A Country of Shepherds* has strong ties to work being done by scholars and government agencies on sustainable practices and the long-term benefits of extensive grazing in Spain, it locates itself within the particular Andalusian social and geographical context. I argue that hearing individual life stories and placing them in dialogue with the broader work on pastoralism reveals a dynamic movement that at once illuminates a rich heritage and suggests sustainable ways forward.

---

2   The Western part of Andalusia tends to be more humid and have a much greater number of *dehesa*s than the Eastern region (Granada, Almería, etc.), where the geography can change from the dramatic heights of the Sierra Nevada to the semi-desert of Cabo de Gata within a one- or two-hour drive by car.

The main interviews offered here were carried out onsite at various farms and pastures from 2015–2018 (with updates in 2021–2022) and took place with my cultural interpreter, María del Mar Torreblanca. I collected the narratives in five different regions of Western Andalusia — within a couple hours' car drive of Seville — which presents a special case within the larger study of pastoralism in Spain. The mountainous terrain creates greater climatic diversity than other regions. Although there are many semi-arid regions, in general it is more verdant than areas of Eastern Andalusia. The ancient landscape is dotted with unique areas of public mountainous pasturelands of the Mediterranean area (*monte mediterráneo*), as well as private *dehesa*s. In addition, the whole region has generally been overlooked by people studying the tradition. The cases I study highlight a range of land types, land uses, and livestock breeds across five provinces in Andalusia. We move from the *monte mediterráneo* of the Sierra Norte (Seville) and the Sierra de Grazalema (Cádiz), to the Sierra de Cardeña y Montoro (Córdoba-Jaén), the Sierra de Jaén, and the Sierra de Aracena (Huelva). We also visit three *dehesa*s in these areas. Here, we see the breeding and raising of protected species that have been developed over centuries to adapt to the highly specific microclimates, including traditional Merino and *Segureña* (Esguerra) sheep breeds and endangered *Payoya* goats.

At the core of this study is a "living archive": the nearly sixty interviews of shepherds, policy makers, educators, community organizers, and landowners. I have distilled these interviews into a handful of in-depth life stories in which we see how none of these Andalusian farms, families, and endeavors exist in isolation. The six case studies offer a glimpse into how those most involved in the ongoing practice, regulation, and celebration of shepherding articulate both traditional and innovative ideas about their work. While most scholarship on the subject maps the routes, economic patterns, and specific historical events or practices related to transhumance, this book presents the varied people, places, voices, and landscapes reflective of a broader pastoral past and present that focuses, in particular, on the Western Andalusian geographies. It is a snapshot in time filtered through the lens of my own experiences and my own process of discovery. At times, it was my very "outsiderness" that seemed to allow people to tell their stories more fully. They often filled in information that may be common knowledge to someone who grew up in the region. They mentioned feeling freed from preconceived notions about their work and lives. Indeed, my presence — and my curiosity as well as my ignorance — often were the source of a good deal of laughter and light-hearted teasing.

I open each case study with an overview of current practices exemplified in the section before inviting readers to join our visits to the places and people who live and work as farmers, shepherds, and landowners. During each visit, we hear how experiences from early childhood influence their chosen vocations today. These personal stories reflect larger forces and constraints, including family heritage, social norms, economic opportunities, and even global climate change. In each chapter, I include short selections that highlight my informants' concerns in their own words. Key to this process, however, was my decision not to carry out formal interviews in a question-and-answer format but to allow farmers and shepherds to show us around their own pastures and farms and talk about their life stories and practices. As we moved about, I recorded our conversations and transcribed them later in order to maintain a strong sense of "walking about" and interacting with other people, the animals, and the landscapes — hiking to an outcrop to see if the goats arrived to the valley, returning to the barn for milking time, driving to remote grazing areas, helping catch a squealing pig that escaped, stopping dead in our tracks when a pair of dead day-old lambs are spotted, and returning to a working farmhouse for a beer and a tapa in the heat of the day.

In each visit, the informants explore fundamental questions, such as: What is my role in keeping this practice alive? What do we gain from it and, just as interestingly and increasingly, what does society gain? And perhaps the most important question of all: How do we see the future, and what do we need to do to keep pastoralism alive and attract new generations to it before it is too late? Finally, every case study ends with a brief update carried out by phone or Zoom eighteen months into the COVID-19 pandemic (November 2021) and, in some cases, a final in-person meeting to go over the manuscript with each contributor in June 2022. The pandemic only further underscored the essential role of these workers and their vulnerability in the current system.

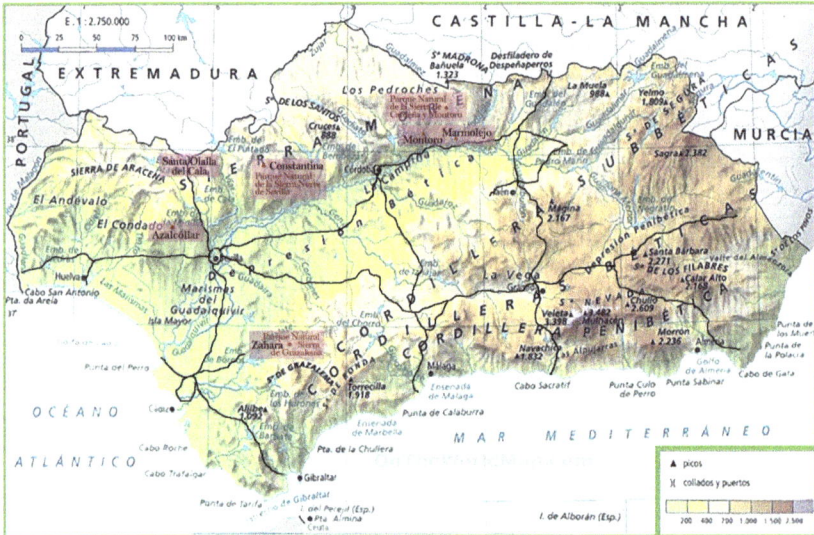

Fig. 0.4 Topographical Map of Andalusia highlighting the regions featured in our case studies. "Andalusia physical map" (2023). OntheWorldMap.com, CC BY-NC, https://ontheworldmap.com/spain/autonomous-community/andalusia/andalusia-physical-map.html Labels added by Licia Weber.

New Pathways: Overview

The six case studies highlighted here reflect an overarching story of people grappling with changes in traditional agricultural practices, changes felt not just regionally but nationally and even globally. Within these limits of time and geography, a surprising richness emerges of both common denominators among people working in pastoralism and the variety of new and innovative approaches to the traditional practice. Taken together, we see transitions from traditional to new models of transhumance, as well as a turn to the importance of extensive grazing in general. We meet a full range of participants, from shepherds to farm owners and their families, and see examples of both generational and gendered change.

The first three cases focus on men who have worked in shepherding for decades, often as an inherited profession. Each has found ways to keep their ancestral practices alive and to bring in family members and others along the way. These cases illustrate entrepreneurial skills that these men and their families use to move in new directions, such as expanding into agrotourism, taking advantage of European Union funds, and exploring new roles with landowners. The two cases that follow focus on women who own *dehesa*s but come from very different backgrounds. One woman is working with her inheritance of a functioning *dehesa*. The other is a foreigner now working in Andalusia on local and pan-European initiatives to protect the natural heritage of the *dehesa* and pastoralism. Each describes the steep learning curve she faced and, in some cases, the challenges of working and gaining respect in a traditionally male profession. The final chapter surveys the collective story told by a wide range of people involved in the social movements and platforms that support pastoralism in myriad ways, including financial backing, knowledge, partnerships, and — ultimately — resiliency. These interviews help us understand the larger context for the individual life stories of the first five chapters.

The first case study explores the story of Juan Vázquez Morán, a traditional shepherd who adopted his own father's profession and practiced transhumance on foot outside of Constantina (Seville) and now has his own small sheep and goat farm. For both of our interviews, Juan's retired shepherd friend Manuel Grillo joins us. Their dynamic banter reveals the tremendous challenges faced over three generations. Even as they often joke with each other, they share stories of the sacrifices they both made — decades of economic hardship, living alone in the countryside for months at a time, and the social marginalization of tending sheep for rich landowners — even as society, in theory, praises the shepherd. The two friends also note, however, the many changes to their way of life. After years of saving his earnings, Juan has been able to buy a small parcel of land on a hilly outcropping where he tends his own animals each day before and after working as a shepherd for a nearby farm owner. He remarks happily: "I'm free, kinda like a snail that carries everything on his back and needs very little. It's not so much that it's good land, but it's your own, and no one around here is gonna tell you to leave." Further, he and his family are now able to live year-round in town, and his daughter is studying for a nursing degree. Juan recognizes how society both depends on his work and often disdains it. While Juan stayed with the family profession, his youngest brother, Patricio, did not grow up with shepherding but loves the landscapes and community they both grew up with. As an ambitious entrepreneur, he has established a gourmet preserves company with the abundant local fruit, which he markets in Seville and London — and to weekend tourists in Constantina. A few years ago, Patricio opened a coffee shop that now serves Juan's cheeses, and he currently has plans for an agrohotel. This current venture will include a partnership with his nephew's family, who recently began raising goats. They hope that within a year they will have enough goats to be eligible for EU subsidies and to dedicate themselves full-time to the business. Taken together, the sons and grandsons of a transhumant shepherd reveal how they have stayed attached to their home region but also made a living for themselves through new practices.

The second case study takes us to an area just outside Parque Natural de la Sierra de Grazalema, near the tourist destination of Zahara de la Sierra. Here we visit Pepe Millán and family, who raise both Merino sheep and *Payoya* goats native to Grazalema. The family demonstrates the highly-developed skills perfected over hundreds of years needed to succeed at shepherding in a challenging environment, as well as the cost — both economic and social — of continuing to work in the profession. Their stories also highlight new roles for people working with livestock. Pepe is now a mentor and spokesman for a new generation of shepherds-in-training and for a broader public that views programs in which he is featured, such as the documentary *La buena leche* and the popular television program *Volando voy*. On the day of our visit, we follow the daily milking routine and the process of resettling the herd through the rocky terrain. We also hear about the challenges the family has faced to keep afloat economically, as well as how things have changed for the next generation. Pepe's daughter Rita did not initially want to continue in the profession, but she is now an entrepreneur in her own right. She has secured government subsidies for their operation, which includes the endangered *Payoya* goats, and has launched a local cheesemaking and delivery service. We hear about the past and the future as the family expands and the world changes.

The third case study focuses on a shepherd, Fortunato Guerrero Lara, who continues to practice transhumance and works alongside his father and son. He also wears many other hats. Fortunato's family raises *Segureña* sheep on public and private land and practices transhumance by truck, moving the flocks from winter pastures of Sierra de Cardeña y Montoro (Córdoba) outside Marmolejo to the summer pastures of the Sierra de Segura outside of Santiago-Pontones (Jaén). On the day we visit, he welcomes us, saying he hopes we get word out "so society will understand what a shepherd does nowadays. We manage land that has high environmental value." As we follow him around during birthing season, we see him working his flocks and meet his own father, as well as his son who intends to stay in the family profession — a highly unusual choice today. We also visit a man Fortunato calls his "collaborator," the landowner Rafael Enríquez del Río, who hires Fortunato to manage and protect his *dehesa* and area of forest. During our visit, we talk with an array of other people Rafael and Fortunato work with to develop a multifunctional *dehesa* beyond shepherding: beekeepers, lumber thinners and harvesters, and hunters. As we listen to their discussions onsite, we hear of the economic-environmental vitality and balance involved in multi-functional land use. Fortunato himself is also a valued advocate and spokesman for shepherds and others in livestock entrepreneurship, and his case highlights the many other tasks that livestock workers take on now because they often can't make a living for a family without outside work. And Rafael, as a conscientious landowner, plays a critical role in stewardship, creating opportunities for professionals with expertise and a shared vision for a sustainable future.

After these first three case studies of livestock professionals (*ganaderos*), who not only tend to flocks of sheep and goats but recently have created their own small livestock businesses, we look more closely at the role of the owners in keeping extensive grazing and pastoralism viable. These cases also highlight a newer trend of women taking a more active role in the profession.[3] Marta Moya Espinosa, the subject of our fourth case study, inherited a *dehesa* in the Sierra Norte and large flock of Merino sheep from her father, but for years she left it in the hands of others while she raised a family and managed one of Seville's prestigious private country clubs. Recently, she made the monumental decision to leave this lucrative, sixty-hour-a-week job and now devotes an equal amount of time to understanding her inheritance and learning

---

3   A recent phenomenon are also studies on women who work in pastoralism and more recently the role of women in pastoralism (Fernández-Giménez et al. 2021, 2022).

to become a conscientious, knowledgeable farm owner. She helps to oversee the day-to-day operations by working alongside her shepherd-manager from dawn to dusk and is exploring new initiatives to revitalize the ecosystem. As we tour this working farm, Marta discusses the many challenges she faces with learning about the daily care of animals, finding shepherds, helping the *dehesa* recover from a damaging forest fire, and understanding often volatile government policies — all while working as a woman in a traditionally male world. Marta works to train and keep farmhands in a radically different society than when her mother was helping run the farm in the 1950s as the new wife of a landowning farmer. To get a sense of life on the *dehesa* in the mid-twentieth century, Marta introduces us to her eighty-year-old mother, Carmela Espinosa. While Marta talks about learning how to work with livestock, finances, and shepherds today, her mother reminiscences about the hardships and triumphs of running a large household with eight children on a rural rustic farmhouse during the difficult postwar years. Both women experienced the privileges of the traditional landowning class of these farms and *dehesa*s, as well as the challenges of trying to both harness and change traditions.

Another farm owner with a very different background and a broad European resonance is the focus of the next chapter. Ernestine Lüdeke was born in Germany, but she has adopted Andalusia as her own. Ernestine began working in Spain shortly before the 1992 World Expo in Seville and soon became involved in environmental issues. By about 2000, she and her husband had established the "Fundación Monte Mediterráneo", an organization dedicated to protecting Andalusia's delicate ecosystem and to championing new initiatives based on traditional practices. They decided to house the Fundación on a nearly abandoned *dehesa* they bought outside of Santa Olalla de Cala in the Sierra de Aracena in the westernmost side of the Sierra Morena (Huelva). As Ernestine walks us around the Dehesa San Francisco, we hear how they have coaxed the *dehesa* back to life with a variety of plantings and raising livestock, centered around a flock of Merino sheep that are raised with transhumant practices. As part of the tour, we visit the educational center on the property and hear about regional and international teaching initiatives. The work of Ernestine and the Fundación showcase the intersection of land and livestock, as well as of traditional and innovative practices with public and private initiatives. Later, we hear from one of her trainees, Daniel, whom she has now hired as her manager-shepherd. Ernestine has the resources, knowledge, and drive to influence a wide circle of farm owners, shepherds, policy makers, and consumers. Her broad-reaching work focuses on practical applications rather than naïve romanticism and resonates throughout the region and even internationally.

Our last chapter shifts gears to follow a narrative thread suggested by Ernestine with her "Fundación Monte Mediterráneo", as well as everyone we interviewed. Here, we take a closer look into the many collective organizations, or *plataformas*, that support the shepherds' work. In our interviews, we hear from people in three main areas: 1) *ganadero*s and other professionals working with collective organizations to support transhumance and extensive grazing; 2) university-trained professionals based at public institutions and working to promote pastoralism through, for example, the use of grazing for fire prevention and the teaching of skills for cheesemaking; and 3) primarily government-sponsored programs, such as the popular shepherd schools, which train a new generation. Among the people interviewed here are a few of the individuals who have been on the forefront of these movements for decades, including Jesús Garzón Heydt, Paco Casero, and Yolanda Mena Guerrero, along with newer voices, such as Maricarmen García and Paco Ruiz. Each works collaboratively with a host of shepherds and *ganadero*s, government agencies, non-governmental organizations (NGOs), and grassroots collectives striving to ensure the resiliency of pastoralism in Andalusia and beyond.

Overall, these case studies offer multiple points of view from both traditional shepherds and the new model of *ganadero*-shepherds, and their families, as well as from farm owners trying to be conscientious stewards of their land and from advocates creating new resources for practitioners of pastoralism. They all play key roles in the functioning and longevity of pastoralism. Together, their stories reveal the hope and frustration, the nostalgia and excitement, of working in a profession dating back millennia and now in the process of profound change. We learn how those working closely with pastoralism are concerned equally about the people, animals, and landscape itself — the elements for sustainable pastoral systems. As they describe their work and lives, they dialogue with cultural narratives about shepherds and Spain that increasingly link them to discussions about environmentally sustainable practices and food systems. All articulate a sense of urgency related to their situation, as well as a set of possibilities for the future.

This project began with myriad preconceptions (mostly my own misconceptions) about pastoralism in Spain. I share here how my perspective has broadened over time — a process that is still ongoing. For this reason, I often use the present tense and a plural form to invite the reader along with me in my journey through different pastoral spaces over a period of about five years. My goal is to bring the human face of pastoralism to a broad audience, allowing the informants interviewed and the images gathered to tell the story of an ancient practice in the midst of transition. My hope is that, as we hear the complex dynamics and practices involved in traditional pastoralism as well as glimpse the broad social movements that support it, we will see how the stereotype of a solitary shepherd working in isolation — or at best with his family — does not provide the full story. A broad range of supporters and organizations have emerged to help sustain the practice. We all have a part in how this story will unfold over the next couple of decades, and as world citizens — and consumers — we will have powerful input into its outcome.

Since many of the first interviews were conducted, life has taken its own twists and turns. In spring 2018, as I was checking back in with informants and planning my final interviews before finishing *A Country of Shepherds*, both my parents died within weeks of each other. I hurried back to Wisconsin and helped my siblings sort through a house full of antique furniture, photos from the early twentieth century, books from our Irish-American grandparents, and a barn full of tools from the original 1880s icehouse and caretaker's cottage my parents had lived in for forty years. Everything else faded into the background as I grieved. Two years later, eager to return to the project, I booked a flight to Seville, only to have it cancelled as the world locked down as the global COVID-19 pandemic erupted in spring 2020. We all waited anxiously inside our homes and miniscule social "pods" for nearly eighteen months. Another plan to return in fall 2021 was dashed to the ground as the deadly Delta variant spread, and the EU placed the U.S. back on its list of countries with travel restrictions. In the end, like much of the world, I turned to FaceTime and Zoom to conduct my work, completing the last formal follow-up meetings with my informants in November 2021. By May 2022, I was able to travel to Spain and share the final draft of this book with them and get their feedback. Once again, I got to see first-hand their resiliency in the face of new challenges with severe climate change and changing markets. Their lives and practices continue to make a strong case for sustainability.

The process of shepherding this book project to completion only further underscores the rapid changes in the world since I first began. The starts and dramatic halts in my work come through in the narrative, reflecting processes of life and dramatic historical change. The uneven narrative threads in *A Country of Shepherds* suggest the on-going impact of individual, regional, and global losses and crises, while also offering examples of the resiliency of individual shepherds, *ganadero*s, and their practices.

Pastoralism: A Contextual Background and Terminology

Pastoralism refers to a wide variety of traditional livestock systems found worldwide and is prevalent in certain regions in the Iberian Peninsula. This study focuses on the specific case of Western Andalusia, which shares characteristics with other regions in the Mediterranean world, and on a pastoralism that includes both cases of transhumance and extensive grazing. For readers less familiar with the subject matter and special terms used in the Introduction (particularly outsiders like me), this section contextualizes terms and concepts used by our informants as they talk about their work. Yet further information about the vitality of pastoralism, both as an agricultural practice and as a cultural phenomenon, can be found in the bibliography.

Andalusia: Cultural Geographies

The southernmost region of the Iberian Peninsula, Andalusia, is rich in cultural and geographical diversity. The province is Spain's most populous, with eight million inhabitants representing around 18% of the national population. Foreigners often think of it as an arid region associated with sunny beaches, olive groves, and flamenco, but it is far more varied than this popular image. A road trip through Andalusia is akin to traveling across several countries: high snow-capped peaks, towns and cities that flourished under Arab and Roman occupation, kilometers of intensive greenhouse vegetable production, and the crowded beaches of the Costa del Sol all exist side-by-side. Two significant mountain ranges run through the region. Outside the city of Granada, the Sierra Nevada boasts the highest peak on the Iberian Peninsula (Mulhacén, at 3,578 meters). The Sierra Morena, meanwhile, runs through the regions of Huelva, Seville, Córdoba, and Jaén. Farther southwest, the Sierra de Grazalema rises from the Costa del Sol to humid Grazalema, which has the most rainfall of any region in Spain. Between the Sierra Nevada and Sierra Morena lies the Guadalquivir River, one of the largest and longest in the peninsula, which flows from the high peaks in Jaén through the ports of Cádiz to the Atlantic Ocean. In the fifteenth century, it was the only navigable river in Spain, famous for transporting early explorers out of Seville on their way to the Americas. Many of Andalusia's cities and towns have rich Muslim, Christian, and Jewish histories. This complex cultural history is still visible in many of the towns we visit in our case studies: we still see evidence of Moorish city planning in the white-washed village of Zahara de la Sierra, and Constantina's and Santa Olalla's medieval castles perched on commanding hillsides reflect an era when this was frontier land between warring regions.

Abundant sunshine has allowed Andalusia to develop widespread intensive farming zones and become the breadbasket of Spain, providing agricultural products to consumers across the European continent. These areas are often known as *campiña*. The lack of water in most parts of Andalusia, however, favors the ancient practices of "dry" farming, in which less water is used to produce a flavor-packed product. In Andalusia in particular, the practice known as extensive grazing (*ganadería extensiva*) utilizes larger pastures for a relatively small production per acre, as opposed to intensive farming practices, which use a small amount of land with large inputs of feed, fertilizer, and labor for a greater yield. Extensive grazing relies on livestock appropriate to the region, primarily smaller livestock (*ganado menor*), such as sheep and goats. These flocks are often moved many kilometers from one area to another based on seasonal climate conditions: the practice known as transhumance. There are various names for the people involved in pastoral practices, including the shepherds (*pastores*) who tend to the livestock, *ganadero*s (a broader term for livestock professionals who often own their own flocks), and landowners who own the pastureland and sometimes the herds as well. As one of the most sustainable food systems in the world, extensive grazing — and especially transhumance — also preserves biodiversity and helps to maintain rural populations.

Migratory Shepherding and Public Lands

Transhumance maximizes the efficiency of shepherding activities since grazing occurs during the seasonal peak productivity of pasturelands. In Spain, the typical movement of shepherds across seasons involves a northern journey to summer pastures with a return to the south in the winter. Transhumance differs from other forms of pastoral non-sedentary systems because people and livestock perform circular movements between specific summer and winter pastures. Thus, transhumance is distinct, for example, from nomadism. Depending on their location, some shepherds only practice transterminance, a shorter movement of flocks (fewer than one hundred kilometers) from low valleys in the winter to high mountain passes in the summer months. There are also *ganadero*s who practice extensive grazing without moving their flocks and herds long distances.

Recently, transhumance has been designated as UNESCO Cultural Heritage of Humanity for over nine countries in Europe, including Spain. UNESCO defines transhumance as a system of people, animals, geographies, practices, and culture:

> Transhumance, the seasonal droving of livestock along migratory routes in the Mediterranean and the Alps, is a form of pastoralism. Every year in spring and autumn, thousands of animals are driven by groups of herders together with their dogs and horses along steady routes between two geographical and climatic regions, from dawn to dusk. In many cases, the herders' families also travel with the livestock. Two broad types of transhumance can be distinguished: horizontal transhumance, in plain or plateau regions; and vertical transhumance, typically in mountain regions. Transhumance shapes relations among people, animals, and ecosystems. It involves shared rituals and social practices, caring for and breeding animals, managing land, forests, and water resources, and dealing with natural hazards. Transhumant herders have in-depth knowledge of the environment, ecological balance, and climate change,

as this is one of the most sustainable, efficient livestock farming methods. They also possess special skills related to all kinds of handicraft and food production involved. (https://ich.unesco.org/en/Decisions/14. COM/10.b.2)

In Spain, the northern territories in the traditional transhumance are known as *agostaderos*. They are generally higher-altitude terrains and are defined by widely spaced trees or shrubs that are often covered with snow in the winter and are moist and green in the summer. The southern territories, known as *invernaderos*, are used in winter. In the case of Andalusia, these pasturelands are often part of the public *monte meditérraneo* or of private *dehesa*s. If the owners of these large-scale farms follow the traditional multifunctionality, the *dehesa* will often combine pastures for flocks, the sale of meat, the use of space for private hunting, and the strategic management of native crops, such as olives and cork. While Andalusia's often hot, dry climate means the farms cannot support crops meant for human consumption, the land provides a wide array of flora nutritious to ruminant species. Even as the pattern of land ownership in Spain is constantly adapting and changing with new social systems and laws, many old patterns of land use still hold when it comes to the practice of transhumance. In this sense, the northern territories used in summertime are, for the most part, still run communally, generally administered by the local province's forest service, while private *dehesa*s host many of the more southerly wintering grounds.

With the rise in cultural interest in transhumance, shepherds have begun to use social media to document their movements and to invite tourists and journalists to join them (see Chapter 6). The last few decades have seen a remarkable growth in public awareness and appreciation of these ancient practices.

Transhumance: Historical Overview in Spain

Transhumance has its roots in the natural migration patterns of many animal species. The practice certainly originated before organized agriculture itself, as hunters made the transition from simply following their prey to directing and shepherding the herd animals, beginning the long process of domestication. Transhumance has been an essential element of the Iberian Peninsula economy for millennia. As early as the twelfth century, when the production of Merino wool became an important commodity, the *vías pecuarias* were formalized under royal mandates. Other products of shepherds and their flocks, namely dairy and fresh meat, also became essential to many local communities. In some especially mountainous or arid regions of the peninsula, shepherding was the only viable economic activity. Due to its cultural, economic, and environmental importance, the organization of land, labor, and trade routes evolved to fit the needs of this activity. As far back as the medieval period, legislation enacted by organizations such as the Mesta offered protection to the systems of transportation and land organization developed by shepherds.

As Spain's infrastructure began to modernize in the nineteenth century, forms of mass transit began to replace the on-foot transhumance. Many shepherds welcomed the ability to send their sheep by rail, relieved from weeks of walking with flocks over mountain passes and across rivers. Without the foot traffic, however, conditions on the ancient droving routes began to decline. More recently, newer legislation has contributed to further declines in traditional modes of transhumance, such as the 1993 law regulating flock management to avoid disease spread. These laws may help maintain livestock and human health, but they add cost and layers of bureaucracy that shepherds and farmers must contend with.

Despite the widespread transition to intensive farming and the abandonment of rural land across Europe, some families in Andalusia have continued the tradition of transhumance. Whether by foot or by truck (train service ended in the 1980s), they have safeguarded this tradition — and with it the trails, the clothing, and even the songs. Yet, while these transhumant shepherds remain culturally relevant, their economic influence has decreased. In the 1990s, there were an estimated 1.3 million transhumant sheep in Spain by 2011, these numbers had fallen to about a quarter of a million. Today, the practice depends largely on trucks. Jesús Garzón estimates that, while are still about 600,000 transhumant livestock and 6,000 transhumant families, only a small percentage move their livestock on foot. He believes that with the steep rise in petrol prices and fodder as well as increased subsidies available for the practice, more people will return to the traditional transhumance by foot (Walker 2021).

As the cost of technology decreases, transhumant shepherds, whether transporting flocks by foot or by truck, have taken full advantage of cell phones to coordinate transport and track weather conditions, as well as to allow communication with teams who organize locations for rest and water. The shepherds and aid groups share information about fences and other obstructions on the *vías pecuarias*. In addition, with the aid from larger organizations, some transhumant shepherds have begun to use GPS trackers on their flocks, and even drones to oversee larger areas. Specialized monitors can help locate missing animals, assess nutritional needs of the flock, and create a digital record of routes and resources for other shepherds, as well as for ecologists working on the restoration and conservation of *vías pecuarias*. The trackers can even monitor an individual animal's temperature regularly and communicate this data back to veterinary teams.

Vías Pecuarias: History and Ecological Benefits

Spain is the only country in the world that has a network of legally protected *vías pecuarias* for transhumance, and they are critical to the long-term viability of the practice and its ecological benefits. While these trails often began by following waterways, they widened as flocks grew. Many date to the twelfth and thirteenth centuries and continue to provide rights of way for shepherds to move their flocks from north to south, or between elevations. In the 1990s, the *vías pecuarias* regained their old legal status as a public good. This means that they cannot be developed for other commercial purposes and are protected for primary use by transhumant shepherds. These laws also render each province responsible for the regulation and maintenance of the stretches that fall within its borders. Today, there are about 125,000 km (78,000 miles) of protected droving roads throughout Spain owned by the state: in Andalusia alone, there are over 32,000 kilometers of *vías* covering more than 45,000 hectares (112,000 acres). This vast network includes *cañadas reales*, which are 75 meters wide, *cordeles*, at 37.5 meters wide, and *veredas*, at 20 meters wide. Much of the background and regulation of these roads is set out in an important, lengthy government document, *El libro blanco* (1993), which is by far the most referenced legislation in the protection of the *vías*.

Since use of these ancient rights-of-way by shepherds has dramatically declined in the twenty-first century, the *vías* have suffered greatly. Shepherds who continue to use them often find that, although the droving routes are nominally protected, neighboring roads, gardens or wilderness have begun to encroach upon them; in some cases, landowners plant along them or even build fences that shepherds must cut to continue their journey. The *vías* have also become popular spaces for outdoor recreation: hikers, joggers, and cyclists use them more and more frequently. Most conservationists acknowledge that tourism, while it can occasionally disrupt flocks in movement, also helps protect the *vías* and ensures ongoing support for their maintenance.

Scientists have begun to study the environmental impacts of the on-foot practice. The *vías pecuarias* act as biological corridors, allowing for the movement of small animals and plants, which hitch a ride between natural areas on passing flocks. Migrating animals transport seeds, facilitating the exchange of species between different parts of the Iberian Peninsula, thus conserving biodiversity. According to Márquez and García (2008), one square meter of a droving road can contain more than forty distinct species. Each sheep transports approximately 5,000 seeds and feeds the soil with about three kilograms of manure each day (Walker 2021). The decrease in traditional on-foot migrations has led to a loss of ecosystem resilience (Manzano et al. 2010). Because of the ecological importance of the *vías pecuarias*, environmental groups have become involved in the protection of traditional transhumance. Some advocacy organizations focus on the practice of transhumance itself, while other groups focus on the ecological health of the *vías* (with an understanding that the primary protector of these routes is the rights-of-way granted to shepherds). The *Asociación Trashumancia y Naturaleza*, for example, advocates directly for transhumant workers, while environmental organizations like *Ecologistas en Acción* focus on the restoration and protection of *vías pecuarias* in general.

Fig. 0.5 Map of the *vías pecuarias* throughout Spain. Map by Diotime, "Principales vías pecuarias españolas" (2009). Wikimedia, public domain, https:// es.wikipedia.org/wiki/V%C3%ADa_pecuaria#/media/Archivo:Principales_ vias_pecuarias.png

The *Dehesa* and Multifunctionality

In addition to the ecological benefits of transhumance for the protection of public lands, the system of extensive grazing in Andalusia includes the key role of the mostly privately-owned *dehesa*s — a farming land-use system that helps both to maintain both a vulnerable ecosystem and to stem rural depopulation. In contrast to intensive monoculture farms typical of industrialized modern farming, the *dehesa* follows a multifunctional model in which the land is managed to support both production and ecological conservation. The *dehesa*s focus on animal products since the dry, hot environment will not sustain most crops without irrigation. Most *dehesa*s raise Iberian pigs, sheep, and some cattle for their meat, but they also produce valuable agricultural specialties, such as cork from the cork oak and oil from native olive trees. Appropriate land-use practices help prevent fires and erosion while also protecting native flora and fauna. The *dehesa* is typically home to a variety of animal species (such as the Iberian lynx, the imperial eagle, and black vulture, among others) and, consequently, draws hunters. The area also attracts tourism thanks to its dramatic landscapes and is a reservoir of traditional cultural knowledge held by the communities that have stewarded these lands for generations.

With the so-called "green revolution" of the 1960s, the transition from extensive to intensive agriculture, as well as a more urbanized workforce and economy, has led to stress on and even abandonment of southern *dehesa*s. In response to this strain, environmental activists, policy makers, landowners, and farmers are looking to revive sustainable agricultural traditions of the past. There is more support for landowners to re-invest in multifunctional farming to restore the health of their land and help sustain the local community as well as the environment. Multifunctionality can create jobs and strengthen the economic viability of rural landscapes, and it has been promoted by politicians, scholars, and farmers alike as the only option for sustainable land use.

Despite these broad-ranging benefits, the *dehesa* system is threatened by the overuse of land and soil, the abandonment of rural lands due to changes in economic conditions, and the devastating effects of climate change. There is insufficient investment to support ongoing maintenance and combat fully the effects of these changes. Government policies and European Union Common Agricultural Policies often fail to recognize the complexity of the *dehesa* system and its special importance to Andalusia. This has led scientists, farmers, and NGOs, as well as some policy makers in the Junta de Andalucía (the executive branch of the government of Andalusia) to found working groups, such as *bioDehesa*, and even to publish a comprehensive document on the land system entitled *"Dehesas de Andalucía: Caracterización Ambiental"* (2006). Along with the *vías pecuarias*, the *dehesa* is a focal point for conservation in Spain. If this sustainable system of land use can be preserved, there is a chance to preserve the ecosystems and livelihoods that have developed along with it.

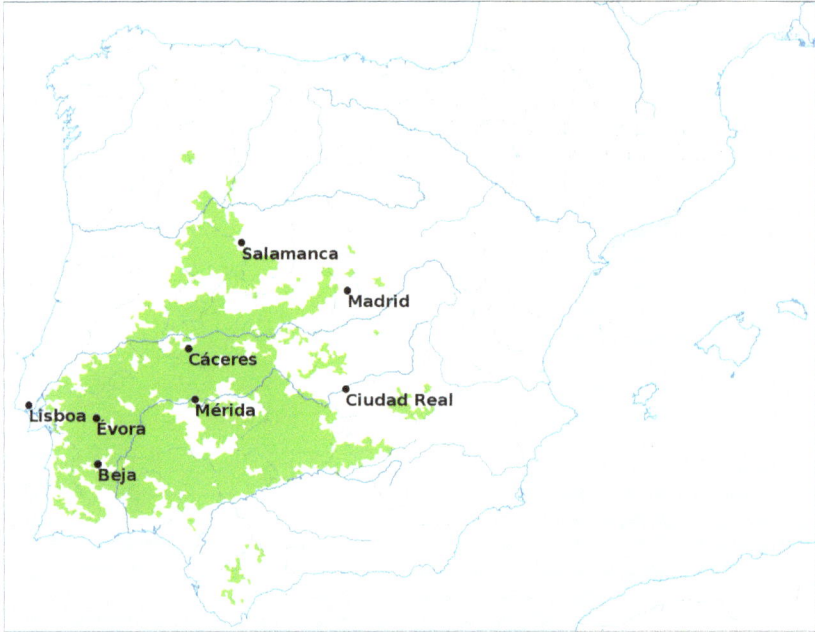

Fig. 0.6 Map of the *Dehesas* in the Iberian Peninsula. Map by El Mono Español (2015), Wikimedia, CC BY-SA 4.0, https://commons.wikimedia.org/wiki/File:Dehesa_in_Spain_and_Portugal.svg

Landscapes and Animal Breeds

Just as pastoralism is linked to specific landscapes and ecosystems, the regional breeds of sheep and goats are deeply intertwined with these geographies. The famous Merino sheep have a long history in Spain, dating from at least the thirteenth century and the important wool trade with Flanders, and have now spread to many other parts of the world. In our case studies below, we will hear about other varieties of sheep and goats, breeds that have been developed not only for the quality of their meat or milk, but also because they adapt well to the terrain, climate, and vegetation of the region. Andalusia itself has six distinct sheep breeds and six goat breeds. There are many more breeds registered for all of Spain. *Ganaderos* who raise these native breeds often receive government subsidies because they help to maintain biodiversity. There is often an official association for each breed that supports the shepherds who raise them. In our case studies below, we hear from each *ganadero* about the importance of the breed, or *raza*, he or she raises, the animals' adaptability to the local conditions, and the high quality of meat or milk they produce. Regional varieties include those raised primarily for meat that adapt well to transhumance, such as *Segureña* lambs, as well as sheep raised for both meat and milk, such as the endangered *Merina de Grazalema*. In the latter case, we see the close link between the place and the breed, which has adapted to the colder humid climate in the Sierra de Grazalema and is not found outside this small region. We will also hear about two local breeds of goats used primarily for their milk to make cheeses: the *Sevillana Florida* and the *Payoya*. The *Florida* is considered a *raza de fomento*, that is, a breed that has been identified as having genetic characteristics that are ideal for helping to maintain delicate eco-systems but is also known for its hardiness and productivity. The *Payoya*, meanwhile, is an endangered breed critical for the continued production of the popular *Payoyo* cheese.

Key to all successful shepherds' practice are their dogs. They are companions and coworkers, ensuring the health and viability of the flocks. The large, often ferocious mastiffs weigh over ninety kilograms (around two hundred pounds) and are trained to guard the sheep at night and to protect the lambs from wolves, wild pigs, and other predators. Herding dogs, usually intelligent and limber breeds such as Australian Shepherds or Border Collies, help the shepherd to guide and manage the flocks as they travel to and from the pastures. After years of training, these dogs acquire valuable herding and communication skills. Traditional *ganadero*s often keep track of the herd and direct the dogs by listening to the *cencerros*, the traditional bells of varying pitch placed on animals at the front and back of a flock. The shepherds can also communicate with their dogs from a distance with a system of complex whistles and calls. Puppies can sell for hundreds of euros and trained young-adult dogs for many thousands. Breeding and training sheepdogs to master these skills is a career in itself.

Changing Markets: Wool, Meat, and Dairy

Wool

The Merino sheep that originated in Spain was bred for its soft wool, which became a key export across Europe in the Middle Ages, and, later, to the Americas and the South Pacific. Centuries before Pacific Island shepherds became experts in its production, Spain and the United Kingdom were the leading suppliers of this variety of wool. Today, most Merino sheep are raised in Australia and New Zealand, which has cornered the global market for Merino wool. China also now exports wool to Europe and beyond. And, as mentioned earlier, many consumers have replaced wool with synthetic fleece for their wardrobes. All these changes have led to a dramatic drop in value and production of Spanish Merino wool (especially since the early 2000s), and recent economic crises continue to slow the growth of this market. Despite the drop in demand, sheep still need to be sheared—at a cost of about €1.50–€3 each. When the wool cannot be sold, everyone involved loses money. Nonetheless, there is a growing demand for high-quality products from a clientele who see social, economic, and environmental value in "buying local" and shepherds working for projects such as "Made in Slow" (http://madeinslow.com/proyecto/transhumance-by-made-in-slow/). Jesús Garzón, director of the Asociación Trashumancia y Naturaleza, credits this trend for the 7.5% increase in Merino wool sales in the last five years.

Meat

Meat and dairy are the primary export products from goat and sheep production, especially since the devaluation of wool in the last few decades. Most meat from sheep and goats is destined for export to the European market. While more than 90% of production is consumed outside of Spain, *ganaderos* who practice extensive grazing often depend on sales of their product to consumers near to home that are looking for a specific origin, freshness, and quality. Within Spain the consumption of meat in general, and lamb specifically, is higher than the EU average. Yet, the cost of production versus the market price over the last two decades has made it hard to make a living. For example, the cost of raising a sheep is about one hundred euros, and the price per lamb fluctuates between six and fourteen euros per kilo, depending on the cut and the time of year. The margin calculations become more complicated depending on whether the shepherds practice transhumance and the number of sheep births per year.[4]

Dairy

Spain is famous for its milk-producing ovines and caprines, and many of the most famous Spanish cheeses come from specific sheep: the *Manchega* sheep produces the renowned Manchego cheese, the *Churra* sheep produces *Zamorano*, and the *Payoya* goat produces the increasingly sought-after *Payoyo* cheese. Even the Merino sheep, best known for their warm wool, are also well-loved in Spain for the creamy *Torta del Casar* and *La Serena* cheese varieties produced from their milk. In addition, many pueblos have their own cheese varieties. The rich history of place-specific food is now protected by European law labeling regulations, such as the European certification known as the Protected Designation of Origin (DOP), which allows producers from certain regions exclusivity rights over some of their most famous culinary products. When it comes to shepherding, a certain percentage of *ganaderos* benefit from the DOP label, but they still compete with industrial production of these foods. *Ganaderos'* local cheese production was severely curtailed by government regulations for some time; however, a recent change by the Andalusian authorities have eased these regulations. Despite the

---

4   Ernestine Lüdeke (see Chapter 5) gives us her numbers: "An organic lamb, for example, that is 26 kilos live weight will be 46% dressing and produce 12 kilos of meat, which the cooperatives pay to *ganaderos* at about €9.-/kilo, but this price can oscillate a lot depending on the time of the year and market demands. Raising a lamb costs about €100, which includes food, manpower, vet, land, etc. Keeping the ewe 'mother' for a year (in our case the ewes lamb once a year only—other farms have three lambing seasons in two years, but then cannot do transhumance with all their ewes; some farmers rotate the transhumance herds and send, for example, only 30% or 60% of their ewes north: the ones who are in a gestation period or the ones who go north with the rams) is €120 in food, not counting the investment of the ewe itself. Market price for various cuts of meat (*'Precios EA group Cordero Eco Semana 2-23 y hasta nueva comunicación'*): *Cordero eco* 10,5/11 kg 10,30 €/kg, *Paletilla de cordero eco* 15,90 €/kg, *Pierna de cordero eco* 12,40 €/kg, *Carré de cordero eco* 13,90 €/kg, *Falda de cordero eco* 5,30 €/kg, *Pierna deshuesada eco* 14,90 €/kg."

subsequent development of a small-scale cheese industry, many say that more and more bureaucracy is limiting its expansion.

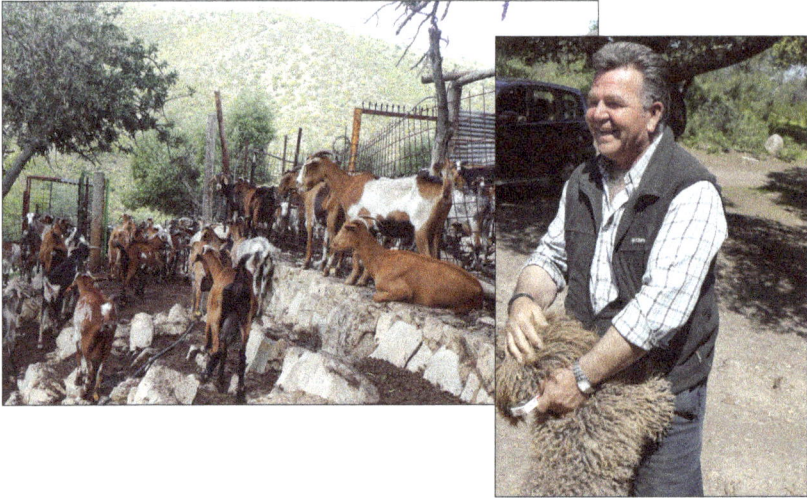

Fig. 0.7 *Payoya* goats in the Sierra de Grazalema (2019); Fortunato Guerrero Lara with his Portuguese water dog, Sierra de Grazalema (2019).

The European Union and the Common Agricultural Policy (CAP)

Given both the changing market and needs of those actively working in pastoralism and extensive grazing, both public lands used for transhumance grazing and private *dehesa*s are now often highly dependent on outside funding and subsidies. The broadest reaching of these is the Common Agricultural Policy (CAP): the European Union program that regulates, sustains, and determines agriculture and rural development among the twenty-seven member states. The CAP policy itself accounts for a large portion of the EU's total expenditure, making up approximately 40% of a €145 billion annual budget.[5] Due to the broad remit of the CAP, many shepherds and farmers in Spain rely

---

5   See European Parliament, 'Financing the CAP', April 2023, https://www. europarl.europa.eu/factsheets/en/sheet/106/la-financiacion-de-la-pac; European Commission, 'Market Measures Explained', (n. d.), https://ec.europa.eu/info/food-farming-fisheries/key-policies/common-agricultural-policy/market-measures/market-measures-explained_en

on it to one extent or another. Either they receive rural development grants for maintaining vitally biodiverse ecosystems, or they receive direct payments for food production. *Ganadero*s and shepherds often find their yearly incomes are impacted by even small fluctuations in payouts from this program. Every shepherd, no matter the scope of their operation, has a story to tell about the payments granted (or withheld) by the CAP.

The market-setting practices throughout the European Union attempt to maintain a difficult balance between vastly different political, cultural, and ecological environments, and these are not always successful. Reforms to the CAP in 2013, for example, failed to incorporate extra subsidies for "High Nature Value" (HNV) farmland. These are spaces where extensive maintenance supports biodiversity and contributes to ecological health and sustainable production; most traditional shepherding land thus falls under the HNV category. As a result of this omission, many farmers in Andalusia lost valuable subsidy monies, threatening the economic viability of their ongoing efforts. NGOs and activists who support shepherds have been pushing for the inclusion of HNV farmland into the CAP, but it has been an uphill battle. Recent revisions, now in force (2023–2027), address some of the concerns about the environment by including new eco-schemes and greening strategies while also continuing preexisting measures and funding to facilitate generational renewal in rural areas in the European Union. Along with this direct income support, the new CAP has attempted to implement a fairer distribution system more generally.[6]

Applying for CAP subsidies is a long bureaucratic process that often takes months to complete and then must be repeated annually. Despite the many criticisms of this unwieldy policy, many view it as a necessary evil. Few shepherds can afford not to petition for these funds, as the changing economy has made it increasingly difficult for them to make a living only from selling their wool, meat, and dairy products on a free global, national, regional, and local market.

---

6   European Commission, 'The Common Agricultural Policy: 2023–27' (2023), https://agriculture.ec.europa.eu/common-agricultural-policy/cap-overview/cap-2023-27_en

Depopulation

In addition to understanding the geography, extensive grazing practices, and economy of pastoralism, it is crucial to understand the complex history of rural depopulation and its relationship to sustainable pastoral practices. A national-identity narrative linked to an idyllic rural existence dates back to early modern times and is featured in many popular pastoral novels of the time. These cultural productions, however, also reveal an emerging discourse about race, culture, and animal husbandry (see Javier Irigoyen-García, *The Spanish Arcadia*, 2013) that continued to develop over centuries. In the twentieth century, this traditional narrative came under scrutiny by the Franco administration, which portrayed the Spanish countryside and its inhabitants as in need of "redemption." Franco's movement only exacerbated flight from so-called "backward" rural areas.

The continuing debate about rural Spain can be seen in the reaction to Sergio del Molino's best-selling book *La España vacía* (2003). The book has sparked intense national debate — and even government action — around the long-term issue of depopulation of the countryside. More recently, rural areas have experienced a "brain drain" as better-educated young people leave home, either to find work in nearby cities such as Madrid and Barcelona, or to leave the country altogether. This global phenomenon has hit hard in Spain, where changing cultural values and economic incentives have made population retention difficult. Young Spaniards increasingly find themselves pulled in multiple directions as their expectations of a role in the new economy are frustrated by limited employment opportunities.

In 2008, as world markets went into freefall, all Spanish citizens, especially those who had made small investments in homes or the stock markets, felt the monumental shift of the recession. Just before the housing bubble burst, many people had invested in extensive development along Spain's sun-drenched coast to reap the benefit of the thriving tourist industry. Much of this infrastructure and building work then stalled for years: buildings remained empty due to high mortgage prices, and the region went into debt trying to pay off the money owed to developers. Soon after this, the unemployment rate began to skyrocket. Within one year, unemployment had doubled, and within a few more years, nearly a quarter of the population was unemployed, double the rate for Europe in general. In Spain, this financial crisis continued for years and is often referred to as "La Crisis."

This long economic crisis hit young people (*jóvenes*, which often refers to people well into their thirties) especially hard, despite this generation having a higher level of education than ever before. Today, some younger Spaniards, forced from their hometowns, families, and traditions that rooted people to place, are working to rebuild connections and systems that will allow them to stay, or even to return to the places of their ancestors that they may have never personally known. This movement, often referred to as *neoruralismo*, increasingly includes people from all walks of life who seem to understand the urgent need to bring a new generation into traditional practices and lifestyles that have been rapidly disappearing. Pastoralism can combat rural depopulation by creating jobs as well as protecting traditional landscapes, culture, and food sources.

Fig. 0.8 "Transhumancia." Photo by María del Carmen García, *vía pecuaria*, Spain (n.d.).

Maps and Resources

Transhumance

Contreras, A. et al. (14 February 2021), 'Trashumancia en ovino segureño: Tecnología GPS para un sistema socioecológico en movimiento.' *Interempresas*. Discusses the advantages of using GPS during transhumance, (in Spanish:) https://www.interempresas.net/ovino/Articulos/315744-Trashumancia-en-ovino-segureno-Tecnologia-GPS-para-sistema-socioecologico-en-movimiento.html

Digitanimal (2017), 'Collares GPS para ganado con ayuda de los fondos europeos'. Promotes taking advantage of European Union funds to pay for sheep's GPS collars, (in Spanish:) https://digitanimal.com/

Grupo Operativo Ovinnova (2020). Offers a guide to transhumance terminology and history, (in Spanish:) https://goovinnova.org

UNESCO (12 December 2019), 'Decision of the Intergovernmental Committee: 14.COM 10.b.2'. The official acknowledgement of the nomination by Austria, Greece, and Italy of transhumance for inscription on the list of the Intangible Cultural Heritage of Humanity, https://ich.unesco.org/en/Decisions/14.COM/10.b.2

Walker, Kira. 'The revival of a historic journey across Spain.' *BBC Future Planet*, 23 September 2021, https://www.bbc.com/future/article/20210923-the-revival-of-spains-epic-pastoral-migration

Vías pecuarias

Caminos Libres, 'Registro vías pecuarias de Andalucía', 23 April 2005, (in Spanish:) https://www.caminoslibres.es/legislacion/REGISTRO%20VIAS%20PECUARIAS%20PROVINCIA%20SEVILLA.pdf

Vela, Juan José Domínguez (2021), 'Mapa de clasificación básica de las vías pecuarias de Andalucía', in Venegas, C. et al, 'Propuesta metodológica para el estudio de las vías pecuarias desde el paisaje. Aplicación al Cordel de Gambogaz (Sevilla)', *ResearchGate*, https://www.researchgate.net/figure/Mapa-de-clasificacion-basica-de-las-vias-pecuarias-de-Andalucia_fig1_350400477

Dehesas

Consejería de Medio Ambiente, Junta de Andalucía (2006), *Dehesas de Andalucía: Caracterización ambiental*. Presents the ecological characteristics of Andalusian *dehesas*, (in Spanish:)
https://www.juntadeandalucia.es/medioambiente/portal_web/web/servicios/centro_de_documentacion_y_biblioteca/fondo_editorial_digital/documentos_tecnicos/dehesas_andaluzas/dehesas_andaluzas.pdf

Federación española de la dehesa, 2017, (in Spanish:)
http://fedehesa.org/

Interempresas, 'El ganado ovino en la dehesa andaluza', 29 August 2016. Discusses sheep herding on the Andalucian *dehesa*, (in Spanish:)
https://www.interempresas.net/ovino/Articulos/277265-El-ganado-ovino-en-la-dehesa-andaluza.html

Iberian Dehesas, 'Breaking barriers: Challenges of rural traditions in the pasture and Iberian montage', September 2017,
https://dehesasibericas.es/en/tradiciones-rurales-ibericas/rompiendo-barreras-desafios-de-las-tradiciones-rurales-en-la-dehesa-y-montado-iberico/#wpfb-cat-5

Junta de Andalucía, *Bio dehesa*, 2013, (in Spanish:)
http://www.biodehesa.es/

Tierra y Mar & Espacio Protegido Canal Sur, 'Los ganaderos de dehesa esperan mayores ayudas en la nueva PAC, la Política Agraria Común', YouTube, 24 January 2021. Presents *ganaderos*' expectations for the PAC, (in Spanish:)
https://www.youtube.com/watch?v=lyvtpvwGNvU

Pastoralism and Food Systems

European Commission, 'Market Measures Explained', 5 July 2019,
https://ec.europa.eu/info/food-farming-fisheries/key-policies/common-agricultural-policy/market-measures/market-measures-explained_en

European Commission, 'The common agricultural policy: 2023–27', 14 March 2023,
https://agriculture.ec.europa.eu/common-agricultural-policy/cap-overview/cap-2023-27_en

Junta de Andalucía, *Portal Ambiental de Andalucía*, 2023. Presents the ecological policies and initiatives of the Junta de Andalucía, (in Spanish:)
https://www.juntadeandalucia.es/medioambiente/portal/home

Varea, Ramiro. "Ovejas con GPS: la trashumancia se digitaliza." *El País*, 19 May 2019. Discusses the use of GPS during transhumance, (in Spanish:)
https://elpais.com/retina/2020/05/19/tendencias/1589907178_447551.html

Fig. 1.1 The town of Constantina, Sierra Norte de Sevilla (2017).

1. New Directions in the Sierra Norte de Sevilla: Juan Vázquez Morán and Family

Every day I get up with the sun, and I always see something new. I get a lump in my throat when I think about all the rough times I've been through. It's not so much that it's good land, but it's your own, and no one around here is gonna tell you to leave. You can't do this alone. I couldn't have done it without my wife.

Juan Vázquez Morán

Overview

When a colleague at the University of Seville, María del Mar Torreblanca (hereafter Mar, who drove and joined me in each the main interviews for Chapters 1–5), suggests that I talk with her friend that grew up in a shepherding family, I eagerly agree. I am up to date on recent media treatments about transhumance, but I want to explore more how people close to the practice live, work, and think about their vocations. I want to understand why it has captured national and international audiences, including myself. Without full awareness of what I am about to embark on, or even how to interview shepherds, Mar and I head to Constantina in the Sierra Norte de Sevilla.

The two shepherds featured in this chapter were the first I met and became my first teachers in what would become several years of changing expectations, understandings, and attitudes about who shepherds are and what they do. I soon realize these are not stories of lone shepherds working in isolation, but rather stories of families, communities, and landscapes. What began as an afternoon interview over a cup of coffee

   https://doi.org/10.11647/OBP.0387.01

turned into a series of on-site interviews with Juan, his wife Manoli, and his shepherd friend Manuel. I also met Juan's younger brother, who, instead of taking up shepherding as a trade, decided to make and market local artisan products. I quickly grasped that to understand the intricate interaction of shepherds, animals, and landscapes in pastoralism, I also needed to understand family and community networks and how these enable shepherding to survive. Through them, I also began to appreciate how everyone has their own story to tell, even in the same family.

These first two shepherds, Juan Vázquez Morán and Manuel Grillo, are as different as night and day, but somehow, like those two natural states, they seem to work in an effective unison and highlight each other's strengths. The two of them have a shared history as hard-working Andalusian shepherds, though played out decades apart. While Manuel (now in his mid-60s and retired) has lived his whole life as a transhumant shepherd and often experienced the prejudices of others, Juan (in his late-40s and still active) is now experiencing a major shift in the cultural acceptance — and even celebration — of his trade, at least at the national level. The two shepherds illustrate the cultural and social shifts across generations. There are very few transhumant shepherds working today in the way that Manuel and Juan used to work; even as the practice is now receiving wide recognition for its importance, it is disappearing from the Spanish landscapes. As a retired transhumant shepherd, Manuel is firmly rooted in the traditional. Juan still has one foot in the traditional practices and has also moved in new directions.

First, we will trace Juan's story and how, as a currently active shepherd, he has transformed a family tradition. He first learned the trade from his father and practiced it with thousands of sheep and goats for decades. Later, he left the transhumant practice to tend to animals on other people's farms, so that he could live in town with his wife and daughter. In the last few years, Juan has established his own small *finca*. Most of his sheep — eighty Merino mixed with Ile de France sheep, known for their good meat production, and a few pure-bred Merino sheep, kept for the milk they produce that makes good cheese — graze on rented pastureland near town, but Juan is most proud of his fifty Seville Florida goats, which graze on the small plot of land he owns. This breed of goats, he explains, adapted over centuries to the extreme heat and cold, lack of water, and rocky outcropping of the Sierra Norte de Sevilla. Juan's career trajectory, from transhumant shepherding, working for hire, and finally to maintaining his own small farm to graze his animals — with no government funding — has not been a common path in the last century. While one of Juan's brothers left shepherding 10,000 animals in Extremadura to buy his own tavern, and another brother never went into the profession to begin with, choosing instead to market specialized local fruit products, Juan's love of animals has kept him in the profession. But, he explains, he is equally motivated by the daily tasks and the educational nature of his work: "I learn something new every day." His story showcases the opportunities and challenges of small-scale shepherding and rural development.

In what follows, I describe two visits with Juan. The first is a sit-down interview with him and his shepherd friend Manuel. The second visit, onsite at Juan's barn and in town, gives us a vivid glimpse of his life and accomplishment in moving from shepherding for hire to having his own animals and land. We also see the importance of family and witness new initiatives in rural development as we meet Juan's wife Manoli and brother Patricio. The last section provides brief updates from November 2021, after eighteen months of living with the COVID-19 pandemic, and a final update from May 2022 that includes a hopeful glimpse of a new entrepreneurial generation entering pastoralism.

Fig. 1.2 Juan Vázquez Morán and Manuel Grillo (2017); Juan on his newly acquired land parcel (2019).

The Visit: Traditional Shepherding and Retirement from Transhumant Practices

Filled with anticipatory excitement about our first trip, I check my recording equipment and hop into Mar's small Fiat at dawn. Leaving Seville's early fall heat behind, we pass the dry, white cotton plains of the intensive farming zones and see Carmona's medieval watchtower in the distance. Soon, we begin the gradual climb into the green Sierra Norte de Sevilla, past grazing pastures that resemble nothing I have ever seen in the U.S. I soon learn that these traditional Andalusian *dehesa*s are large expanses of land that mix groves of olive and cork trees with grazing lands and low forest holm oak, hosting a variety of the distinctive black Iberian pigs, sheep, and occasional cattle. *Dehesas* are the essence of biodiversity and sustainability, new buzzwords for ancient practices. We pass at least six flocks of sheep herded along dirt paths and fields by shepherds carrying their traditional *cayados*, a long, curved walking staff, and accompanied by their dogs. The shepherds' earth tone clothes blend with this landscape and are a stark contrast to the neon yellow jerseys worn by the occasional cyclist on the road. We pass a sign for a *vía pecuaria* — the Cordel del Herrador that starts in Carmona and passes another important *vía* (the Cañada Real de Robledo in Constantina), finally ending in Extremadura — marked with a red triangle with an image of a cow in the center. The wide dirt path passes through areas filled with cork (*alcornoques*) and holm trees and continues into the horizon. It eventually will lead to Carmona. As my guide Mar describes the stringent requirements that govern the production of the prized *"Pata Negra"* ham (it must be produced from 100% Iberian pigs, which are 100% acorn-fed), the hilltop ruins of a castle come into view, looming over the white-washed village of Constantina. This castle was built by Muslims in medieval times during their long occupation of the area but was Christianized by Fernando III in the fourteenth century. Like much of Andalusia, this was frontier land for centuries. Small castles in various stages of disrepair dot the landscape.

We arrive at the small town's center and enter the restaurant, which specializes in local grilled lamb and pork. Here, we first meet Juan Vázquez Morán and his coworker and friend Manuel Grillo. They invite us into their world as they alternately joke and recount experiences of a lifetime of working together as shepherds. As they talk, I sense they enjoy having an audience with which to share stories of hardships, along with moments of levity. Juan is clearly the "man in charge" as he still is actively involved in shepherding, while Manolo is clearly the "man of experience" with the flexibility that retirement has afforded him. Their easy camaraderie is contagious, and we spend hours talking as servers and locals look on with more than a little surprise. I'm guessing that it isn't often that a foreigner shows up in the restaurant with a video camera to interview a pair of shepherds. In fact, after an hour there, the owner sends over a second *café con leche* "on the house." Although my own inexperience shows — the battery fails on my recording camera, and I have no backup for the last part of the interview — this first foray into such a radically different world from my own leaves me eager to know more.

As we talk at the restaurant, Juan recalls his childhood as one of eleven children growing up in makeshift huts built out of local vegetation while his father moved flocks of sheep and goats from Constantina to Marchena, Lora del Río, La Campana, Écija, and beyond. Juan was an early initiate into the world of transhumance: he remembers being just eight or nine on night watch, struggling with fear as he listened to night sounds in the pitch black before dawn. He vividly recalls one of his early experiences with another challenge of animal husbandry: by age ten he was expected to kill a goat he had raised as a pet

> When I found out they were going to kill it, I got up, took my little goat, put it under my bed, and crawled under there with it. And my dad said, "Where's Juan?" He pulled me out from under the bed and slapped me. After he hit me, he said, "You're gonna have to see this so you'll believe it." And he killed the goat. So, every time I kill a goat or a sheep or any animal, I remember that story. "You're gonna have to see this so you'll believe it." When an animal looks at me, I just can't kill it. I'm incapable. What hurts the most is killing a goat. They cry like people. You can see the tears fall from their eyes. You always learn new things.

Although he can laugh now as he tells the story, Juan becomes somber when he confesses that it is still hard for him to kill the animals he raises. He prefers raising goats for their milk.

Though the life of a shepherding family was never easy, things got much harder for his large family. One night, they awoke to a fire in their hut, and all their belongings burned. But, as word of the disaster spread, nearby shepherd families brought food, clothing, and materials for shelter and cooking. He observes: "You don't see that level of solidarity today." Although the other families had little, they shared what they had. The community of shepherds was strong, but Juan shares painful memories of the more general social stigma of being the son of a shepherd. Echoes of the shame he felt as a boy seep through the story as Juan recalls being an outcast. One year, for example, when Juan's family was living and working as shepherds on a private farm, the owner prohibited his own young boy, who was vacationing at the farmhouse, to play with Juan and his siblings.

> The truth is, when I think about it, I get emotional. I got so tired of crying. Just remembering it.... And it's not that I don't think about it now. It's just that so much has happened in town and out in the country that you feel powerless and looked down upon. Now, anyone can have access to a degree. It used to be that that wasn't the case. It used to be that whoever could go to college was some rich kid's son. And the shepherd's son, on the other hand, had been born to raise sheep, pigs, goats, cows.... I was born to do that. I was a shepherd's son and was thought of as an insignificant little animal.... One time, the boss came and locked my mother and us up in a room so we couldn't play with his children. They treated us like we were little animals. He came in from Córdoba to spend the weekend at the farmhouse.

Later, when Juan began to date, girls refused a second date when they found out he was a shepherd. He adds, in a voice quiet with indignation, that some people in town still will not talk to his friend Manuel because of his profession.

Juan left the shepherd's life for his mandatory two-year military service. Upon his return, he decided to work in construction but found himself looking at his watch all day long. So, he decided to take up shepherding again as his true vocation. Juan says that he loves tending to animals, being out in nature, constantly learning new things, and having a degree of freedom. Today, he does not own a watch, and, though he works longer hours, he loves his work.

Juan and ten other men used to be away for months at a time, moving 3,000 sheep from the Sierra Norte to rented lands in the plains of the Guadalquivir, an area where cereals had been harvested and the fields needed to be cleaned and fertilized. He notes that he still works from sunup to sundown seven days a week, but at least he is never away from home overnight. He chokes up and his eyes glisten as he recalls years of ill treatment and the sacrifices he and his family made to buy their small parcel of land:

> I get a lump in my throat when I think about all the rough times I've been through. It's not so much that it's good land, but it's your own, and no one around here is gonna tell you to leave. You can't do this alone. I couldn't have done it without my wife.

While on the one hand Juan is forthright about very real sacrifices they endure, he explains that he perseveres because he loves his work and has fulfilled his own vision of becoming a small farmer raising his own livestock. He credits his wife Manoli, more than government funds or helpful employers, for helping him in his life project. His face softens as he describes how Manoli has always supported him. "We have always been a team," he repeats often through our interviews.

Whereas Juan stopped living as a transhumant shepherd years ago, Manuel spent over half a century in the countryside, often for up to ten months a year with only brief visits home. He jumps into the conversation and exclaims with a wide smile: "I've been a shepherd since the day my mother bore me." Five years ago, he retired to live in town with his daughter's family. He now enjoys walking down the street for a cup of coffee, sitting in the town's central square with friends, and having a cell phone. But his face still lights up with delightful nostalgia when he describes his feeling of freedom spent camped out under the starry night skies in his little pop-up tent where he slept during his long months away from home. He acknowledges the difficulty of having a family life when he was gone so much of the year, but he knew no other life than that walked by his father, grandfather, and even great-grandfather. The years of being out in the countryside with little pay or access to health care show in Manuel's toothless smile, but his quick, agile movements and gestures reveal a strong vitality. The two men have worked together closely for many years: as Manuel talks, Juan finishes some of his sentences. In between laughter and jokes, Juan recalls bathing with his brothers in the Guadalquivir River one warm night, while their clothes floated down river, leaving them in shorts as a mean bull chased them off the land. As the two friends continue their banter, they describe half a dozen close calls: tending to the birth of a Siamese lamb, performing emergency surgery, and carrying out other work that most people would need an advanced veterinary degree to perform. The skills they have acquired and the range of life-and-death issues they have dealt with are just part of life as a transhumant shepherd. The bond formed over years of shared experience is deep but playful.

When Manuel retired, Juan continued tending the livestock of wealthy farm owners from Seville and Córdoba. But many things have changed. Where he was once "looked down upon" as a shepherd and treated like an "insignificant little animal," he now demands respect and is given it by many. What becomes clearer with each story and quick-witted comment is that Juan actively models the dignity of his vocation and the parameters for building and maintaining mutual respect between himself, livestock owners, and townspeople. When I first met Juan, he was tending to 1,000 sheep for a wealthy Sevillian man, but this particular owner does not treat Juan as if he were a possession. The man is about Juan's age, well-mannered, and regards Juan's work highly; however, Juan remains vigilant after seeing too many situations in which he or his family were not respected. One landowner even insisted that Juan always address him with the honorific title "Don." Juan says that if this owner now slips into using the informal "*tú*" to address him, Juan reminds him to keep things formal:

> Some of them make us call them by the title "Don" or "Sir." Once, one of them used "*tú*" with me and said, "Hey you, Juan." I corrected him: Let's keep things formal. We're not on a first-name basis. If I use "*usted*" and "Sir" with you, you use "*usted*" and "Sir" with me." He was shocked. Now we respect each other.

As part of a generation that came of age during the transition to democracy, Juan has participated in a social movement that has challenged unwritten rules about social class. Now, more young people — even his own daughter, the daughter of a shepherd — have access to higher education and can choose their own career path. Juan announces with fatherly pride that, although his daughter loves tending to the livestock, she is now studying for a career in nursing. Juan, and even more Manuel, represent the old guard of shepherds who have watched democracy change the political landscape and still fight to conserve the cultural and ecological landscape of shepherding.

Increased social status and mobility have been accompanied with another significant shift for Juan. After decades of making sacrifices, Juan and his wife bought a small parcel of land a few years ago in the hilly countryside outside of Constantina. Now he has a small barn for livestock and poultry, which he tends to daily. As our interview wraps up, Juan invites us to visit his *parcela* [plot] and animals in a few weeks when the late fall season brings less work with the animals.

Walking Around the *Parcela*: From Tradition to Private Ownership

Three weeks later, on a chilly November morning shortly after dawn, we meet Juan and Manuel again at the town's center. Mar and I are on our second cup of coffee and bundled up in layers of fleece (and we soon learn we are contributing to the problem of the declining market value of wool). Juan pulls up in his 4x4 truck with Manuel in the passenger seat. "Hop on in and pardon the smell; this is a farm vehicle," Juan jokes. His big warm smile and twinkle in his deep brown eyes let us know we are in for a treat. As they banter back and forth, Juan impishly tests his friend's knowledge: "How can you tell a Merino sheep at birth?" Manuel does not recall and Juan laughs good naturedly but waits to give us the answer. That comes about an hour later when we look in the mouth of a sheep and Juan states: "You can tell by its black tongue."

As we wind through *dehesa*s and pastures, we pass a flat, lush green field enclosed by a stone wall. Juan slows and points to the field: "I rented that for years, it was beautiful, easy land, and it was for sale, but I didn't have the money to buy it. I knew how to keep the land in good shape with grazing, but they only wanted money." As a shepherd, he earns barely enough to build a small house for his family and make ends meet. We then stop at the entrance to a small grassy plot with cork oaks where Juan hops out and opens a gate to introduce us to his sheep. He explains that he has a variety of breeds (known as *razas*) and jokes with word play: "I'm not a racist" (*"No soy racista"*). Juan then makes a trilling sound that I recognize from watching shepherds moving sheep through Madrid's central streets at the Festival of Transhumance. About a dozen sheep come running when he shakes a blue plastic bag, but they stop suspiciously when they realize the bag is empty and does not contain feed. "They know when you try to trick them," Juan explains, "they're smart." We climb back in the truck and hang on as it climbs a steep, deeply rutted 300-meter dirt road. As we pass a family shaking an olive tree, letting the black ripe olives drop to a blanket below, Juan gives a friendly wave. We climb through the holm oaks, olive, and fruit trees, to a small plateau where the road ends. A small new barn is tucked into the hillside on the 20 × 50 meters flat niche that now holds Juan's earnings and dreams. He bought the parcel a few years ago. His eyes tear up when he reflects on years of hard work that he, his wife, and daughter have performed to achieve their dream of private ownership of land. He comments that they never have a day off: "I've only got my wife and my daughter, and I can't go anywhere. Saturdays, Sundays, holidays.... I've got work to do every day."

Despite difficulties raising money to start his own small livestock business, Juan has never applied for government funding. The grant process favors those who already have time and money, he says. As we will hear in other chapters devoted to people who moved from traditional shepherding to owning their own livestock business as *ganaderos*, the amount of paperwork and ever-changing rules make it extremely difficult for a working farmer to apply for funds. Juan cites examples of farm owners who own an *explotación* of sheep or goats — that is, a herd consisting of at least two hundred animals — and receive subsidies from the European Union's agriculture and rural development funds. Although these owners receive relatively large sums of money, they continue to pay shepherds very little to take care of their livestock and often do not follow the European Union's own guidelines. Many people I interviewed also mentioned that most of the CAP monies to date had not gone to small-scale landowners for sustainable shepherding. I soon learn in subsequent interviews that there is deep disagreement about these funds between those who support and depend on them, and those who disdain the way they are set up to favor people who already have more resources (see the "Contextual Background and Terminology" section of the Introduction for more on CAP funds).

As the sun warms the hillside, the early morning mist gives way to blue Andalusian skies and reveals miles of valley below. Juan describes how at night from this vantage point the lights of Córdoba — even sometimes Granada — twinkle in the distance. This morning there is a commanding view of the rolling *monte mediterráneo* countryside. This steep semi-arid plot for grazing his animals is a stark contrast to the grassy, wooded land he rents for his sheep below, but Juan now owns this land, the barn, and all the animals he raises here: a few sheep, dozens of goats, a few pigs, and the ducks, chickens, and geese in the coop out back. While Juan talks, Manuel quietly begins pulling a weed that looks like thyme but that neither sheep nor goats will eat; even after five years of retirement, his hands aren't accustomed to being idle.

The first animals to greet us are Juan's dogs, a mastiff and a Saint Bernard, who follow us everywhere. Shepherds' dogs are expensive — often over 300 euros to purchase — and they require breeding documents and take up to two years to train. Juan loves working with his dogs and gives a command to the Saint Bernard to show off just how clever this canine is. He names a certain lamb and asks the sheepdog to retrieve it. Juan is delighted when the dog chooses correctly. But Juan's face turns grave as he recalls how another mastiff was gravely wounded. Rather than directly report the story, Juan becomes vague about the details, but he concludes: "It was a crime committed by a two-legged wolf [i.e., a human]."

Another incident illustrates the often-uneasy coexistence between shepherds and their neighbors. When a neighbor's Chihuahua came on his land and barked at the sheep, Juan's mastiff charged. When the small dog's owner put herself in between it and the much larger dog, she was bitten and had to get fifteen stitches in her arm. Even though the neighbor had trespassed, Juan still had to get rid of his valuable dog. He shakes his head, saying, "See what bad luck I have?" The mastiff was just doing its job, but Juan still had to pay the price. Finishing the story, his wry sense of humor about his profession emerges again: "Just like I told you, every day there's something new." Even though his dogs do not work as hard as they used to when he practiced transhumance and had larger flocks, they are still essential, and their loss threatens both the livestock and the shepherd's livelihood.

As we near the barn, a sheep retreats in a frightened panic, and we see its still blood-stained side. This is a sheep that was attacked several nights ago, even though there was a guard dog standing watch. Wolves and wild boars are the usual culprits. We then walk inside the barn to meet some of Juan's goats and sheep, and even a baby pig. Juan's lively wit and knowledge show themselves as he intersperses a discussion of the genealogy of his prize Merino sheep and the life cycle of his goats with gripping tales of delivering a crossbreed goat from a miniature goat. He also dispenses practical advice: always look at a sheep's teeth to determine its true age before buying it; they grow a pair of teeth each year, accumulating them until they have a full set, around the age of four. As we continue walking around the stable, Juan tenderly picks up a dwarf goat, explaining it is his favorite. Next, he cuddles a baby lamb, describing its birth two days earlier. He has a story for nearly every animal in the barn: "See that sheep with the goats?" he asks. "She thinks she's a goat because when her mother died, she nursed from a goat." A lifetime of learning and dedication pour through his words and gestures.

Juan's extensive experience is well known and respected locally. Friends, farm owners, and the occasional veterinarian consult him when they cannot solve a livestock problem on their own. Recently, he recounts, a friend told Juan that his flock was going lame and the vet had not cured them. The long-time shepherd easily diagnosed the problem as "foot rot" (*pedero* or pododermatitis) and prescribed bathing the animals in sulfur. The sheep were soon walking again.

Even after decades of working, Juan remains an eternal student of his animals and is generous about sharing his knowledge with others. He observes:

> When you're working with animals, it's not about theory, it's about practice; theory is not the same as practice. I've studied through practice, experience. Every day you learn something new. It's practice that's valuable.... You have to live it. And besides, you have to pass it down from generation to generation. You can't learn it from a book.... Now they've even got shepherding classes. It's the strangest thing!

Part of this knowledge includes what seems (to an outsider) a secret language between Juan and his animals. After our tour of the livestock in the front barn, we move back outside to a small field adjacent to the barn. Juan laughingly invites us to give a shot at calling to the animals grazing nearby. Though loud enough to be heard, our calls and whistles do not provoke even a momentary raised head or glance from the animals. But when Juan emits a peculiar "rrup," the sheep reply immediately with a series of "bah bah" (although not a single goat responds). He then uses another distinctive call for his goats—a clicking of his tongue. They respond with a succession of bleats. Later, another *ganadero*, Pepe Millán, explains this ancient shepherd language to us (see Chapter 2). We have just glimpsed an elaborate art form, learned and practiced over centuries, highly effective for herding many animals with just a few people and dogs.

Next, we move behind the main barn. Here roosters, peacocks, ducks, chickens, and rabbits greet us. Juan again smiles, saying "I've always been someone who really likes animals." He tenderly talks about sharing this world with his daughter as she grew up. "My little girl has been raised around country life. Farm-raised chickens, farm-raised eggs." She had fresh meats, eggs, and milk and learned the "language of the countryside." He continues, saying that it is worth the price he has had to pay in hardships. Juan begins another story of a former employer cheating him before cutting himself short and turning back with joy when a sheep comes up to him and bleats. He reveals again, "if an animal like this looks me in the eye, I can't kill it for meat." Juan uses this prize Merino, like most of the ruminant animals in the barn, for milk and cheesemaking.

Every day — sometimes twice a day — Juan milks each animal by hand instead of with a machine, saying it causes less suffering. He gets about 100 liters of milk per day. The animals eagerly come to him for milking, knowing that his hands notice when the milk is gone. This trust between Juan and the animals is critical for good quality milk and for the welfare of the animals, he explains. Machines can continue to milk goats even after the milk is gone, and people using the machines can often be inattentive. "They'll give more milk if I milk them, and I do it more for them than for me, so they don't suffer too much." He laughs, saying he likes to see his animals "fat and happy." The animals may suffer less, but Juan pays a deep price: his knuckles are swollen and cracked from decades of milking. Arthrosis makes his hands ache, and he has another doctor's appointment the following day for cortisone shots. It is clear that Juan loves his work and wants others to appreciate that it is a choice, a vocation, one that is valuable — and that should not bear a stigma. There is dignity in what he does, and it should be neither minimized nor idealized.

After this comprehensive tour, it is time to head back into town. As we pass the Cañada Real del Robledo that Juan, Manuel, and Juan's father have all traveled, he reflects on why they stopped practicing transhumance: they had to make too many sacrifices with family life, social status, and physical hardships. According to Juan, too much "has happened. [Transhumance] has been damaged. A small-scale shepherd can't do it." There are too many obstacles today. Each animal, for example, must have an identification document and pass a blood test to be bought or sold, and a shepherd can't have more than a few animals unless they have property or a landowner who will give them a license. If a shepherd is caught moving livestock without identification documents, there is a heavy fine. "They ask for this form, that form, and more forms on top of that. You've got to get a guidebook before you start doing transhumance, or they don't let you do it." What is more, the droving routes that leave from Constantina are impassable, overgrown with underbrush and spiny bushes from lack of use. Recounting the new trend of everyone saying these droving routes can be saved through hiking (*senderismo*), Juan is highly skeptical:

> Now everybody's talking about *senderismo*, but it won't work. Nobody clears the routes. Not even a mouse can get through. The routes are all going away because livestock doesn't come through here anymore to eat any of the brush; you just don't see any animals come through to clear anything.

Instead of using the droving routes and needing so many papers to use roads all too often blocked or overgrown, shepherds and owners have turned increasingly to the trucking industry to move their animals: "They bring them in a truck from another *finca*, and it all happens in one day to avoid fines." While activists like Jesús Garzón and other shepherds who carry out longer transhumances further north are having a degree of success with keeping the droving routes clear and alive, the practice of shorter movements of livestock in Andalusia (transterminance) seems to be disappearing at record speed, even though the region has the most kilometers of officially protected routes.

When I ask about the future of transhumance and extensive grazing, Juan's and Manuel's faces grow grim. The efforts to train a new generation of shepherds, they believe, do not go far enough. These two lifelong shepherds believe that if those who have not grown up with this tradition will always be looking at their watches. Juan elaborates, observing that not many people have a vocation to work with animals in this way and the few that do must withstand economic hardship, oppressive restrictions, and continuing prejudice. Just the previous night, he recounts by way of offering a practical example, he went home to shower and eat after a long day tending to the animals but then returned to work at midnight: Juan had to move a sheep about to go into labor to an enclosed corral so that she and her newborn lamb would be safe from outside attacks while in their weakened states.

> There are very few of us. Who wants to work on a Saturday night? Who likes that? You have to be ready, always ready. Sheep are not like cars that you can park at night. If you don't like doing this, it doesn't work. That's why there aren't any new shepherds. There just aren't any more of us. There are people who want to have sheep, and then they call me because they don't want to take care of them.

In addition to the long hours and the need to be available seven days a week, Juan describes how many landowners of pasturelands and large herds have made things worse by continuing to mistreat shepherds and pay them poorly. Juan gives the example of a man promising a "big" bonus for him and the other shepherds who moved a large flock, but Juan was given just fifty euros to pay all three of his men. He forfeited his third to give the other two a better bonus. "It's just not worth it," he and Manuel say in unison.

On our way back to town, we pass a house on the outskirts with no electricity or running water. Juan tells us that his family moved there when his father fell ill and left transhumant shepherding. We pass two large semi-trucks labeled "livestock transport" on the edge of the road into Constantina. It is November and time for flocks to be moved from summer to winter pastures. The flocks that used to be herded along the Cañada Real are now loaded into trucks and driven to the winter pastures further south. We are witnessing first-hand the huge change to the ancient transhumant tradition.

Before arriving at Juan's house, we pass by two key centers for this centuries-old village known for livestock: the town's farming collective and the meat processing plant. Juan wants us to meet his wife Manoli and to sample the cheeses she makes by special order. We step inside their house in town and gather close under a traditional Andalusian *camilla*, a heavy cloth draped over a table, with a heater underneath it to keep us warm in the late autumn chill. No longer in constant motion as he was on at his barn, Juan relaxes while Manoli shows us a striking 1954 black and white photograph of a handsome, strong, young man shearing a sheep (see Fig. 1.3). This is Juan's father. It is not the stereotypical image of shepherds with weathered faces. Next, she proudly shows us miniature cork carvings of villages that Juan delicately crafts as a pastime, as his hands permit. I realize the bookshelves display many of these traditional artesian cork villages. While once common, they are rarely found outside of private homes now. As Manoli showcases her husband's past and current work, I recall his story of meeting her in a night club and how she did not flinch at dating a shepherd. After decades of marriage, she still wholeheartedly supports his vocation.

Fig. 1.3 Juan's father shearing a sheep (1954). Courtesy of the Morán family archive.

Juan, in his turn, is eager to show us his wife's work. He ushers us into the kitchen to taste the small, home-batch cheese Manoli produces from the liters of milk Juan gets each day. First, we try a creamy fresh goat cheese made the previous night, then another highly flavorful goat cheese she has stored in olive oil for two weeks, which gives it a hard, dry consistency. For our final local treat, we try the Merino sheep cheese, which is the couple's favorite. We see a variety of cheese molds, hear about recipes, techniques, and how Manoli handcrafts cheeses for individuals who have placed special orders. Tasting these high quality, very local products make us all consider how much could change if policies about cheese processing and marketing better supported small-shepherding farmers and producers. As we will hear again in the case of Pepe Millán and his daughter's *Payoyo* cheeses, there is every possibility for better cash flow, better use of local milk production (instead of export sales to France), and, ultimately, a bit less depopulation of rural areas.

Branching out with Local Products and Stemming Depopulation: Patricio Vázquez Morán

To further our understanding of the broader dynamics of rural life and pastoralism, we meet later with Juan's youngest brother, Patricio. I am curious why he did not follow in his father's footsteps. He is the only brother in the family who never took up the family profession, and his story and memories are markedly different from Juan's. Patricio recounts that, as the last of eleven children, he was only five years old when his father became debilitated with cirrhosis of the liver — a disease associated with the drink that often accompanies the solitude and hard work of shepherds — and moved the family into town. He has only vague memories of their life in the countryside, but he has some fond memories, for example, of the bonds formed while sharing Christmas with other shepherd families. Patricio also recalls growing up in town, hating school, and learning to work in the kitchen at the nearby convent. Years later, when his mother suffered a stroke, he began making preserves so he could work from home and care for her. He slowly built up this new business thanks to innovative combinations of hazelnut jam, dried oranges dipped in chocolate, and lemon-orange marmalades. Soon, Patricio expanded the business with his sisters and nephew and began selling products to tourists escaping the Seville summer heat for a day in the picturesque castle town of Constantina, to consumers at Seville's outdoor organic market on the Alameda, to shops in the international airport in Seville, and even to a handful of restaurants and shops in the United Kingdom.

Patricio may have broken from family tradition, but he has stayed in Constantina and continued to expand his multifaceted business ventures. After his initial success, Patricio opened a beautiful modern café, *Cafetería Obrador Valle de la Osa*, boasting an outdoor patio right on the Alameda, a store full of his handmade preserves and pastries, and an inviting upstairs area tastefully decorated for breakfasts and mid-day snacks (*meriendas*). After touring a smartly organized kitchen outfitted with stainless-steel fixtures and filled with fresh vegetables in preparation for the day's dishes, we sit by the large modern wood-burning oven (*chimenea*) upstairs as it removes the morning chill. Here, Patricio serves abundant platters of fresh, local cured serrano ham (*jamón*), artisan breads, a few of Juan and Manoli's goat cheeses and a Merino sheep cheese — all paired with his own homemade jams.

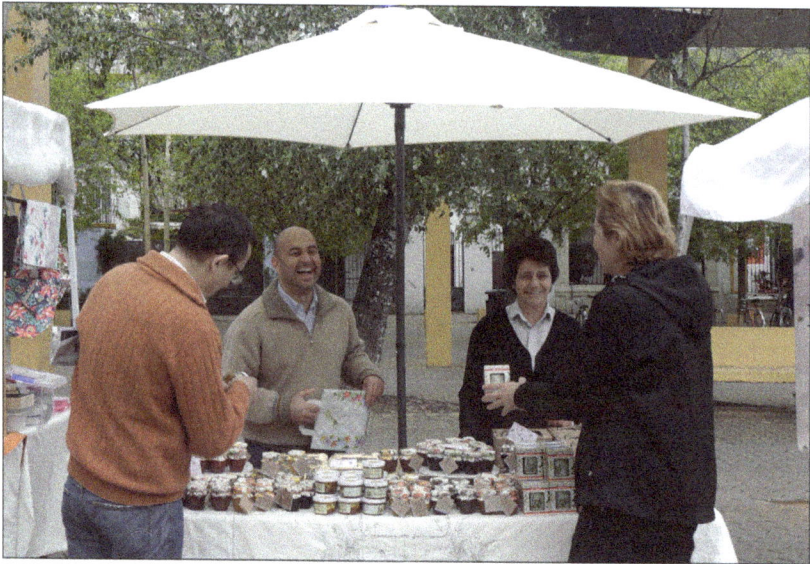

Fig. 1.4 Patricio Vázquez Morán and his sister, Conchi, selling homemade preserves at the Organic Market in Seville (2019).

A savvy businessman, Patricio reports that he now also serves late-night pizza to bring in more young customers. Business is picking up, he says, and he looks forward to the summer tourist season. Patricio hopes the café will become a new hub of activity for the town. What began as a strategy to work from home is now a booming family business. Having the vision, talent, and local support to open a place like the *Café Obrador Valle de la Osa* is one of the best ways to help remedy the trend toward depopulation in the area.

While townspeople are proud of Patricio's work, and he has received an award for being an outstanding entrepreneur in Andalusia, it is typically the tourists who visit Constantina and Seville who are willing to pay for the added environmental and nutritional benefits of locally sourced and high-quality artisanal products. Patricio points out the ironic contrast between his own success and the fact that his brother cannot sell his local milk products to tourists due to the numerous and often costly bureaucratic regulations.

> It is crazy that livestock farmers cannot do the same thing I've done. Rather than sell milk to the co-op and have them re-sell it to industrial markets to make cheese, local farmers, who have cheese recipes and practices that go back generations, should be allowed to sell their own cheeses to local markets without so much expensive and time-consuming bureaucracy blocking their efforts.

Patricio tells the story of the local cheese business his nephew's family attempted to start but that was quickly shut down because of these stringent guidelines. Patricio's husband, who is also present for our interview and very attentive to the discussion, now interjects his own story. Having grown up on a farm that raised cattle, he remarks:

> As for me, I escaped country life as soon as I could; studying set me free.... We need to support people like Juan and Patricio who want to stay in Constantina and other rural areas. We depend on them to maintain our ancient landscapes for the future and our own leisure.

If towns like Constantina are going to survive — the population has dropped 14% (from 7,400 to 6,100) in just ten years — new solutions need to be implemented, and soon. "This is the future," Patricio observes. He and his husband believe that the way to stem rural exodus is to ease regulations and support the production and marketing of local foods, as well as to raise awareness about the added environmental and nutritional benefits these provide. A fair market price for such products would provide rural communities with more economic stability and help them preserve their populations.

Before leaving Constantina and returning to Seville, Mar and I decide to try a short hike along the official droving road that leads directly out of the city center. We soon find that Juan is right: we have to pick our way through deep underbrush for half a kilometer and then come to a field that has encroached so far into the *vía pecuaria* that it is hard to see where the ancient droving route is. After more laborious attempts to stay on a narrow path, the growth is so thick that we recall Juan's description of the droving route: "Not even a mouse can get through." Where once these rights of way were well transited, they are no longer used by shepherds like Juan and Manuel, and they have fallen into deep disuse and, at times, overplanting; the undergrowth has become a fire hazard throughout Spain, especially in these hotter (and, at times, more arid) regions of the Iberian Peninsula. Yet, as we leave Constantina, we cannot help but reflect on how Juan and his brother Patricio have made a successful transition from being the sons of a shepherd who lived on the social and economic margins to local businessmen who enjoy their chosen vocations. This shift has, nevertheless, come at a great, ongoing cost — especially for the shepherd brother — and, as Juan reminds us: "You can't do this alone." Strong family and community support is critical. These two brothers are modeling a future by choosing to stay in their hometowns, adding to local sustainable food production, and owning their own businesses and land.

A mixture of old traditions and new beginnings permeate the stories heard in Constantina and the precariousness of life in this small Andalusian town. Although Juan believes in general that the hours "just aren't worth it," he is still dedicated to his chosen vocation and enjoys the learning it affords him. After completing these interviews with Juan, and later other shepherds and landowners, I began to understand the challenges of personal sacrifice, economic viability, new levels of paperwork, poor land, and deteriorating access to droving routes as some of the many roadblocks to traditional pastoralism in Andalusia. But I also see hope as a few young people take the profession in new directions and a larger system of support emerges.

Updates and Conclusion

Several years later, in November 2021, I check back in with Juan by phone. We are a year and a half past the onset of the global COVID-19 pandemic that rocked the world. He reports that his family became nearly destitute when the main buyer of his animals' meat and milk stopped buying from one day to the next. Juan had nowhere to sell these products; the milk went bad, and he still had to feed his 150 animals daily. Markets crashed for shepherds' products, as we will see in interviews below, but, in most cases, they bounced back quickly when science had swiftly proven that coronavirus could not be transmitted through animal products. Shepherds suddenly became "essential workers" who were depended on by local supply chains. In Juan's case, however, the situation took longer to bounce back. When his in-laws fled the stricken city of Madrid to stay with Juan's family, they unwittingly brought the COVID virus with them. Juan himself fell ill. Being an honorable man, he told his buyer. Even though he reminded the buyer that milk could not spread the disease, the buyer refused any form of contact for a drop off and cancelled the contract. "It was a dirty trick," Juan says, and we hear the hardship still on the tip of his tongue.

> It hit us hard, really, really hard. We were on the brink of tears. Thank God we're alive, but it hit us really bad because the animals have to eat every day. You have to pay the bills. But you can always find friends and a little bit of help.

Juan and Manoli closed up the house in town and moved to the country. Friends helped them get through the period, loaning things they hardly could afford to loan. I cannot help but see a parallel. Juan, the son of a shepherd whose family had all their belongings destroyed by fire and survived because the support of the shepherd community, has himself survived a different disaster, again with the help of a local community. The continuing precarity of the profession (along with an ongoing stigma of it as unsanitary) is still present despite national campaigns promoting pastoralism as both a treasured patrimony and the key to a sustainable future.

Notably, just a week before our call, more than eighteen months after the pandemic, the buyer who canceled his contract asked to purchase

Juan's products again. Juan flatly refused. With the loosening of government regulations on local cheesemaking and sales over the prior year, Juan had found other markets and now sells all of his cheeses and milk directly to consumers through home deliveries. What began as a crisis has turned into a more profitable business — a middleman no longer cuts into Juan's profits.

Next, I check in with Patricio, who, as an adept businessman, was able to pivot to a carry-out menu for his cafeteria when the pandemic hit. In fact, he is still growing his business and plans now to open a rural hotel that will honor Constantina's pastoral history, where visitors can experience nature and develop a keener awareness of local landscapes and ecology. He has been granted a license to convert an old army building located at the highest point of the Sierra Norte de Sevilla into a hotel with a restaurant and a farm school. His nephew, who now has a few animals, wants to leave his trucking job to make a full-time living raising goats. The nephew plans to establish a small livestock farm on the land adjoining the hotel, tend goats, offer rural tours of the farm's sustainable practices, and provide fresh milk and meat for his uncle Patricio's restaurant. Together, these enterprises can bring employment to Constantina by expanding markets for local products. They plan to educate tourists from larger cities in the area about the role of pastoralism in the countryside. No one in the family is interested in reviving the transhumant practices of their ancestors for themselves, but they are finding new ways to keep extensive grazing going. As Patricio observes, they are finding their own way of passing the legacy from one generation to the next. Juan and his wife, Manoli, Patricio, their sister, the nephew and his wife, are all finding ways to stay in Constantina and keep alive the traditional forms of production as well as the products themselves.

In June 2022, I returned to Constantina one last time to share a draft of *A Country of Shepherds* with Juan and Patricio. Ever the great host, Patricio and his sister Coronada turned the visit into a delicious early summer meal of fresh tomatoes pureed into a cold soup called *salmorejo*, pig cheek, and a sampling of their in-house marmalades and Juan's fresh goat cheeses. As we were finishing our meal, yet another family member, Patricio and Juan's niece-in-law Vanesa and her youngest daughter, Paola, stop by. In her 30s and energetic, Vanesa explains how, as a result of the 2008 recession, her husband (Patricio's nephew Juan Carlos) lost his job as a highly trained carpenter. To make ends meet, he started as a truck driver transporting goods across Europe. After years of this grueling work and being on the road much of the week, they devised a plan to raise goats that would allow him to stay in Constantina. Although neither Vanesa nor Juan Carlos had any experience in raising livestock, three years before our meeting they bought three goats with their savings. Now their native *Florida Sevillana* goat herd has grown to 120 goats. If all goes well with birthing season, Vanesa continues, they will reach 200 by fall — the magic number needed to establish an *explotación*, a herd size which makes them eligible for substantial government subsidies. Once that happens, Vanesa's husband will quit his driving job and work full-time on the farm. Vanesa laughs as she describes the steep learning curve and the five or six days a week she works hands-on to manage its operation while Juan Carlos earns the necessary capital to grow their investment. She tells us about spending nights out in the rain tracking down sick goats, liberating goats caught in wire fences, milking a hundred goats by hand when the machine broke down, and aiding in difficult births — all stories of sacrifices made for this profession that parallel Juan's own. She laughs now, saying:

> It's very hard, and I've shed a lot of tears.... the goats can be really sweet, and really mischievous and wild. I've got enough to write a book. But now I just have to laugh.

Her own "book" about pastoralism, she notes, also includes what she has gained as a person from doing this hard work:

> I'm super happy. I've gotten into shape in the country. I'm nervous sometimes, and being in the country relaxes me. It's another world. And it gives me another outlet as a mother.

She likes the physical nature of shepherding and having her own work outside of the home. Vanesa's nine-year-old daughter Paola now jumps into the conversation, enthusiastically listing all the pets she gets to have now that they have a country life. Besides four cats, a dog, and several rats, Paola has her own goat that she likes to ride.

Fig. 1.5 Caring for their growing herd of *cabras floridas sevillanas* are Juan Carlos Vázquez Morán (2022); Vanesa Pablo Fernández (2022); their daughter Paola (2022).

The family's new venture, Vanesa emphasizes, requires dedication and the understanding that "you need to be always looking out for the animals and aware of the time implications," as well as the need for a sense of ownership in pastoralism. "It has to be your project," she insists. She and her husband developed a five-year plan to expand their herd to a sustainable level. Having a personal investment in pastoralism helps support you when the risks are overwhelming, and the situations are volatile. Just last month, for example, they had to find new pastureland for their goats because the owner of their existing pasture decided to repurpose it for housing horses instead. Enlisting Patricio's help, Vanesa and Juan Carlos then asked permission from city hall to graze their goats for a month on city land just up the hill from Patricio's shop. The city accepted, wanting both to support a new business venture in Constantina and to have the land cleaned by the herd. As we talk, she points to their goats, which are visible from the terrace. Next month, the herd will move to a higher elevation — an elevation above which all land is public — but they are still searching for a longer-term solution until they can open their agrotourism hotel at the old military installation near town. It will have plenty of room for grazing, a rural hotel with great vistas, and the separate areas required by law for making cheeses for market. Access to pastureland and a good business plan go hand-in-hand, remarks Patricio, who now chimes in. He explains that any strategy should always evaluate the "payoff" of investing in expensive machinery if the work can be done easily by hand at first and, also, should always include efforts to sell directly to the consumer with no middleman involved. These two precepts have worked for Patricio, as he reminds us: "My father was a shepherd, and I didn't inherit anything. I started from zero.... You have to start bit by bit." This family's observations encapsulate many of the issues and trends in pastoralism now: the challenges of a changing economy in a global market balanced against the new opportunities for direct-to-consumer marketing and increased demand for agrotourism. Even still, the support of a strong, multi-generational family network cannot be overestimated.

Fig. 2.1 The town of Zahara de la Sierra, Cádiz (2017).

2. Teacher of Tradition: Pepe Millán and Family (Zahara de la Sierra, Parque Natural Sierra de Grazalema, Cádiz)

That's why I've collaborated with a variety of people... because you can see what's written down, or your grandchild or your great grandchild can see it. These rural traditions aren't written down, and that's what we're losing.

Pepe Millán

My idea is for all of us to change how we do things; to get rid of the middlemen and make direct sales to the consumer.

Rita Millán Luna

Overview

Chapter 1, on Juan Vázquez Morán, illustrates how transhumance in many cases is transitioning over time to an extensive grazing model in which shepherds own their livestock and family members look to other ways to develop markets for their products. In this chapter, we meet the livestock professional (*ganadero*) Pepe Millán, who first took up shepherding in the 1960's out of economic necessity. Today, he owns his own farm, grazes his animals on common land within the nature reserve (*parque natural*), and teaches his vocation to others. Pepe and his family raise goats and sheep native to Cádiz, and their story showcases how an integrated landscape, people, and animals can lead to a successful livelihood, even in a region not well suited to agriculture.

https://doi.org/10.11647/OBP.0387.02

As I get to know Pepe, I realize that he understands his animals to a profound extent and wants to share his passion with everyone around him. A dedicated shepherd, he believes in the old ways — the same methods for success that got him to where he is now. Disapproving of young people who don't have a connection with the land or even any understanding of where their food comes from, he laments: "it's not like it used to be." This observation has served as a catalyst for Pepe to share widely his traditional knowledge of pastoralism. He is devoted to maintaining the genetic purity of species native to his region, breeds developed over centuries to adapt to the steep, rocky landscape. He raises *Payoya* dairy goats (considered endangered), as well as *Merina de Grazalema* sheep on his farm nestled into the boundaries of the Parque Natural Sierra de Grazalema. For Pepe, the land, native breeds, and his own native knowledge of the mountainous pasturelands are inextricable. Animal varieties bred for the region, good shepherd dogs, and a shepherd with intimate knowledge of the ravines and outcroppings of the landscape fit together like a puzzle.

Pepe's dedication to and hope for the future has recently brought him wider recognition and a second chance to fulfill an early dream to be a teacher. For nearly a decade, Pepe has mentored students at the *Escuela de Pastores de Andalucía*, teaching new entrepreneurs and shepherds at the school crucial skills for the profession. He has also collaborated with the University of Seville on a documentary, which caught the attention of the celebrity TV show *Volando voy*. Recognition for his work as a mentor and teacher helps to buoy Pepe's sense of a mission with his work. In the case that follows, we watch Pepe in action as a master shepherd-*ganadero* and hear about his mentoring. We also glimpse the life of his daughter, Rita, who is working on the farm during our visit and reveals the struggles ahead for someone of her generation.

The Visit: Guardians of Tradition and Ecosystems

A well-published scholar-activist in the extensive grazing movement, Dr. Yolanda Mena, encouraged me to call Pepe. On my first try, he is out in the pastures, and the signal keeps dropping. I call again in the evening when he is back home. Like Juan Vázquez, he immediately extends an invitation to visit him at the farm. On the appointed day, María del Mar and I leave Seville, once again at dawn, this time heading to the Sierra de Grazalema in the Province of Cádiz. As we turn onto a road that narrows and winds through the Sierra and around one final deep curve, Zahara de la Sierra comes almost magically into view. A car full of English tourists has pulled over to photograph the white-washed village tucked into the shade of a commanding outcropping. A fourteenth-century frontier fortress perches on top of the highest peak. Verdant grass speckled with the reds, purples, and yellows of April poppies, lupine, and mustard line the shore of El Gastor, the deep blue reservoir at its base. We pass a shepherd herding a few dozen sheep on the side of the road, leave the lane that climbs into the picturesque historic town center, and turn onto to the gravel road that leads into the Sierra de Grazalema's Natural Park, an area recognized as an important biosphere reserve by UNESCO. The road narrows further and begins to bottom out from the abundant spring rains, so we tuck our car into a niche carved into the limestone outcropping and walk the rest of the way. Following a trail through oak groves, olive groves, and the brushlands of Mediterranean riverbank forests in Cádiz's Garganta Verde, we easily hike the last kilometer to the Millán farm, which stands out on a rocky plateau in between the limestone ravines and riverbanks.

The busy daily morning work routine is in full swing when we arrive. The family raises 350 *Payoya* goats for their milk and 250 *Merina de Grazalema* sheep that also must be milked and put to pasture. But there is a bit of drama this morning: when the border collies return with the family's goats, ten are missing. While Pepe's wife, Isabel, and their two adult children begin moving goats into stalls equipped with machines for milking, Pepe swiftly grabs his shepherd's staff, whip, and binoculars. He whistles for his dogs and heads back over the mountain to bring back the missing goats. It is a rigorous hike through the *monte mediterráneo*, a deep and rocky terrain filled with brushlands of carob, wild olive, and lentisk trees and bushes. But even at 57, Pepe still has strong, fast legs.

Fig. 2.2 Pepe Millán (2019) and his farm in the Parque Natural Sierra de Grazalema (2019).

Later, when the wayward goats have been brought back and milked, Pepe and Isabel funnel them through a series of gates into the barn; the only sound is the clank-clunk of metal gates being opened and closed. Then Pepe, stationed by the barn door opening to the pastures, begins rapping a series of patterned signals with his staff against the metal barn door and adds a few verbal commands. Like Juan, Pepe is fluent in a rapidly disappearing language of communication with his dogs, sheep, and goats. Observing him in action is akin to watching an accomplished artist perform a highly choreographed event.

Isabel, who is positioned in the back barn, begins nudging goats toward the door, silently fanning them with the traditional, large, and palm-shaped fan woven out of reeds. The air fills with a chorus of *cencerros*, the variety of bells worn by certain individual goats that aid the shepherd in determining, simply by the sounds, where the herd is located — and even in moving them about with the aid of well-trained dogs. We are witnessing a traditional practice essential to the shepherd's livelihood, finely tuned over centuries and still performed daily. Movements, sounds, and smells permeate the scene. This is an art form that a camera can hardly capture.

When the last goat is out, Isabel returns to the kitchen, and Pepe follows the goats, moving easily through the boulder-studded path to his lookout post. He picks up a sturdy branch — now turned into a walking cane — and hands it to us as we follow him to a perch overlooking the deep ravine to the stream below. He points to a smooth deep rock wedged into the steep hillside and invites us with a good-natured joke: "Go ahead and sit in the rocker. You'll be more comfortable there." He leans easily on his staff, surveying his land and the Parque Natural as he begins his story about becoming a shepherd. Suddenly, he emits a long, loud clear whistle that echoes back from the hills across the valley and shouts: "Dale! Dale!" (C'mon!). A series of a short, a couple long, and one very long "hidooo" follow. Then, a moment of silence. A second loud-yet-whisper-toned whistle and another command: "Pst! *Oye!* Candela! Come here! That's right!" We hear a bark from below but see no dog. "Go!" Pepe listens again. The chorus-like song of the goats' *cencerro* bells leaving the barn is now a distant murmur. "Hear that?" Pepe asks. A raspy, muted bell faintly sounds. With his experienced ear, Pepe can tell that the lead goat has not reached the river about a kilometer away. Four more distinct whistles and several more commands. Silence again. Another whistle. Another silence. We hear nothing, but Pepe insists: "Hear the little tinkling bell?" That sound signals that the last goat has reached its destination, where the herd will graze the rest of the day and spend the night until milking time tomorrow morning. In a poetic language, Pepe compares the sounds of these traditional bells to the strings of a guitar: each has its own distinct sound.

> Most people see the specialized *cencerro* bells on the goats and sheep, and they don't have any idea what they are. If you pay a little attention, you'll hear two kinds of *cencerro*s, one's a little bigger and one's smaller. Did you hear that *cencerro*? It's the one the goat's wearing. Did you hear the deeper, raspier one? And the little, tiny one? Right now, they're all up in the corner, you can barely hear them. Did you hear the bigger sound? It's like a guitar string. Each one has its own sound. The *cencerro* bells are telling me where the animals are and where they're going. And, in the mornings, when I head out for the sheep, I hear the *cencerro*s, and I know each one is going to a certain place. And then something happens: the sheep's bell sounds a certain way, the goats' another, and the cows' have even another sound because sheep eat and move one way, and goats eat and move another.

Without moving from his command post overlooking the valley, Pepe has orchestrated the movement of 350 goats as they make their way down the ravine. The intricate call-and-response ritual and joint effort of shepherd, dogs, and goats takes less than twenty minutes. One dog returns briefly, and Pepe nods, "Look at this one. He's tired. He's worked hard this morning." He explains the difference between moving sheep and goats, as well as the all-important natural surroundings:

> Sheep are easier to herd in the open field. But then, here, inside the barn, goats are easier to herd than sheep. With sheep, if you tell them "Go," they might go in, but then one sheep will try, and you'll see it can't get through. So, you'll try to grab it, but it won't like that. Then the others will want to get by and go in, and that's when you'll have real chaos on your hands. The only way to herd them is with dogs.

The *Payoya* goats, he explains with pride:

> are native to the Sierra de Grazalema; they are adapted to this terrain, raised in this area. They fend for themselves very well. The Sierra requires skills that don't come easy to everyone. The land will condition you and the animals. I grew up in the Sierra, and I've learned about all its special bends, ravines..., all the things that will trip you up. If you're not familiar with the Sierra, it won't let you make a living from doing this.

We realize we have been privileged to witness an ancient practice that happens every day, 365 days a year, shifting only as the seasons change. Now, with the goats in place, Pepe can settle in again, more comfortable leaning on his staff than sitting on the rocker he has offered us. Before returning to his story, however, Pepe insists that he is not the "protagonist." He wants to tell us his story so this way of life, this knowledge is not lost. "That's why I've collaborated with a variety of people... because you can see what's written down, or your grandchild or your great grandchild can see it. But these rural traditions aren't written down, and that's what we're losing." He is part of a millennia-long tradition of pastoralism that has molded and preserved the biodiversity of this natural area, which includes the engendered *abies pinsapo*, a rare Spanish fir that has survived here since prehistoric times. Shepherds are now being called "environmental forest rangers," he reports, suggesting an expansion of stewardship to include not only fauna but flora. At heart, Pepe sees himself as a caretaker for the legacy of this ancient practice and rural landscapes. He doesn't want to see it lost.

Pepe's entire life story is literally visible from this strategic vantage point. He points out a house on a hill facing us, some five kilometers away as the crow flies, but over an hour away along the Sierra's winding roads. "That's where I began," he says plainly. Raised by a single mother and his maternal grandmother in the 1960s, Pepe grew up knowing the threat of hunger and how his grandmother's goat (and the high nutritional value of its milk) kept his belly full.

> I was raised without a father, and I was left on my own like a ball thrown out on the field. It's not like it is now. When I grew up, if they saw you doing something wrong, they'd slap you first and ask questions later. I lived with my mother, but it wasn't like it is now. First off, there was no food. So, when you wanted to earn money to buy food, you had to work for it and spend more hours than are on a clock earning it. When I was a boy, I was in a country school that's back behind that hill. Do you remember that man that was out there with the sheep? Well, that man's son and I went to the country school. And at eight years old I knew how to multiply and divide, but now I can't even remember how to do all that. They gave me a scholarship.
>
> If I'd gone away to school, I would've had to pay, and my mother said no. So, I couldn't go. There was just no way. If my father had been there, I would've been able to depend on both of them for support. The economy might not have been that good, but maybe something else would have happened because some people from my generation did go away to school. Not many, but some went to get an education. Not to be lawyers and such, but they went to teaching schools and became teachers.
>
> After I turned eight, I didn't go anywhere else. I grew up here, in that house [he points to the house in the distance]. Ever since I was a boy, a little boy, I've always been around animals. I even fed from a goat like a kid! That's the truth 'cause I like milk. Back in those days, we didn't have yogurt; we didn't have a lot of things. So, at least I had my belly full, although it was just milk. But it was goat's milk, and they've shown it to be one of the best foods there is.
>
> I learned to love goats 'cause of my mother's mother, my *abuela*. She had a goat. She died with a goat in her bed that was keeping her warm. She loved living in the country, and I keep that tradition alive because of my *abuela*. I've got cousins who've retired and others who've already passed on. They worked with livestock. I've got a brother who worked with livestock when he was a child, and a nephew too, but not now.

Pepe recalls his upbringing with a mixture of fond nostalgia and clear-eyed acknowledgement of the poverty-stricken reality of rural Andalusia during his youth. Then, he repeats a message we have heard from many shepherds: others have left the profession because it is relentless, requires great personal sacrifices, and is still largely unprofitable. He notes that few family members or friends have chosen to continue as farmers.

> Here's the thing. Either you like it, or you don't. Let's just say, you can like it a little, but to be here where we are, you have to really like it. If not, forget it. This is 365 days a year, 24 hours a day, one day after another, one year after another. Me, thirty years ago I was selling sheep for more than they sell them today. I've stayed with it because I've liked it ever since I was a boy, and I had the dream of having my own herd of goats.

For Pepe, though, both economic necessity and his love for his vocation have kept him at this work. Every time he has left shepherding — for mandatory military service and, later, for work in France and Switzerland because jobs in Spain were scarce — he has returned to start from scratch again with just two goats. Each time he slowly rebuilt his herd, always looking out for new opportunities. He explains that after decades of foiled attempts to keep make a living, he was able to secure a loan, buy his own herd, and graze it on land he had rights to.

> When I did my military service, I already had sixty of my own goats. You started your service when you were older back then. I was twenty-one. I came back when I was twenty-two. I was in for longer than most, eighteen months in total. After that, I worked a couple of years, and I had to sell the goats when I went away. I kept two goats. And when I got married, one of those bad spells hit like this economic crisis that stopped people cold. I went to France and Switzerland because there was no work. Finally, over there at the foot of Prado de Rey [he points to a house], some land with goats became available. So, I picked up and went. And over in that house, there was a man who helped me take care of the two goats while I was working outside of the country. Once I returned, I'd spend the weekends working with him, after I had gotten seven or eight goats. I was on a farm for four years, working with a herd of goats. Then I looked for a place to share half with someone because I said to myself: "I'm running this farm that's not mine." After that, I spent the next thirteen years sharing half of what I earned.
> I got a loan to buy a herd of goats, and I went to another farm. Then things with the owner began to get complicated. So, I put the goats up for sale. I had a big herd. At first, I had 600. Then, I sold 200 and kept 400. I said to myself: "400's a lot," so if anyone had wanted to buy 200 of the

goats I still had, I would've sold them and kept the last 200. And that's how things stayed.

Often, Pepe's attempts to establish his own farm were foiled by greedy employers, an all-too-familiar theme we heard earlier from Juan Vázquez. Many landowners do not respect the shepherds who care for the proprietor's animals alongside their own, nor do they offer fair prices for grazing rights on their land. Here, Pepe tells us of a landowner who demanded payment of half of Pepe's goats in exchange for grazing them on his land. While Pepe describes the often-contentious relationships between farm owners and workers, he also sees himself as fortunate. His entrepreneurial skill as a shepherd and the community's high regard for him, as well as his family's contributions, have helped him turn adversity into opportunity more than once. Shortly after the abrupt change in the contract with the landowner, another local shepherd who was retiring sold his 70-hectare farm on the edge of the Parque Natural to Pepe. With the help of a local banker, Pepe invested his life savings into the land and went deeply into debt to establish his own goat farm, where he has now been for nearly twenty years. He recalls the events leading up to his big decision — and the heavy interest rate he was charged.

> I couldn't come to an agreement with the owner. So, I told a cousin of mine who came through here, and my cousin told the owner I was interested. I said to myself, "Pepe, don't do something crazy, but if you can get a reasonable deal, go ahead. Give it your all." And that's why I'm here. I had the dream, and I worked hard too, but someone threw me a lifeline. We got this place going for four million pesetas, my hard work, and my wife's. And two children.
>
> It would be like you sitting right there and asking right now, listen, you want this jacket? You've got to give me 1,000 Euros. But then you say, I don't have it right now. Well, then, I'll have you sign this paper that states that tomorrow, the day after, whenever, you'll pay me. That's just how it happened. That man knew me, and I had done him favors without asking for anything in return.

Despite being charged an exorbitant interest rate of 18%, Pepe still feels lucky: in many places such a large loan would never have been offered. Banks normally consider the risk too great with a livestock farmer who has no guaranteed income or equity. With the loan and family's hard work, they now own a house in nearby Zahara de la Sierra while still spending days, especially in the busy spring season, on the farm. But the steep interest rate on the mortgage weighs heavily on their profits and constricts the family's dreams of expanding the business or taking vacations. The ever-increasing cost of "middlemen" impacts the bottom line for the family, as he comments wryly: "There are a ton of people who make a living off of what we pay." Prices for meat have hardly kept pace with inflation, and a family now needs at least 200 goats and government subsidies to make a basic living.

> I came here fifteen years ago. I used to sell young goats for 500 pesetas, which is three euros now. And I've got a few young goats that I still have to sell. Very few, but now they'll only pay two and a half. You see, I sell to you, you sell to some other woman, and that woman sells it to the consumer. And when it gets to the consumer, that's where the real money comes from. So, you have to be happy with half, otherwise the consumer won't have it, and I won't get paid. There's a family here in Zahara that's been waiting all their life, wanting a little herd of goats. For example, in town, they had a corral; and with thirty or fifty goats, the family could get by. Now they'll need at least 200, and they have to be good goats. Not to mention how much land they'll need for 200 goats. You've got to get subsidies. If they don't give you subsidies, forget it. There are a ton of people who make a living off of what we pay.

In addition to paying for the farm building and land that he owns (along with the bank, as he never fails to add), Pepe rents land in the public pasturelands from the Andalusian authorities. Every five years an auction is held, and a point system determines, at least in part, the outcome. Pepe is ranked highly because he earns points for living onsite and raising the highly prized native *Payoya* goats and *Merina de Grazalema* sheep. In the end, however, he says with resignation, money usually wins out, but now there is a new, bittersweet new reality: fewer people want to use the land for shepherding because there are fewer shepherds, and so there is less competition. The number of bidders has dropped dramatically in the last five years.

Economic constraints frame every aspect of the Millán family operation, starting with his family's inability to pay room and board so that Pepe could study to become a teacher, and later to pay for the needs of his own growing family. Both financial hardships kept him in shepherding as a career, but "it's cost me a lot," he repeats several times. Later, when we talk to Pepe's wife, Isabel, she quietly but firmly states:

"I don't like working with animals. I do it to support Pepe. I wasn't raised like this. I was raised in town. I was an orphan living with my aunt and uncle," an orphan without family resources. After Rita and Pepe married and unemployment was still rampant in Andalusia, they decided to begin a farm life together so that Pepe would not have to work abroad.

In the early 2000s, as the economy began to improve in southern Spain, both of Rita and Pepe's children left the farm to work in Andalusia's booming construction market — one as a construction worker and the other as an administrator. But with the 2008 global economic crisis, the industry came to a screeching halt and remained stagnant for nearly a decade thereafter. While Pepe still hopes that his children will be able to carry on the family legacy, he sees the challenges that continue to arise. People want and expect more now than when he grew up, when poverty was widespread, and it was enough just to "eat and that was it." Despite his established herd of goats and flock of sheep, land, buildings, and access to the public pasturelands, he repeats the common phrase we have heard from other shepherds: "It's just not worth it." Increasingly strict and costly government regulations mix with the tantalizing promise of new sources of aid, but obtaining this support is often difficult for a working farmer with little time or money to hire professionals to help understand and apply for these subsidies. In particular, he laments the challenges that his daughter faces when contemplating how to make a future for herself in extensive grazing.

> It would be a good solution of course, but you have to get everything together, and the government gives you a world of trouble. There's not a lot of work, so for people who want something, the government will first tell you they'll give you the money; that there's money reserved for new entrepreneurs; and who knows what else, etcetera. But, when they get involved, they just give you the run-around: "This has to go here; now you have to do that; you have to come here." My daughter's been in the middle of doing the never-ending paperwork for quite some time now. If things go well, she'll be able to spend a year and a half with no problems, maybe two years, doing something half-way legal and without worries. But then, sometimes, when you have almost everything ready, they'll say, "No, this doesn't work; you can't do that because who knows why." It's sad because she likes working with animals. She gets it. You have to understand it, and she likes it. She has the dream that she can work for herself. That's why she's hung in there.

Things are much harder now than when he began, and people have lent him money simply because they knew him and the cheeses he sold:

> Man, it's difficult on two fronts: they won't give you a loan now unless you have ten times more money than what they're going to give you. If she had started when we came here fifteen years ago, it would be different.

Ganadero and Teacher

But rather than delve further into the difficult reality of his profession and his struggles to help his children, Pepe now refocuses the conversation. From the same vantage point where we can see the rustic farmhouse where he was born, Pepe points to another farm that tells a different story, a story of Pepe as a teacher (though not as the public-school teacher he once thought he might be). For the last several years, a young shepherd has lived on this farm. Pepe mentored the aspiring shepherd, teaching him the art of listening to the *cencerro* bells, milking, training dogs, sanitary regulations, reading the pasturelands' temperament, and, critically, helping him gain access to land to graze his animals. Today, the young man is making a living raising livestock like his teacher. Pepe is quietly proud of his work, and there is now someone to carry on the tradition who lives just across the valley.

Pepe's work as a mentor has grown steadily since he first signed up in 2010 for the local-government initiative to pair well-established shepherds like him with students in their then newly formed *Escuela de Pastores* (Shepherd School). He speaks now with both pride and conviction, comparing the importance of teaching a new generation of shepherds to teaching people how to drive:

> This way of life is getting lost. It's like getting your driver's license. If someone doesn't teach you how to drive, you'll never learn. You can watch cars go by all day long, but you won't learn that way.... People need to see the benefit in the sacrifice. It's very nice. You get here, and you say, "This is really nice."
>
> I go there [to the *Escuela de Pastores*] when they call me. I give a talk on whatever they ask, and then, I bring them up here too. In fact, I'm the one who's had the most students every year since the first class came through.

Every year. Since the school began, they've come here every year. There are some who want to have an *explotación* [a herd large enough to attract subsidies]. I see a future for some, yes, but not for others because some just come to spend a little time here, like they're going on a field trip or to the disco. On the whole, the percentage of students I work with is more positive than negative. In fact, right now there's a student who's working up there in the *monte*.

Every spring he lectures on goat farming at the school — as well as his specialty, the art of *cencerro* bells — and then hosts students-in-residence at the farm, mentoring them for several weeks of hands-on training. Although he sees a future in some trainees, he also recalls the first one he hosted, who spent two months as an intern with his family and treated the time like "he was going to the disco." With more interest among youth today — and more rigorous screening by the program leaders — recent applicants have been very good, he remarks. Both he and the students have benefitted from rebalancing the time spent between classroom theory and on-the-job practice. His current mentee is from Madrid, and even though he admits she was "a little lost" in her first week, things are going well because "she really wants to do what she's doing."

Even as he describes the hardship of his profession, Pepe exudes a clarity of purpose and commitment that are reflected in the urgency he feels to continue to teach others. This drive to teach does not only cover the training of new shepherds but also the raising of general awareness surrounding the environmental and nutritional impact of land use, animals, and food sources. The *ganadero*-teacher acknowledges that he keeps going because of an ignorance he perceives in city folk.

Someone who's studying in Seville graduates; they're 24 or 25 years old and don't have a family working in a rural area. They like the idea of country life. They've even seen goats or sheep as they are herded down the droving routes, but they don't have any idea about what these animals are really like. The goats go by, and they don't know if they're wearing a *cencerro* bell or why they're wearing it, or if the udders have milk or not; if some goats are bigger or smaller. They have no idea. That's for sure. They're not going to value this. It's something that practically no one knows about.

He spends hours that he can scarcely afford to talk to people, even a curious "*norteamericana*" (North American woman) as they liked to call me, and educate them about traditional shepherding practices. Last week, for example, Dr. Yolanda Mena came to the farm with her students to learn about the Millán family operation and the high nutritional value of goat's milk. Pepe was surprised at how little young people, even these educated university students, know about their food sources, farming life, and the countryside in general.

> The main objective is for people to learn what we do. I've been surprised to find out that a ten- or twelve-year-old child comes here and doesn't know that goats give milk. This child thought cheese came directly from the big *supermercado* [supermarket]. You're at the University of Seville. You know Yolanda Mena .... Well, she has been here, and she was even here when the goats were about to give birth, during the birthing season when we get new offspring. She just said she wanted to come sometime; she gave me a date; and she came. She was here on a Saturday or a Sunday, and she went back excited about what she had seen and eager to explain it to her class. And you know, we're not talking about children anymore. These people are eighteen years old or older. We're talking about men and women.

Pepe continues to broaden his educational reach through mass media. Several years ago, he allowed a filming crew to make a documentary that featured his work and conveyed the high nutritional value of goat's milk, *La buena leche* (2015). Co-sponsored by the Andalusian local government and the University of Seville, it showcases the family's daily routines and explains the ecological and nutritional benefits of the Millán family's traditional method of raising goats. Years later, he reached a much broader audience when he was invited to participate in the popular TV series *Volando voy* (2018). He joined the show's celebrity host Jesús Calleja and journalist Mercedes Milá not for the notoriety but, rather, to draw attention to climate change and "raise people's awareness about the small collective acts they can do to help preserve the environment." The episode focuses on the Parque Natural de la Sierra de Grazalema where Pepe's family works, focusing on the threats to the ancient *pinsapo* fir trees. The show highlights the importance that Pepe's extensive grazing plays in the ecosystem. His animals clean the pasturelands of underbrush, fertilize it, and make it easier for the rare Spanish fir to thrive. As Pepe interacts with the media stars, his keen sense of humor enlivens a lesson: as he shows the host how to milk a goat, he has him begin by first practicing on Pepe's fingers! His playful personality and inspirational teaching reached thousands of viewers. As Mar and I learn about the delicate ecosystem of the pasturelands, we see a parallel between the endangered *pinsapo* of the Sierra de Grazalema and Pepe's own guardianship of the land — both are vestiges of the past, and both need our support to survive.

> They need to know what they're eating and where it comes from. It's like the chicken you buy from the rotisserie shop. It can be raised in a month, a month and a half, and it's ready to eat. But for one of these chickens running around here, the little bitty ones, it'll take a year at least before you can make chicken stew. For the chicken to grow to the size you'll need, it'll take even more time for you to make a more-or-less good chicken stew. You'll need a year.

Now Pepe turns the tables on our interview, with one of his characteristic teaching moments. He asks us: "If you had to move goats, how would you do it?" Luckily, his mobile phone rings before we can answer, and we are off the hook. The organizers for this year's *Escuela de Pastores* are calling to schedule a lecture on *cencerro* bells and to send another set of interns to the farm. Pepe's dedication to his art and desire to pass it along make him in high demand in the emerging world of new pastoralism training.

It is time for the mid-day meal, and we head back to the farmhouse. As we first pass through the milking barn, Pepe points to the array of traditional *cencerro* bells hanging there and rings the loudest, then the softest. We get one last audiovisual lesson on the artful mechanics of what we witnessed from the hilltop. One last look at the pasturelands we leave behind makes it obvious that no machine could clear this rugged land as well as his herd, and no shepherd, no matter how fit, could climb it as often as needed to graze the animals and still bring them back for milking. The bells and dogs — and the knowledge of how to use them — are crucial (and this, of course, is the answer to his earlier quiz question).

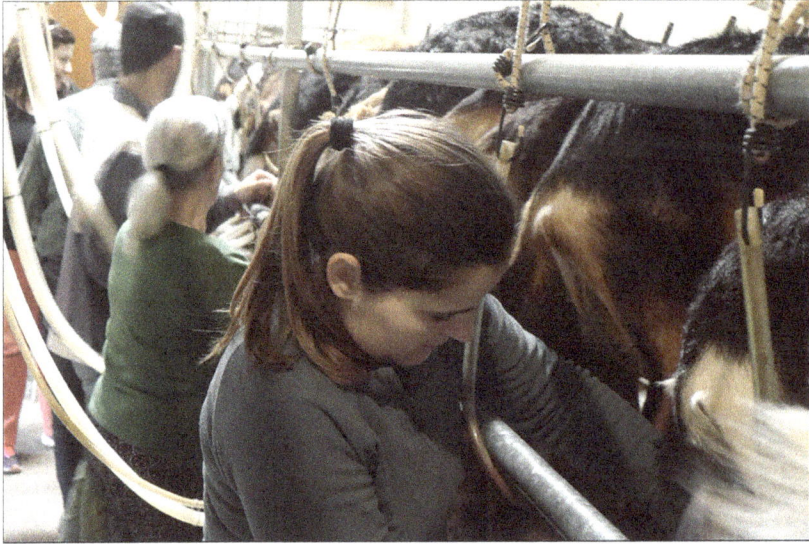

Fig. 2.3 All hands on deck as Pepe and his family work together at milking time (2019).

In Between the Changing World of Pastoralism: Rita Soledad Millán Luna

My idea is for all of us to change how we do things; to get rid of the middlemen and make direct sales to the consumer.

Rita Soledad Millán Luna

Although Pepe has good access to the rocky pastures of the mountain, use of the public lands comes often with regulations that restrict many possibilities for making a good living and limits his ability to bring his daughter Rita on board to expand into the popular *Payoyo* cheesemaking business. So, while he is rounding up the wayward goats, his daughter Rita invites us into the farmhouse to tell her own story. As a woman in her thirties, she adds another perspective to this case study. Rita makes clear that she loves working with animals, a love learned early as she worked alongside her father. She recalls a childhood filled with time outside, animals, and never needing anything. She smiles as she recalls how her father even built them a pool. And yet, there were "other things." They never had a vacation, and she grew up being keenly aware of how cruel society, and especially school children, could be in the face of stereotypes about the children of shepherds.

> Well, I remember a nice childhood. The thing about living in the country is that it demands 24-hour-a-day, 365-days-a-year dedication. If you want to have fun, you have to have it in the country. Right now, we're not living here. We're here all day and go to our house in town to sleep. But before, until I was sixteen, we did live in the country, in the real country, the real rural country. Not here. On the other land. We've been here for fifteen years. The other land is on the road from Zahara to Prado del Rey. There we really were in the middle of nowhere.
>
> You see, I like animals, so when I was going to school and I'd come back from doing my homework and everything, I'd go out to be with the animals. We always had to help our parents, that's for sure. And also, that's probably why we know how to do so many things these days.
>
> But, yes, it was good. It's just that there are many things that aren't easy to do. I remember my childhood as very happy. Country life can really be enriching. I don't doubt that, but there are other things that aren't so good, and kids can be cruel. They make fun of you because you come from the country. I haven't had problems, but it's true that kids are very cruel. The truth is that I never had problems because I always really loved living in the country. I had all the animals I wanted. I didn't have any problems. Maybe the other kids couldn't have a dog at home, but I had seven in the country, and cats, and rabbits. But that's because I really like animals. So yes, it was good, I'm happy.
>
> Then there's this, for example, my friends would finish school in the summer, and they'd go to the pool and do other summer activities. I couldn't go. My dad made us a little pool so we could play and such, but it's not the same, and it keeps you from having certain things. You have many other things, and they're very rewarding, but you don't live like the rest of society lives or like children live nowadays. It deprives you of other things. Especially when you're a girl. Later, when you're more mature and conscious about things, you start having your own personality, and you don't really care. But especially when you're a kid, it can be difficult. Yes, children can really be cruel.

Clear-headed and articulate, Rita explains that working as a *ganadero* or *ganadera* was neither her nor her brother's dream. She had left to study and got a job helping to run an office, where she worked for eight years. The job vanished with the economic crisis, and she could hardly pay rent, so she had no choice but to return to the family business. She clearly states, "I went to school so I could have a day off," but in fact

she spent most of her weekends and holidays returning to the farm to
lend a hand.

> I'd ask to take my vacation time when there was more work to do here.
> So, I didn't completely cut ties. My parents have lived their entire lives
> here. When the whole country got into this crisis and everything went
> upside down, I said, "Look, instead of being away from home and not
> in the best of conditions, I'll go back home. I'll have more than enough
> work, and it's work that I like." I'm trying to get ahead and continue what
> my parents have done for so many years.

She is searching for ways to incorporate shepherding into a new life for
herself. She first tried to open a cheese shop, but government restrictions
curtailed that enterprise. Her story illustrates the often-conflicting
policies about extensive grazing. On the one hand, individuals
can apply for funds to clear, fertilize, and promote biodiversity on
public lands, but, on the other, they are prevented from pursuing
opportunities for expansion and renovation. A growing family can
rarely all stay in the family business. After nearly six often-frustrating
years back on the farm, Rita took on an administrative position in a
farm association that promotes the native *Payoya* goat species that her
family raises. Her goal of building something for herself, of doing
creative and meaningful work, and of amplifying the work that her
father set in place could only be done by working away from the farm
for a few years. Clearly a *ganadera* cannot afford a middle-class lifestyle
without supplemental income.

Rita takes us into a 30m × 25m × 8m cement building attached to the
barn and milking areas. Furnished in a rustic, practical, and appealing
way, this spacious building is set up for a family of four to use as a
base of operations on the rocky pasturelands for up to twelve hours
a day. Red gingham sink skirts brighten the kitchen corner, and the
open cupboards are stocked with spices and preserves. A rustic pine
dining set holds places for four, and a comfortable grey sofa floats in
the middle of the room, separating the kitchen from the facing wall in
which a corner stone fireplace still holds embers from the early-morning
fire. Cast iron pots hang on the hearth. Rita's younger brother, nearly
hidden in the shadow of the chimney, sits on a stool, quietly listening
to his sister.

As we talk, Rita unwraps a checked cloth to reveal a perfectly round white *Payoya* goat cheese. The firm rind surrounds a semi-soft, rich, and tangy cheese. Her voice now bubbles with enthusiasm for the first time as she recites her recipe, which mixes *Payoya* goat milk with *Merina de Grazelema* sheep milk for added richness. In a lively lilt, Rita talks about her hope of developing new markets and revenue by publicizing her gift for making savory goat cheeses on the internet. Rita sums up what would be needed to make a decent living in pastoralism: pacing production of meat, which doesn't keep as long as cheese, and establishing direct sales with no middleman.

> The market for meat, lamb, as well as goat, is down. So, the costs are much higher than just production costs. It's very hard. You have to be on the lookout for subsidies; you have to make sure the animal is fed for enough time in the country; you have to consider many different alternatives so you can meet your bottom line and then some. And even then, it's very, very hard.
>
> One option, which also is my idea, is for all of us to change how we do things; to get rid of the middlemen and make direct sales to the consumer. So yes, then you can make a profit. If not, it's very, very, very hard. It depends on feed prices, if you have a good year. It depends on many, many things, and then, on what they want to pay you.
>
> Nowadays you have to work with the internet. It's easiest, and apart from being easy, it the most economical and fastest as far as costs and many other things. The problem we have in Andalusia and in Cádiz is that we're not aware of what we have. The clients who come from other places tend to understand things better and can be better clients than the ones from around here. So, when you think about selling both meat and cheese, you have to keep that in mind, because the whole online thing is very important.
>
> Also, the products are perishable, and how do you deal with that? Meat is more complicated because, right now, we only have one birthing area for both sheep and goats. So, we have all the births at once because the market we have now demands that. Since we sell wholesale, we have to produce many at one time. If we were the point of final sale, it would be different. We'd have to change how we manage the animals. Instead of having everything all at once, we'd have to always have product ready to sell. We'd have to stagger the breeding and everything else so that you could have meat every two months for market. Your clients need to know that they can buy every two or three months. If you make things clear from the beginning, then there's no problem.

That is, if you're organized. With cheese, you have a little larger margin of time for production because there are different cheeses. Some are aged; some are fresh. With all the different kinds of cheeses, you can play around a bit.

My idea is to plan out how I can arrange to sell meat directly to the consumer because we can't sell milk, cheese, or meat directly. I need to figure out how to do direct sales so that if you came here and you wanted a liter of milk or a lamb or whatever, I'd be able to sell it to you. So, I'm looking into how I can manage all that.

Soon Rita's eyes cloud again with concern about the future. Disillusionment seeps back into her voice as she outlines the hurdles to opening a cheese shop. For one thing, situated in the Parque Natural, the farm must be managed in accord with strict regulations. The family must rely on a generator for electricity as solar panels are prohibited. In addition to needing a better power source, she explains, they would also need a better water source but are not allowed to dig a well. Thus, in order to set up a business, Rita would need to rent a place in town and bring it up to standards that would meet sanitary requirements. In town, however, construction is also limited because of the historic designation given to the downtown area. Echoing not only her father but also other people we have interviewed on all sides of extensive grazing, the situation boils down to a bureaucratic challenge that can easily overwhelm individuals and families working on a relatively small scale.

I reflect on the irony of the French, who buy raw sheep and goat milk from Andalusia to make their world-class cheeses yet whose laws require public institutions serving food to purchase a certain percentage of it from local, organic farmers. As in many parts of the world, people in Spain either cannot afford or are not willing to pay the real cost of good organic milks, meats, and cheeses. If the government changed its regulations, shepherd-farmers might be able to stay in business. As a woman deciding her future, Rita's bottom line is the time-investment. She repeats, "I went to school so I could have a day off," but, now, what she wants is to have her own place and to be able to enjoy it. In slower times, she and her brother could "take turns," but even with all four of them working, there is not enough income to sustain three separate households.

As a young farmer-entrepreneur like her father was, Rita is always looking for ways to move forward. She is tempted by the government subventions offered for new ventures in farming, but she also sees how they are a sensitive subject for her family and often a double-edged sword. Subsidies look attractive, but they can sink you further into debt as you try to meet all the criteria, and they sometimes take up to one year to be approved and released. The system favors people who already have money and time to invest in the lengthy, costly application and certification process.

> The subject of aid is a little delicate. I've learned from the people I work with and others who've shared their experiences with me that it's better to come up with something on your own without any governmental start-up funds. If later you ask for it, fine, but you can't count on it in advance because it changes with the wind. It may or may not happen. There are times when you ask for some start-up, and then, you have to meet certain requirements that end up costing you even more with the assistance than if you didn't request it. There are a lot of factors. This whole topic of aid is a long story. If you can do it without it, all the better. If I can meet all the requirements, fantastic, right? But I don't plan to start out with aid.

As Pepe's wife Isabel begins preparing the family meal, we say goodbye and hike the kilometer back out, taking a last look at the farm as we close the gate to the Parque Natural. We drive another kilometer, and the fairytale image of Zahara de la Sierra comes into view again. Signs point to the historic downtown area with access to shopping and restaurants as well as cycling and hiking routes. I recall Rita's disgust that the famous commercial brand *Queso Payoyo* is in fact not made with 100% milk from *Payoya* goats. A local cheese shop offering the family's authentic local cheese would have a ready-made market for times when the town swells by the thousands in high tourist season.

Fig. 2.4 A Family portrait, Sierra de Grazalema (2019).

Conclusions and Update

Soon after our interview, we learned that Rita took an outside job working for a collective, the Asociación de Criadores de la Raza Caprina Payoya, which helps protect and promote the native goat species the family raises. The daunting reality of regulations and start-up funding had delayed Rita's dream of opening a cheese shop. When we check back with Pepe in fall 2021, however, Rita was back working at the farm and developing local production of cheeses — though mostly by special order, as we saw in Chapter 1 with Juan's family. He also reveals that his own mother worked as a goat herder (*cabrista*) and goat cheese-maker herself as he tells us that Rita has inherited the "gift" for working with the farm animals and producing good cheeses. Nevertheless, and although government regulations eased during the global pandemic, opening a larger cheese shop is still out of reach for her. Instead, Rita dedicates her energies and employs the new skills she acquired in her administrative post to help the family. She learned her way around government forms and regulations and has now applied successfully for CAP farm subsidies. Pepe tells us with a smile that he is very happy with this new division of labor. His daughter is now the family administrator, doing all the paperwork to keep funding and regulations in order.

With Rita back on the farm full-time, Pepe reports that he decided to sell nearly half of his Merino sheep and keep his prize *Payoya* goats. "I'm getting too old for this rough terrain." He admits that his once-strong legs are aging and the deep ravines are more challenging to climb daily. As we talk just a year and a half into the onset of the COVID-19 pandemic, he describes the frightening spring months of 2020. Like Juan Vázquez, Pepe experienced a huge drop in income with plummeting milk and meat prices when the initial global shock paralyzed markets. Fortunately, in Pepe's case, it was a relatively short time before he was recognized as an "essential worker" and enjoyed new respect and a freedom few others had in town. He describes how the local guards stopped everyone, asking for their papers and fining anyone who was moving illegally through town during lockdown. When the same officials saw Pepe, however, they gratefully waved him on through, thanking him for providing milk and meat for the community. If only briefly, the pandemic showed the world that shepherds are truly essential in times of global crisis.

Pepe and his family represent resilience and dedication over the decades of challenges. The shepherd acknowledges that, although he loves working with animals and being his own boss, he might not have chosen this lifepath if he had been born into another socio-economic class. Still, he took what he was given, educated himself on the art of shepherding, and built a business out of it. He has helped to protect a native species and ecosystem, as well as created his own legacy both with the farm itself and with his teaching and mentoring of the younger generation. Pepe had been able to become a successful farmer because of the economic and social structures in place decades ago, when banks still took a chance on small-scale farmers, albeit at a steep cost, and before government subsidies were offered. He is an entrepreneur who has taken great risks to reap modest gains for himself and his family, but he has achieved much larger gains for the surrounding environment and the sustainability of food systems in Andalusia.

We meet Pepe Millán one last time at an outdoor café in May 2022 to show him a draft of the book and get his blessing for publication. As Pepe tries to place us among the dozens of researchers and students that have worked with him, he says it looks good. He then recalls a good-humored and instructive story about one university-trained collaborator. Pepe roguishly asked him: "How many years did you study to learn your trade, to be able to work in the country?" To the collaborator's response of "eight years," Pepe laughed and added "Well, I've studied all my life. And I wasn't taught by a professor or a father, only by watching. You have to watch nature and learn from it. My daughter Rita has that gift too." Pepe chuckles again recalling the man's response: "Well, you got me on that one!" *Ganaderos* like Pepe are natural scientists whose curiosity, patience, and natural intelligence allow them to observe and learn from the complex patterns found in nature. Although his cell phone keeps ringing now, as people at the farm contact him to help with a delivery, he cannot resist a final hands-on lesson. Positioning his finger as though it was the tail of a goat, he demonstrates how in pregnant goats there is a certain point that he can feel to see if the offspring will be male or female. He concludes: "You can study all you want, but you have to watch and learn."

The era in which Pepe could start with two goats and find a local banker willing to gamble on a shepherd with nothing but a good reputation has long passed. Rita wants to make her own contribution through cheesemaking but is still battling roadblocks. Pepe's son still helps with the farm operation, but he also must supplement his income at different times of the year with construction or harvesting local crops like olives. The family continues to sustain what they have built, but it is unclear how much longer this can last. The fundamental question remains: Who will take over for Pepe when he retires, and can it succeed without the support of a whole family system?

In 2018, Pepe confessed "the future looks a bit dark to me," but, in 2022, he is guardedly optimistic. Rita's success in taking advantage of subsidies and new guidelines as well as her willingness to take over part of the family business offer hope. Having hiked some of his land, I wonder more broadly: if no one grazes animals on the land, what will happen to the health of this unique biosphere reserve with its endangered *pinsapo* and fauna, as well as the tourism that protects Zahara from depopulation? The next few years will be telling. In fact, as I later find out, Pepe was featured in the closing session at the *Escuela de Pastores* 2022, "What is the Future of Extensive Grazing?" His story reveals his determination to work hard and invest fully in his career with the hope of passing his knowledge, and perhaps his farm, onto the next generation. I am left with his own words, which he has repeated often "That's why I've collaborated with a variety of people... because you can see what's written down, or your grandchild or your great grandchild can see it. These rural traditions aren't written down, and that's what we're losing". Pepe continues interviewing with people like me to ensure this way of life gets passed along.

Fig. 3.1 A view of the barn and sheep in Sierra de Cardeña y Montoro (2018).

3. Transhumance, Diversification, and New Collaborations: Fortunato Guerrero Lara (Sierra de Cardeña y Montoro [Córdoba] and Sierra de Segura [Jaén])

I've been at this for thirty years, but it's still the same. More new things to do, paperwork, registrations, land problems.... Young people have it really hard. We're fighting with our lives.

Fortunato Guerrero Lara

Organic practices are our future, especially if we want to live in a world that's not so cruel.

Rafael Enríquez del Río

Overview

When I interview Paco Casero, a life-long activist for agrarian reform and the environment, I ask about two key issues in pastoralism today: land usage and generational turnover. Instead of answering me, he just picks up the phone and calls Fortunato Guerrero Lara, a shepherd and land-rights leader who straddles tradition and innovation. After we are introduced, Fortunato extends an invitation to visit his family-based operation near the Parque Natural de la Sierra de Cardeña y Montoro (a nature reserve between Córdoba and Jaén provinces), which combines private *dehesa*s, mountainous pasturelands, and pine forests boasting diverse flora and fauna. Along with his father and son, Fortunato, raises three flocks of *Segureña* lambs, a

https://doi.org/10.11647/OBP.0387.03

breed developed both for its frequent birthing of twins and for its easy adaptability to high altitudes. In summer, the family practices transhumance. They move their 1,200 sheep from Sierra de Cardeña y Montoro, where I interview them, to pastures in the high Sierra de Segura near Santiago-Pontones (Jaén). These latter pastures are on land that Fortunato helped to negotiate collective rights to for shepherds in the area.

In this case study, we first visit his family's sheep operation and talk with three generations of shepherds. Next, we follow Fortunato to a *dehesa*, where he introduces us to Rafael Enríquez del Río, a landowner he collaborates with, and Rafael's daughter Isabel. As he says, "they are one of the few conscientious landowners" in Andalusia. Rafael, who inherited his *dehesa* after the Spanish Civil War, actively works to maintain its biodiversity and has hired Fortunato as his part-time foreman to oversee these efforts. The two men have distinctly different lifestyles and personalities but are united by a shared passion for their cultural and ecological heritage, evidenced by the way they care for the natural landscapes where they work. Through Fortunato, we will explore relationships between families of different socio-economic classes and the systems that support or restrict them, as well as glimpse what biodiversity on a multifunctional *dehesa* means.

The Visit, Part I: A Family of Transhumant Shepherds in the Sierra

On the appointed day, Mar and I drive nearly three hours from Seville to the edge of a small farming town, Marmolejo (in the province of Jaén), to arrive at dawn. Fortunato Guerrero Lara and a jovial crew, including his father and son, a long-time colleague, and of course the family water dog, are waiting. They instruct us to follow them, and we wind through 20 kilometers of rocky pasture, deep into the nature reserve. As the spring mist lifts, signs warning of lynx crossings become visible in the early morning April light. Turning onto a gravel road, we climb higher to a plateau tucked between ravines and rocky land planted with olive trees. A white barn stands on one side of the plot, and a makeshift corral with several stalls stands on the other side. A red plaid wool blanket and sleeping cushion hang from a tree, drying after the morning dew.

Fortunato's co-worker Juan García Pastor enters the corral to check on the new mothers enclosed with their lambs. It is birthing season in Andalusia, and they have to train some ewes to accept and nurse their own offspring and, sometimes, other lambs who have become orphaned: "It's like taking off one sweater and putting on another," explains Fortunato. The individual stalls help encourage acceptance. This bonding and nursing process is critical: if the newborns are not suckled soon, they won't survive when the summer heat arrives and their transhumance begins. While Fortunato's 18-year-old son, Javier, helps, Fortunato's 87-year-old father, Manuel Guerrero, dons his traditional shepherd's cap, picks up his shepherd's staff, and moves sure-footedly into the rocky pasture area, disappearing down a steep incline.

With everyone engaged in their daily routine, Fortunato begins to take inventory of his flock. Abruptly he stops and, without a word, also disappears down the ravine. A minute later, he shouts back to Juan: "We're missing three lambs!" A quick, efficient search ensues, and, within minutes, Fortunato climbs up to the plateau holding the body of a bloodied, mauled lamb only hours old: "It's a wild boar," he shouts and angrily continues, "only a wild boar would kill just to kill. A wolf would have eaten his kill." All hands search along the fence line and soon find the predator's point of entry. Fortunato explains: one glance at the ewes with remnants of birthing blood on their wool and a quick count of newborn lambs didn't add up, particularly because *Segureña* ewes often birth twins. His mastiff, who had always guarded the sheep at night so Fortunato could sleep in the village with his family, was stolen several weeks ago. Fortunato is training a new mastiff, but it is too inexperienced to be left to guard the flock all night alone. This *gadanero*'s skill in training dogs becomes clear when his herding water dog fetches a bottle of water and tobacco from the truck for him. But while the water dog is smart and a good herder, Fortunato explains, he cannot offer the protection of a mastiff and is not powerful enough to ward off nighttime attacks by wolves and wild boars. The plaid blanket hanging at the entrance is now explained. Fortunato and his son took turns two nights ago sleeping next to the sheep. They have killed one boar already. It is clear that today's massacre was the work of another.

Fig. 3.2 Fortunato and his water dog, Sierra de Cardeña y Montoro (2018).

Fortunato now moves quickly to pair the ewes with other newborns. The precariousness of life here dampens the early-morning optimism. As an outsider to this life of shepherding, I am struck by how quickly an idyllic spring morning can change and reveal the dangers of the trade. There will be no comfortable bed in town tonight as they are forced to keep vigil again.

Tradition and Transhumance: Manuel Guerrero

While Fortunato leaves us to address the new situation and set up plans for the ewes left without lambs, we interview his father Manuel Guerrero, who has been quietly watching the drama unfold. Under the shade of his traditional cap, his weathered face looks out over the flock. He leans easily on his staff as he settles into a morning watch. Manuel and his generation are the image that most of us have of a shepherd. Now, in what a government official referred to as a "dialect of an old-time shepherd, a language of few words," the spare conversation of some old-time shepherds when they talk to outsiders, the octogenarian who has spent all his life as a shepherd outlines his life story. His own father was a shepherd, and, as a child, Manuel worked alongside him on the transhumant process. When he came of age and married, poverty was widespread. Opportunities were few in a largely rural, post-Civil War Andalusia. There was no choice involved in becoming a shepherd, Manuel explains. "Here, you either picked olives or worked with livestock." He chose his father's profession and lived for decades as a transhumant shepherd, tending others' flocks. He was away from home six months out of the year. "I don't know what it's like to be in town for winter," Manuel remarks matter-of-factly as he briefly describes his transhumant lifestyle.

> I did transhumance from Pontones to a *finca* called Centenera. You can get to it in twelve days walking. I went on horseback. There weren't many cars back then, and I'd be there half a year. Six months away from home. That's a lot, but it had to be done. There was no other way to eat. I didn't have sheep. The sheep were somebody else's. I stopped doing transhumance on foot when life got better, and there were cars, trucks, and trains. But I started out bringing them in on foot. Ten, twelve days on the trail. If you got tired, you had to sleep. If it was raining, you pitched a tent. If not, well, if you didn't have a tent, you slept outside with all the other shepherds. Sometimes there were three, four, or five others, depending on how many sheep you had. Some of us would sing. We'd get a little sunburned... And the family? My wife was used to me being gone. What are you gonna do?

For years, Manuel worked for landowners. He would lead their flocks and a few horses, each summer, on a twelve-day trek by foot to higher elevations. Bit by bit, one sheep at a time, he also built his own flock to a few dozen. It has been about fifteen years since Manuel has completed a full transhumance by foot.

When Fortunato rejoins us, both father and son talk together, saying they would like to once again perform a complete transhumance. The distance to Santiago-Pontones is just 198 kilometers, so walking with the flock would be cheaper than renting a truck, which now costs well over 5,000 euros. Even with their large herd, they would not have to buy feed or worry about scorching heat in the summer. They do still complete a shorter seasonal migration using two pastures:

In the summer, we go to the pastures ... that are 80% public *monte* along with some rented fields. In winter we go to rented *finca*s where there's a lot of rockrose shrubs, rosemary, thyme, the *monte mediterráneo*.

Much of this movement is performed by truck but, whenever possible, they undertake part of the trip by foot:

[We sometimes move the flocks by] taking advantage of the planted fields, the roads, and the trails. In summer, we see a lot of brush and meadows, and we have two spring seasons. We leave when the lower spring ends, and we go up higher when the mountain spring begins [in Santiago-Pontones].

New highway construction and housing projects, however, have cut off continuous access to the *vías pecuarias* (droving roads), which would make the longer journey more challenging. In addition, recent laws requiring blood tests to aid disease control, birthing and death licenses, and other restrictions make the traditional transhumance by foot logistically difficult and expensive. Transhumance by truck only cleans and fertilizes their two pastures, which means the ancient routes are no longer kept clean.

Fig. 3.3 Manuel Guerrero watches over the flock, Sierra de Cardeña y Montoro (2018).

Here, Fortunato and Manuel remark on a positive change in their own lives: after doing transhumance by foot throughout Andalusia and La Mancha for decades, they can enjoy their own houses, one in each town. As his own family grew, Fortunato explains, he needed a stable home in town so his three children could attend school and have access to career opportunities that were not available to a shepherd's children when he grew up. Father and son split their time between Marmolejo and Santiago-Pontones, and Fortunato has worked on his own at the same farm for twenty years. Yet Fortunato states that this relatively new way of doing transhumance and making a living has its own challenges: "At least we haven't had as many problems. It hasn't been as stressful. But as we've gotten more ambitious, life's gotten more complicated."

Shepherd and Land-Use Expert: Fortunato Guerrero Lara

With the morning routine reestablished, Fortunato invites us to walk with him as we talk further about not only his family and shepherding, but also his advocacy in pastoralism and land use. Fortunato notes that, although he learned shepherding from his father, many significant changes have occurred since he took the leadership of his father's carefully built flock. After studying the complex and ever-changing government funding opportunities, he became adept at navigating bureaucracy, especially the CAP of the European Union and its funding for entrepreneurs in extensive grazing. With this funding, he acquired three *explotaciones*, flocks of about four hundred sheep — one each for himself and his wife, and more recently his son, who decided to carry on the family tradition of shepherding. Due partly to the new opportunities of the maturing democracy, his own life has improved upon the static traditional role of an Andalusian shepherd left to live in poverty much of his life, working in isolation for a landowner. These positive changes have allowed him to support a better lifestyle for his own family. Besides having a house in town, he proudly notes his children can study at the university. Nonetheless, he admits: "It hasn't been easy to send my children to college. One daughter's a civil engineer, and the other one's a social worker. Both of them are working." As I soon learn, even though shepherds increasingly own their own flocks, many must take on extra jobs in order to support a more middle-class lifestyle.

As we continue touring Fortunato's farm, watching him set new *Segureña* lambs to pasture with their mothers, he talks about his advocacy work. He describes the complex web of relationships that those who work with sheep and goats must navigate and expands on his role in leading this dialogue. For years, he has been a spokesperson for the fight to increase access to pasturelands. He once worked with the "Cooperativa del Cordero Segureño" (named after the Río Segura in Jaén) established by his ancestors as a collective for shepherds raising traditional livestock in the region, yet it was through his work as president of the "Sociedad de Transformación Pastos de Pontones" that he and others successfully negotiated for access to both public and private pasturelands. Working with both park officials and private landowners, the collective helped them all understand the benefit extensive grazing offers to the value of land. Fortunato's extensive knowledge of shepherding and the landscapes that maintain his own flocks drives his collaboration with associations, collectives, and landowners to help people see how land use and shepherding practices go hand-in-hand. The sheep keep the fields and pasturelands well fertilized and clean of dry (and flammable) underbrush, and the olive trees provide much needed shade in the hot, arid summers. In the mountainous pasturelands of Andalusia, he frequently repeats, sheep and olives go together.

As Fortunato talks, he often uses a key phrase to describe all aspects of his work, philosophy, and vision: "We're collaborators." He is an articulate advocate for his profession and understands at a practical, as well as visionary level, what must happen with both private and public lands in Andalusia for their way of life and their precious natural environment to flourish. Nonetheless, he knows all too well that there are frequent misunderstandings between the different parties he mediates. Even shepherds compete with each other, he explains, when bidding for pasturelands:

> It's an area where all the pastures are communal, so you can graze different flocks there. And then, you pay according to land use. The objective is for *ganadero*s not to outbid each other. There are some statutes and some rules to follow so no one individual can establish his own pasture.

His experience has convinced him that the competitive relationship between landowners, the government, and *ganadero*s must change so that everyone comes out ahead. Indeed, while the collective was successful in attaining a handful of public lands near Pontones, where he now grazes his livestock in the summer, the program failed to expand into other regions:

> There were great results, at least for the *ganadero*s. For my land, I don't think it was that beneficial. I left as president right after we came to an agreement, and then, it all stopped. It hasn't started up again. Nothing's come of it. I left my position because it makes no sense if they don't value the Sociedad's communal pasturelands. And I don't think either side was willing to negotiate. Neither for the *ganadero*s to keep using the communal pasturelands nor for the government to keep offering them, which, in that aspect, is unfortunate because it could really benefit both. So surely, if we sit down together and negotiate and talk it through, then I think we can reach some type of understanding. It's for everyone's benefit, especially the livestock, which brings profits for everyone.

He primarily blames some of the greedy landowners in the area, who still fail to see the mutually beneficial dynamics of pastoralism and good land stewardship. Worse yet, some of these same landowners receive valuable government subsidies to allow grazing but refuse to provide a place for livestock farmers to live. They expect sheep and goats to clear unusable land of overgrowth but then want to charge shepherd-*ganadero*s excessive rent to do this work. For its part, the government did not help move the program forward; instead, it taxed shepherds 3,000 euros per flock to use the newly available public lands. He paints a grim picture as he speaks on behalf of all shepherds, switching to the collective "we" form:

> There are *finca*s where it's impossible to put a program together with the landowners because they charge outrageous prices. Some friends of mine are paying unreasonable prices for using the *finca*s for four or five

months. And these are places where there's no equipped housing, so *ganadero*s are living in the farmhouses because what else are we supposed to do? Stay out in the snow? There's nothing left but for us to leave. And the landowners know it, and they pressure us with costs that are way out of reach for us.

Although he is disappointed that the program did not develop further, he still holds out hope for future dialogue and mutual understanding. In the end, he still believes that if people can understand how the practice benefits everyone — shepherd, farmer, private landowner, government (*La Administración*), society, and most importantly, the future welfare of the land — change can happen. Mutual, collaborative efforts are the future for a more productive, sustainable agricultural and livestock ecosystem, he insists, yet this work requires that all sides understand the unique conditions and contributions of the rocky Andalusian pasturelands and how it differs from the lowland agricultural lands.

> To raise people's awareness, you'd have to say to the landowner: "Look, this is a *finca* with organic olive trees. If you graze sheep here, you get a bonus." In fact, it should be required because these native olive groves are compatible with the native sheep who graze here. The landowner should consider this and say: "I've got a *finca* with organic olive groves, and as part of the environmental awareness I've been developing for years, I acknowledge that the olives I grow here on the mountain alongside grazing livestock are more profitable than the ones I have in lowland farms." That all seems clear, but how do you get people to see it?

While many shepherds are increasingly active in collectives, Fortunato has worked at a level that many shepherds have not, negotiating with a broad range of stakeholders. Through his work, he has developed concrete ideas about how to improve land access issues at a systemic level. He believes one effective way forward is to provide more official mediators who can help shepherds apply for and acquire rights to public lands for grazing. "I'd say that now it's due to a lack of understanding between the government and us. I think it's a mix. We need people to negotiate for us."

Transhumant shepherds need even more support, he argues, because they work in two distinct geographical regions, each with its own set of regulations for pastoralism. That, and being absent six months out of the year, can often result in lack of access to the best land. Lands rented sight unseen may end up being in poor condition. Good lands may be offered one year only to have the rent double the next year. Fortunato describes the dizzying and discouraging array of roadblocks to land access, especially for transhumant shepherds:

> So, what's the problem? Well, we have to manage the communal pasturelands in the Santiago-Pontones region. We're the ones who do the transhumance, so, we should work together with landowners because one person has a *finca*, but another person doesn't have access to land. And then there's someone else who doesn't have the right licenses, etc. But with public lands, if you could come to an agreement with the government, and say, "What *finca* is available?" Or, so there's access to all *finca*s, "What *finca*s do you have?" Then, that's it. They open it up for competition and say, "we have this *finca* here and that *finca* there." But some of those *finca*s aren't ready for the best use by the *ganadero*s; they have a lot of brush; there's no access; they've got pine groves that don't make good pastures for livestock. So, if the *finca* isn't worth saving, why should they want to preserve it? It just remains out of use.
>
> So, we know which *finca*s are the good ones, and those that are good for us are also good for livestock. We want the ones that suit our needs: this one and that one. The others can be used for wood, or they can be left for the *monte*, or even some other *ganadero* can use it. Landowners could say, "I'll give you a five-year contract, and you do with the *finca* whatever you want. I'm not going to charge you anything. You clear it, get rid of the brush, and if you want, you can plant something on it for your animals, and you give me some." And then, even more important, there are individually owned *finca*s that are not used, and that's simply because they're privately owned, especially in our area. But then again, there are *finca*s where due to the nature of the terrain, the rocks, and the ravines, it's impossible to use machinery. Manual labor is extremely expensive.
>
> So, then, what's happening? These folks own their *finca*, but on top of that, you pay them money, and on top of that, you pay them to get their land in good condition for fire prevention. We create a benefit for them by grazing our animals and clearing the land, so we should also receive a part of that benefit. We collaborate with them, and we do it for free. They need a fire prevention plan, which costs a fortune, but isn't that what we do for free? Yet, we still end up paying to graze our animals on top of everything else, and they get fire prevention too.

Beyond the complexities of land access, in the end, Fortunato echoes what every shepherd, farmer, and *dehesa* owner experiences: the harsh economic reality. The price of lamb plateaued for years at fifty euros in the early 1990s. During the following years the price of land, food, transportation, licensing, and veterinarian costs nearly quadrupled, and unlike other products, fresh lamb has short shelf life. Considering the added ecological and environmental benefits of sheep grazing, with its cleaning and fertilization of vast regions of the countryside, a fair market price would be at least double the hundred euros it is today. Although the prices of Spanish lamb briefly approached this target price in recent years, Fortunato notes that he still can't keep up with inflation due to climate change, skyrocketing energy costs, and market speculation. He has had to change his business model to just one birthing season per year rather than two. New market models need to be developed.

> You can't break even. I no longer do August birthing. I don't think it's worth it for what it costs. So now I just do spring birthing, and only with financial assistance. The whole food sector is like that. It's a big imbalance. The wholesalers buy cheap grain from the farmers, but they sell the feed to us, the *ganadero*s, really high. The costs of energy are going through the roof. Lamb is at 110, but you don't know when to buy or sell. And to add to all of this, there's the drought, and up until last week it hadn't rained. The only good thing, and the reason we keep going at it, is because the *ganadero* works so much that he doesn't spend anything. He doesn't have time to spend.
>
> You have to keep in mind exports because if you don't, it doesn't make sense. Outside of Spain they already pay a higher price for lamb. That's a very important point in the sales process because it makes you lose money if you don't keep that in mind. With better management, it could turn out better. The whole market thing is very complicated. When you have a product like, for example, oil, you store it in a barrel, and you sell it whenever you want. When you have canned or frozen goods, which have a time frame in which to sell, the market gives you a certain amount of time to negotiate. But our product is different. Meat has to be fresh. With lamb, you have to eat it when it's ready. With *Segureña* lamb, which is free range, in order for it to have its true delicious flavor, you can't freeze it and eat it as a lamb chop three months later. It's not viable for all the work it takes, for all the sacrifice. You're raising it organically, and you should enjoy it at its best for many

reasons. Get it today and eat it right away. What's happening? When you produce a fresh product, you have less margin for maneuverability. And then there are the speculators who are in the mix who say: "I buy, I owe, I have my grain seller, I sell it just a certain way...." People need to be more aware of what's going on.

I have heard this observation in every interview so far: "People need to be more aware." The public must be willing to pay fair market value for sustainable food production and back government policies that support this. It is Fortunato's passion to inform others in the face of huge challenges that drives him to take time to talk with people like me. Like Pepe Millán's dedication to teaching a new generation of shepherds and public (see Chapter 2), Fortunato believes fundamental change can only happen with more public awareness and new models for marketing.

> Everything can always get better in life. That's what we've always said. This could be a very, very long conversation, and we could talk about a lot of things. We wouldn't stop until tomorrow. There are always more things to improve. For the government's part, there's a lot to be done in the livestock sector. They're always doing some things, but everything could be improved. We also are very beneficial for the monte. Livestock greatly benefits the monte for its biodiversity, for its fertilization, for sowing seeds. Livestock has alleviated the fire threat greatly. Pasture density is reduced in the summer where livestock grazes. In fact, where there is livestock, there's a smaller percentage of fires. On the lands where I have grazed flocks, there haven't been any fires in the last forty or fifty years. If they could compensate public *fincas* without charging us for the pastureland, giving us a little assistance, it would help out a lot because this sector is now on the edge of disappearing. In just twenty years, livestock on this land, our land, has disappeared. Just twenty years; I'm not exaggerating. I've worked at it for a long time. What's happened is that the *ganaderos* who have stayed, we've stayed because it's what we love. You've been raised around this, it's what you love, and the truth is it takes a lot out of you. It's no longer about what you earn or don't earn. We make the sacrifice, and sure, we live with the costs of the sacrifice we're making.

Fig. 3.4 Fortunato Guerrero Lara with son Javier inside the historic farmhouse (2018).

Generational Legacies: Generational Renewal and Javier Guerrero Vilches

Later, resting for a moment in the shade of an old oak tree, Fortunato talks about another major challenge: the unmet need for more shepherds as his father's generation retires. Fewer than 2% of his partners are being replaced by a new generation. Although he is concerned about the survival of the profession in general, he admits to mixed feelings about the unusual choice his youngest son, Javier, has made to follow in his father's footsteps:

> One thing is very clear, families who are retiring aren't leaving a new generation. My case is an exception. My son continuing to do work like this is an isolated case. And I'll tell you something else, I didn't want my son to be a *ganadero*.

Fortunato and his family are from a town that depends on *ganadería* to survive, yet even though Fortunato loves his work, he still urges his children to complete their education and prepare themselves for another vocation. He knows all too well the precariousness of birthing season, the social marginalization, the economic hardships, and the instability of travelling seasonally with the flock. He understands the need for more shepherds so that this way of life and this ecosystem can survive, but he also wishes an easier life for his own family.

Fortunato describes his views about the decrease in shepherds throughout Spain, as well as his own feelings about his youngest son's determination to work as a shepherd.

> I didn't want my son to be a *ganadero*. I did my duty: the best inheritance I can leave him is his career. The best inheritance is for him to get something out of this because I don't have anything else to give. His inheritance is his training. The future of *ganadería*, at least on land around here, has a tendency to disappear because there's nobody left. When the *explotaciones* let up and the older folks start retiring, there's no generational renewal. It's only by chance when a child comes along like mine and stays and becomes part of the legacy. It's a coincidence. Maybe there are two percent or less of *ganadero*s who retire, and their son takes over because the *Junta de Andalucía* has motivated them to do it with assistance that's there for new or young farmers. They give them some subsidies that they don't have to repay. They help them out some. That's motivated them a little.
>
> My son was going to finish his last two years of high school to earn his *bachillerato* [high school advanced diploma]. He had already started his second year, but suddenly, overnight, he tells me he wants to be a *ganadero*. I tell him, at least finish the *bachillerato*. "Dad, I'm not gonna need it because I want to work." So, since he dug in his heels, I discussed it with him since he seemed 100 percent set on doing it. He knows what he wants, and he's not a kid. He doesn't want to spend all day out driving around and wasting all his time in town. He works just like me. He gets up at the same time I get up. He works some weekends if he wants, but not many. He worked yesterday and Saturday too. I don't know what time he'll work tomorrow. He was taking night courses to finish his *bachillerato* so he could be in the fields during the day. He's eighteen. He had a birthday in December. He was very clear about it. The idea came to him as a child, and it just kept growing on him. He knew his dad didn't have weekends or vacations or anything like that, but look what he's gotten himself into. He knows what he's doing. And he works every day with me. He gets up and goes to bed when I do. He went out last night, but he knew he had to work the next day, and he was in by 12:00.

So, when Fortunato heads over to consult with one of the other shepherds, I interview his son, Javier, who is determined to work alongside his grandfather and father. Javier says when he finished his last two years of high school, he decided to carry on the family tradition. He is well aware that he is the key to keeping the family legacy going because his older siblings chose other vocations. Despite his parents' hopes for him, Javier is both clear-sighted and practical about his choice. He loves animals and the outdoors and spends all his weekends and vacations working with them. "If you like it, it doesn't sting so much," he smiles. The sting includes the teasing he has endured from classmates, who see only the stigma and hard work of the shepherd's life, and missing out on college life, parties, and freedom. Still, he firmly repeats his choice: he'd rather be a shepherd — and after all, he jokes, he can still go out on a Saturday night.

> I like this, and I always told myself that when I grew up, I wanted to do something that I liked. I like this a lot because I've grown up doing it. On vacation or on the weekends I always come here with my dad. In general, I like being in the country, and I like the animals. I have no doubts. In Spain right now we're still feeling the effects of the economic crisis. Things are bad. I'd like to have some training for a career, but even if I had it, I'd still want to do this because it's what I like. Already at eighteen I know what I want. If you have a career, people judge you better than if you don't have one. In life it takes all kinds: construction workers, engineers, shepherds. And *ganadería* is at the base of it all. If that goes away, then everything goes away.
>
> I had to go about convincing my family a bit at a time. It wasn't hard to convince my dad, but my mom was a little harder, although now she's gotten used to the idea. If you're not doing what you like, it's better not to do anything.
>
> Society looks on people who work out in the country as village idiots, but you can have just as much culture as anyone. You read, you watch movies etc. I don't see why going to school is any better than not going to school. I see what a student's life is like, and I don't like it. I might get home tired, but it's something I've chosen. If you're doing something you like, then time goes by really fast. My dad's been doing this for 25 years, and I'm eighteen. The image people have of someone who works in the country isn't completely right. People don't know what it's like to take care of sheep. Not everybody values it. The trick is knowing your sheep. What's nicest, and hardest, is what's coming up now in April, during the birthing season. You've got to be up all night keeping guard.
>
> Besides, even though my dad lets me do whatever I want, I'd rather work than go out partying, and eighty percent of my social life is with my dad. We work together, and we have a beer together. It's a special

relationship, and your friends don't understand sometimes. I'm doing what I like, and I don't care what others think.

Javier has also closely observed the life of friends who dedicated years preparing for a career only to be unemployed. For nearly a decade after 2008, Andalusia's post-crisis job market remained stagnant, with an approximate unemployment rate of around 40% for young adults aged eighteen to thirty. Most of the work they can get is part-time, low-paid, and often precarious. His generation has lived half of their lives in the grip of "La Crisis," a situation that had started to improve just as the COVID-19 pandemic hit in spring 2020. More than a few university-educated friends, Javier admits, are now looking to return to the land to find work and meaning in what some refer to as a neo-ruralism. And, he continues, why would he leave what he loves? He repeats with a smile: "If you like it, it doesn't sting so much."

Javier admires how his father is working to transform shepherding. He points to what Fortunato himself has described going from "being a shepherd for the landowner" to "owning an *explotación*" (a sheep herd large enough to attract government subsidies), from "being the son of a transhumant shepherd" to "owning a nice little house in town". It has been a transition from a solitary pastoral life to being a key organizer in a collective effort to improve the precarious economic conditions and relationship to landholders that have been part of a long history of marginalization. Although Javier is just starting to establish his own *explotación* as he works with his father, he also has his eye on the future. Javier is also working to help increase land access and promote a better understanding of pastoralism in general. In the meantime, however, the 18-year-old is focused on starting his own business as a shepherd. He has inherited his grandfather's simple philosophy: "You have to live."

As we wrap up the morning interviews with three generations of shepherds, I recall Fortunato's joke about his name and his good fortune to work alongside his father and son. I too feel fortunate to have witnessed their work with them and to have heard their stories. Together they demonstrate the resiliency of a family who works to protect tradition but also to accommodate new realities.

The Visit, Part II. Dehesa la Rasa and Multifunctionality: Landowners Rafael Enríquez del Río and his daughter Isabel

As we have seen, the economic reality of shepherding for Fortunato and his family, though limiting, has also been a catalyst to seek out new opportunities so they can afford to continue doing what they love. Fortunato not only manages his flocks and actively advocates for pastoralism; he also works part-time to manage a nearby *dehesa*. While it is difficult to find landowners who understand the delicate pastoral ecosystem and value Fortunato's expertise in good land management, Fortunato's drive, clear-sighted vision, and experience as a negotiator are appreciated by some. He has teamed up with one of these local landowners, Rafael Enríquez del Río, on his private Dehesa la Rasa. Rafael, Fortunato emphasizes, is "someone who's aware of what works. He's seen the benefits thanks to livestock grazing. He doesn't have to use fertilizer, and the sheep keep his *finca* cleared. But it's only one case. It's an isolated case." Fortunato is now equal parts shepherd and businessman in a productive collaboration with this landowner to diversify the *dehesa* and the mountainous pasturelands through sustainable practices.

So, as noon approaches, and just as I think we have wrapped up for the day, Fortunato invites us to join him at this land-management, his second, job. To reach the *dehesa*, we wind back through the hills, turning toward Cardeña as the landscape of mountainous pasturelands and olive groves become intermittent pine forest. We enter another part of the Parque Natural Sierra Cardeña y Montoro that adjoins the Parque Natural Sierra de Andújar. Almost 80% of the 38,500 hectares in this area are privately owned because the land was designated as a park in 1989, and many landowners were able to have their property legacied to keep in the family. We soon pull into the driveway of a nineteenth-century farmhouse where we meet our host. Rafael proudly brings his guests on tours through the small house and invites hobbyists and professionals to use the space for a variety of projects. Perhaps that is why, when curious academics like us arrive, the locals barely bat an eyelash. No one seems surprised that we had traveled across the Atlantic to visit Fortunato and

Rafael, as they appear to have a constant stream of visitors — though most come from across Andalusia.

The people who surround Fortunato and Rafael, two practitioners of the socio-ecological system of *ganadería extensiva* (extensive grazing), are also brought together by the land — both public and private — that they carefully cultivate. Beekeepers, wood processors, shepherds, and hunters all benefit from the bounty of this land. Rafael controls his property with a vigilant eye for monetary value. Without making some profit, the land would have to be abandoned, but his multi-use approach has made the vast land surrounding the *finca* even more valuable for its natural production.

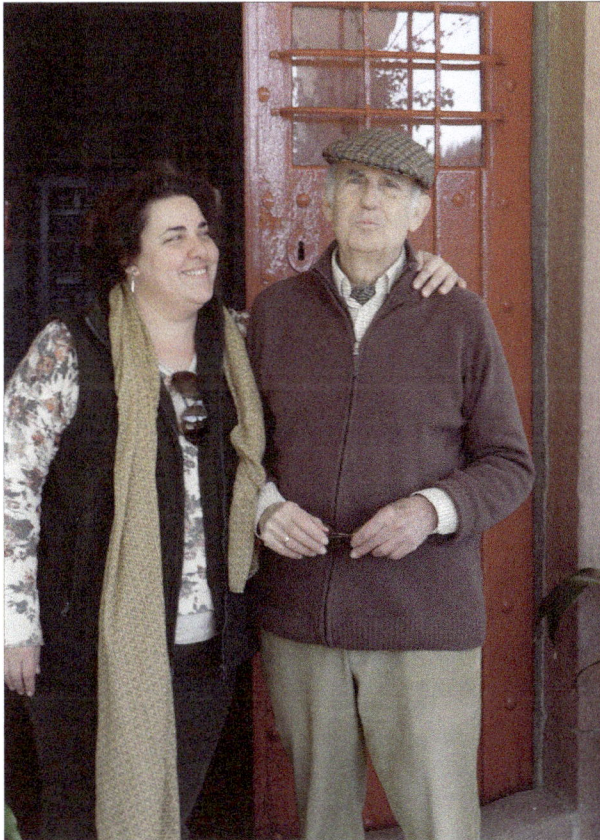

Fig. 3.5 Rafael Enríquez del Río with his daughter Isabel on their Dehesa la Rasa (2018).

As Rafael shows us around, we come to understand how the history of twentieth-century Spain, the *dehesa*, and Rafael's own personal story are intertwined. He recounts how the farmhouse dates to 1897, when his grandparents bought it and some of the surrounding land. The family lived in Posadas, Córdoba but spent vacations on the nearby farmhouse. Everything changed with the Civil War. Rafael was born in 1937, just months after a group of militants shot more than twenty townspeople, among them his father: "They killed him in the war. He was a judge; the reds, the commies, killed him early on. The anarchists, the reds, all those kinds of people, killed some twenty some odd people in the town. He confronted them." By age eight, Rafael had also lost his mother and was living with his grandmother. He remembers spending hours by himself hunting and exploring the mountainous pasturelands surrounding the farmhouse. It was this childhood love of nature, and in particular hunting, that formed the basis for his later vision of stewardship.

When Rafael came of age and inherited the *dehesa*, he began to buy up adjacent parcels of land and learn more about the local trees and animals. As a keen observer, he also witnessed many, at times illogical, laws and practices governing the area that were mandated by the Franco regime. Rafael offers the example of the planting of pine forests that were meant to protect the land but also disturbed the natural ecosystem of the area. Nevertheless, the practice contributes to his income and continues to be part of his overall business plan. Rafael points out another difference from the earlier era. Franco's prohibition of hunting did not represent good stewardship of the land, he feels. Today, selling licenses for controlled hunting, he says, helps to balance the ecosystem and to maintain the economic viability of his land.

Although he spent much time on the *finca*, Rafael was a full-time company owner in town until his business collapsed with the 2008 crisis. At the age of seventy, he retired and dedicated ever more time to his farm. Now, he and his daughter Isabel, together with Fortunato, are setting an example of good private-land stewardship, applying a well-informed multifunctional approach in which pastoralism is a key to stabilize the natural environment of the *finca*, as well as the surrounding rural area. From the veranda, Rafael expands on his vision of sustainable diversification and the proper resourcing of land. We gaze out over the *dehesa* and level pastures of about 1,200 hectares, green from the spring rains and home to sheep and Iberian pigs that graze under olive and cork trees. Rafael explains that, while normally the *explotación* (herd) numbers around 150–200 sheep, recent wolf attacks have devastated the flock. Only about sixty sheep remain. With resignation, he awaits the lengthy reimbursement process from the EU, which he hopes will be in the thousands of euros. He is encouraged that there is now support from the EU for keeping sheep. Rafael's bank has also become more receptive: if at one time they only made fun of sheep-keeping, the bankers now see the value of his flock not just in potential for profit but in its recognized value to the environment. The bankers have heard of the government program that pays shepherds and flock owners to graze animals and clean public lands to prevent forest fires. The last time he went to the bank, Rafael recalls how his banker said appreciatively: "You guys are the firefighters for our forests."

To help make his *finca* economically sustainable, Rafael now harvests cork bark and has 100 hectares planted with olive trees. He points towards an extensive, hilly forested area just beyond the pastures. There he maintains a varied habitat for big game hunting; it attracts wildcats, deer, and boar, as well as partridge. People pay a good fee to hunt there, yet these initiatives are still not enough to make a reliable profit now:

> Right now, it's not organized very well because if you have a *finca*, you don't make much money, and it's even harder to make it an organic one. Nevertheless, organic practices are our future, especially if we want to live in a world that's not so cruel.

Still, Rafael sees benefits beyond trying to make a profit from his land. He is at heart a true conservationist. Proudly, he enumerates to us the wide variety of species his land supports and describes his active cultivation of autochthonous varieties of oak trees. He wants to leave a lasting natural monument to Mother Nature through good land stewardship, as well as through working with community members involved in rural development. Land ownership, he argues, cannot be driven solely by "big bucks". Like another landowner we will hear from later, he recognizes that mountain pasturelands depend on adopting systems for an ecologically sound future not because it is trendy now, but because it is the only hope for the future.

Rafael has remained a good steward of the land he inherited as a young man. He is a traditional landowner who has contributed to the continuation of a large functional *finca*, but, unlike many other landowners of his generation who abandoned their land in favor of jobs and higher incomes in cities, Rafael still spends much of his time on the *finca*. His approach today falls somewhere between micro-management and delegation: he stays involved in every aspect of the *finca*'s production but depends on Fortunato and other workers to take on the responsibility of day-to-day tasks.

Site for *Empresas Agrícolas Familiares*

Rafael and his daughter Isabel are also the beneficiaries of a law designed for *empresas agrícolas familiares*, that is, family farming businesses. The law encourages local collaboration with a wide range of small businesses, including beekeepers, wood processors, shepherds, and hunters. Fortunato helps Rafael and Isabel to manage these new initiatives. Today we meet two new families working on Rafael's land.

The first pull into the *finca*'s driveway in a sleek, black SUV. A stylish woman dressed in a black leather jacket, Ester Vázquez Estela, steps out along with her husband, José Martín Pérez García. Fortunato calls this couple from Cazorla in the Sierra de Jaén the "timber folks" because of their interest in harvesting the farm's non-native pines—a legacy of Franco's 1960s policies that have not been helpful to the natural ecosystem. Some years ago, the couple began in the wood-chip business, harvesting pines for both planks and biomass for renewable energy. They work with a collective and a forest ranger all over Jaén, Granada, Almería, and Córdoba. José Martín explains that, after two decades in restaurant work, the financial crisis led him to team up with his business-minded wife. Needing a stable income to support their two kids at home, he and Ester began a new initiative in the area that just five years earlier would have been unheard of — especially with a woman heading the business. He recounts with satisfaction his journey from restaurant work to working in the countryside:

I worked for twenty-six years in the hospitality business. Let's just say from the time I was born. My father had a wedding hall, and we'd do weddings. It was a restaurant and a hotel too. Part of it I liked, and part of it I didn't. It's a life that wears on you. When there are a lot of parties, you have a lot of work. The hours are hard. And dealing with people..., there are some clients who come in, and you say, "crap, these folks are really nice and polite." But there are others who are just shameful. You have to put up with the drunks. You have to put up with people on drugs. Things can get pretty bad at the bar.

When I turned twenty-seven, I decided to follow my own path. I bought equipment and put together a small business. Then I was self-sufficient, but something happened, and I went a year without pay. I lost everything. I was ruined. They took away all my equipment; they took away everything. I had a *finca*, I had a place of my own... everything..., but then someone threw me a lifeline. And since then, we're getting along a little better. Slower, but a little better. The truth is I'm not interested in having a huge business. With my experience, I prefer to have something that I can handle on my own, where I can control everything, because I prefer to have equipment on one *finca* and not more than that because you can't control it. I'm a worker. I'm a businessman, but I'm a worker too.

Now I have a better quality of life. Even though I have to be away from home from Monday to Friday, and I don't get to see my son or my wife, I come home on the weekends, turn off my cellphone, and completely disconnect. Two whole days to be with my kid and rest. You enjoy the days you spend at home relaxing more than during the week when you can only be there for a little while in the afternoon.... Working with my wife has been the best thing that's happened. I used to have a partner who took me for seventy thousand euros and wiped me out. So, since my wife is now my partner, I'm in heaven because we're both on the same page. And things are working well for us. I don't take advantage of her, and she doesn't take advantage of me. We're both going in the same direction. That's the formula for a high-quality business. I'm sorry I didn't do it ten years ago. What happened wouldn't have happened. I'm in heaven now, and it's great. Just here working. No one bothers me. No one comes by. I'm all by myself. I'm in heaven. I've got incredible inner peace.

Like his collaborator and farm manager Fortunato, Rafael has also enlisted the next generation in his family enterprise. His daughter Isabel del Río, a trained biologist, now runs the vast farm alongside her father and continues to develop his vision of a sustainable multifunctional farm. Isabel now joins us and leads our caravan up into the deepest part of the pine forest, which needs to be thinned so that other growth can flourish. After both owners, Fortunato, and the husband-wife team survey the area, Isabel and Ester strike a deal over the pines and report the transaction to Fortunato. We have just witnessed the kind of negotiation that Fortunato says must happen more frequently with land use in these rocky pasturelands: multiple interests can be served at the same time. Rafael needs to thin his forest to prevent forest fires, the new company needs raw materials, and the biomass will help with the production of sustainable energy.

As they close the deal, two people in full beekeeper suits seem to appear out of nowhere. Rafael and Isabel have recently opened access to their land to beekeepers further down the ravine. Victoria Gámiz is a beekeeper at the University of Córdoba, who also works in the area with the hives she is developing along with her business partner Enrique Medina, who learned the trade from his father. Victoria hopes that, within three years, this part-time venture will become full-time business. For them, beekeeping is integral to extensive grazing and essential to the health of the ecosystem. Both are trained scientists; they respect and utilize traditional knowledge but are willing to experiment with new techniques and with varieties of hives. Enrique, who works part-time in nearby La Mancha as a forestry engineer, sees the need for increased coordination between landowners, shepherds, beekeepers, businesspeople, and government. With all but 4,000 hectares of the 35,000 in the Parque Natural in private hands, its future depends on partnerships with owners like Rafael and Isabel, who, as he says, "know how to and want to diversify" their land. More landowners need to understand how critical biodiversity is to "better resource everything in the *monte* to make it profitable and sustainable." A lively discussion continues among all the people gathered in the pine forest mixed with rocky pasture: multiple generations of landowners and shepherds, beekeepers, and wood-processing partners. My colleague from Seville, Mar, even jumps in to discuss the future, the need for government support of small family projects, greater recognition of the key role of shepherds, and collaborative work to encourage biodiversity. I just try to listen and learn. The owner of the biomass company explains:

Many times, hunting management doesn't let shepherds in. There are very few people like Rafael who bring both together; they're completely compatible. High pasturelands can be very big. Let's say you've got 1,000, 2,000 hectares. There's enough space so we don't have to be at the wrong place at the wrong time. It's a matter of organizing and coming to an agreement with all involved. When you better resource the pasturelands, the more profitable they become and the more biodiversity you're going to have. It just works better. And at the end of the day, it's better for the pasturelands too because they're being used and cared for, not abandoned. If it has a use, it works well, and the *monte* stays in good shape. It's what you have to do. It has to be that way for it to be sustainable. And the biomass will be profitable when the processing happens here and stays here in the region.

He agrees that many interests can be served by adopting multifunctional approaches to land management.

With a simple statement, Rafael summarizes the role of local workers in the formula for encouraging biodiversity and resisting rural depopulation: "A fundamental building block are the people who live on the land." Rafael and Isabel's avid interest in collaborative projects has helped several groups of people find a livelihood in post-crisis Andalusia and contributed to the sustainability of a fragile natural area at risk for massive forest fires, the extinction of flora and fauna, and desertification. Rafael has long been a guardian of this corner of the natural park. Now, he actively seeks out new ways to diversify and develop his rich natural patrimony by encouraging at least three families to use these resources to develop their own visions of a future in the countryside—entrepreneurs who respect the land as more than just a means to make a living. Rafael sees pastoralism and extensive grazing as critical to stop, or at least slow, the acceleration of rural flight and the deterioration of culture:

We can debate about the whole idea of going back to the traditional way of doing things. Transhumance has always happened, but now it could easily fail because there isn't a population who gets their products from transhumant livestock. Now there can't be millions of transhumant sheep. Hundreds, yes, but it's not the same. In the past, there were people who'd buy goats and meat and related products, and the shepherds sold everything: sheepskins, milk, etcetera. When people leave the rural areas, what happens? You lose your culture.

As a conservative landowner, Rafael also looks to the past to understand the age-old problem of maintaining the economic viability and local culture of the countryside. He tells us that, over five hundred years ago, Carlos V "solved rural problems with the countryfolk by sending his administrative advisors into the area." If only society still listened to the elders, he muses: "One of the worst things that's happened to our civilization is that the counsel of our elders has disappeared." Poking fun at his own nostalgia for the distant past, Rafael wryly quips: "Let's buy ourselves an old man, eh?", but he still relates his own work to an ancestral history that goes back millennia in the region. He offers the tradition of hunting on his farm as an example of historical continuity: "Just look at the Roman mosaics that depict partridge hunting." Even with his nostalgia for the past, Rafael realizes that "organic practices are our future, especially if we want to live in a world that's not so cruel."

It is now well past the usual dinner hour, and we head back to the farmhouse, where Rafael insists that we have a fuller tour of their small, meticulously maintained home, an integral part of his vision of bringing together tradition with innovative sustainability. We step inside a turn-of-the-century house which is, quite literally, a movie set: the film *Entrelobos* (http://www.imdb.com/title/tt1417582/), among others, was filmed here. All along the hallway and into the receiving room, the mounted heads of deer, bear, and antelope overpower us with a sense of man's dominance over, but ultimately reverence for, the natural world. Moving into the dining room, antique, green-patterned Córdoba ceramics line the cabinets. An ivory-carved cross with a disfigured Christ hangs on the center wall. With a mixture of bittersweet nostalgia and family pride, Rafael explains that the crucifix dates from the Golden Age. His ancestor, one who had made his fortune in Mexico and returned to Spain as a man from the "Indies" (an "Indiano"), brought the cross with him. When Republicans assassinated his father, they also defaced the cross. The family keeps it prominently displayed as a reminder of their resiliency throughout a difficult history.

Moving through the kitchen with its large fireplace, wood-burning stove, and well-stocked shelves of preserves, honey, olives, vinegars, oils, and meats — all produced on the farm and conserved by Rafael's wife — he leads us into the kitchen courtyard. Chickens roam freely there, but his focus is the new water-collection system and solar panels installed to power the entire house. Even in an impeccably maintained traditional farmhouse there is room for new innovations. Moreover, his motto, "make the best of everything," includes renting out part of the farmhouse as a "country home" to avid bird watchers.

Once we are in the kitchen, Isabel switches roles from businesswoman to traditional host, inviting us to taste the products of the *finca*. Noting how she has prepared herself to carry on her father's work on sustainability of ecosystems and rural populations by studying complex laws and funding structures surrounding land use and farming animals, she goes into the pantries and quickly puts together a delicious mid-day meal from the pantry stores: cured meat, grilled pepper salad, and stewed pork. She offers us a cold regional Cruzcampo beer and homemade *picadillo* made from garden-fresh ingredients after our foray around the property.

As the food is served, the friendly banter between Fortunato and the *dehesa* owners continues. The shepherd-manager repeats his tribute to Rafael as "a visionary entrepreneur," and Isabel in turn calls Fortunato "her best partner." I realize that we are witnessing a team: a shepherd-businessman and landowners with very different backgrounds and personalities yet see life through the same lens of the land. Rafael and Isabel challenge the popular stereotype that most landowners have abandoned good stewardship of land, animals, and rural communities. For their part, Fortunato and Javier dispel the image of the shepherd as the "village idiot." Rafael protects the land, property, and the natural world and exudes a deep respect for all the participants in the setting. As an orphan of the Civil War and a child of the Franco era, he draws on history and the traditional culture of the farm while providing access for a new generation of entrepreneurs in a rural setting. On the other hand, Fortunato is both the ideal of a "man of the people" in his passion for his family, home, and animals, and the astute business entrepreneur whose deep knowledge, insight, and intellect is moving pastoralism to new models. The stakes are high, but as Fortunato notes (and just as Javier had earlier echoed): "If you like your job and you do it with love, it's not so hard. If you're bitter about life, everything's hard."

As we drive back to Seville this spring afternoon, the sun is already hot, dry, and relentless. It is hard to imagine this landscape and sun in July, when it turns brown and arid, making it impossible to graze livestock. Rafael and Fortunato are lucky to have children who are following in their footsteps. Together, they are fighting a global trend toward urbanization and intensive grazing that, if unchecked, threatens the survival of the delicate *monte mediterráneo* and the rich culture of the people living here. In our one-day visit we have witnessed a family of shepherds working in the rocky pasturelands of Córdoba and Jaén, as well as *dehesa* owners actively engaged in good land-use through multifunctionality. Each group cares deeply about the environment, and each contributes their own vast experience and skills to a shared endeavor. Their story is not just about pastoralism and multifunctionality but also the multigenerational and multi-family teams of people that work together in the country to make a living — and to make a difference in environmental sustainability. On this trip and during later interviews, I continue to hear the recurring challenges of increased costs, lack of access, and oppressive regulations. Already, I am discovering how complex pastoralism is and how it involves a much larger community to keep land healthy so that flocks and herds can safely graze.

Conclusions and Update

When I call Fortunato in November 2021, he immediately answers, only to say he'll call back after the conference he is attending in Córdoba. A few days later, when we do talk, it is clear that his optimism has waned since 2018. He reports that it is not because his collaborator Rafael has passed — there has been a successful passage of the family legacy onto Isabel, who continues to be a good steward of the land and continues to collaborate well with him. Nor is it the effects of the pandemic. Like Pepe, it had little effect on their lives after the first couple weeks. He admits:

> It's almost like it didn't happen. We still got up in the morning, and we spent all day on the land. We came home at night, and we'd see it on TV. We were carrying on in the same way. We probably even worked a little

> more peacefully. The Guardia Civil didn't stop us or anything. They'd just wave, and that was it.

Continued problems with government bureaucracy, however, have made things harder each year. Although his family could not continue shepherding without government aid, he says (echoing Pepe Millán) that with the amount of paperwork, documentation, and ever-changing regulations it is impossible to make a living just by shepherding. For example, the new law protecting wolves threatens his livelihood. They have lost 180 sheep to recent attacks. When Rafael's herd of sheep was decimated by wolves, he expressed resignation as he waited for reimbursement from the government. For Fortunato, however, who has fewer resources to support his operation, the loss threatens his livelihood. He reports that he and his son have spent the last four nights sleeping out in the fields because the solutions recommended by the government are useless in their region. Radios, lights, and fencing are not practical in the steep ravines and in an area without electricity. The government will eventually reimburse them for the sheep killed, but the amount of paperwork, documentation, and the lengthy process of receiving payment are only part of the problem. It takes time and energy to replace good breeding sheep that will allow them to re-form and retrain a flock affected in this way.

> I'm fighting with the government for some compensation, but it's hard, and you have to be persistent. It's like we don't exist, the government doesn't do anything. They ask for a lot, but they don't give anything in return. Just bureaucracy, paying self-employment taxes, a lot of regulations — like microchips for the sheep — , paperwork, and more paperwork. There's no time for anything else. They're constantly changing the rules for the animal well-being certificate. If it weren't for the assistance, this would not be feasible. There are more and more requirements for new businesses to get aid and lands.

Fortunato offers another example of how new laws can stifle traditions and even threaten livelihoods. As a shepherd, he and his family can no longer perform the traditional *matanza*, the essential practice of slaughtering and preparing a full range of meats, fats, and byproducts from a sheep for family consumption over months.

Disgusted, he says: "I can't even kill and eat a lamb I've raised for my own family."

When I ask about the conference in Córdoba and his advocacy work, Fortunato explains that the discussions had been focused on the funds of the CAP and on the "transferring of grazing lands, expenses, costs, drinking troughs, and managing aid." Yet, even as the EU offers these initiatives, he says:

> It's impossible. There is no time. New things are always coming out, and more paperwork. It's a complete mistake forced on us by the politicians.

The irony here is striking. When I checked back in with researchers and government officials in fall 2021, many commented on the good progress in a general awareness of the plight of the pastoral ecosystems and the families who have worked within them. Meanwhile, every shepherd I interview continues to struggle.

Today, Fortunato's disillusionment runs deep: he sees a future with fewer shepherds, more rules, and poorer cost margins. As I listen, my own hopes dim for a brighter future for *ganaderos*, even though we heard good news from Juan (see Chapter 1) and Pepe about a new generation taking up the profession.

> I see the future as very bad. There are no new generations coming up, no compensation, despite the high unemployment rate. You've got to be out in the country with the livestock. When you go to a rented *finca*, the farmhouse is in bad condition. There's no running water; no electricity to charge your cellphone; no internet. The house doesn't have anything in it. It takes a small investment: a water tank, a solar panel for your basic needs, and an antenna for cell coverage. It costs a lot, and it's not profitable. It's not worth it! I see the future as very, very, very bleak. I've been at this for thirty years, but it's still the same. More new things to do, paperwork, requirements, land problems.... Young people have it really hard. We're fighting with our lives.

Fortunato also points out a more general, societal loss of a sense of interdependence: "We all need one another. We're losing certain values in life: communication, closeness, family, contact with other people. We must meet our obligations, not just be free to do as we please. Traditions and customs are disappearing." He does realize he is "fortunate" to have his son join the family tradition. The situation this month is dire for him with the recent loss of so many sheep, but some of his hope remains as he states: "We're waiting for the calm after the storm." May it be soon.

Fig. 4.1 View of Marta Moya Espinosa's *dehesa* and sheep near Castillo de las Guardas, Seville (2018).

4. Inheriting a Farm: Marta Moya Espinosa, Castillo de las Guardas (Seville)

The days of near-slavery are long gone — as it should be — people don't want to sleep under trees in rough conditions. As a landowner, if you're not on top of things 100% of the time, you pay a price.... You have to be on top of things every day right along with the shepherds.

Marta Moya Espinosa

Overview

When a friend comments that he used to help another friend on an annual transhumance nearby, I ask if I could meet with the shepherd. He laughs at my assumption that the friend is a shepherd — it turns out that she is a landowner. Marta Moya Espinosa manages a *dehesa* she inherited in Huelva, but she lives in downtown Seville. Having seen the multifunctional approach in Fortunato Guerrero Lara's and Rafael Enríquez del Río's collaboration and land use (see Chapter 3), I decide to call Marta to help me understand from a landowner's perspective the key role of land use in sustainable pastoralism.

This case is about a woman of privilege, who, after working and raising a family, came to a personal and professional crossroads. When I first meet Marta, she acknowledges that a "romanticism" obscured the numerous farming challenges she would face—ones that, after several years of working either full-time or part-time on the *dehesa* every week, she can now quickly list: increased government regulations, the retirement of the family shepherd and the difficulty of replacing him, natural disasters (including a recent wildfire), volatile markets, and,

 https://doi.org/10.11647/OBP.0387.04

finally, absentee landownership. Many people simply criticize owners who are "absent" or try to manage their farms from afar as contributing to a fundamental structural problem in Andalusia, but Marta has acted on the problem. She understands that such landowners can be looked down upon, and she worries about the current state of farming. Her story reveals the complexity of the changes and challenges that landowners face, as well as the arduous work required to revitalize not just a family business but the ecosystem itself.

Marta helps us understand the difficulty of being an urban career woman with little practical experience, faced with reviving her *dehesa* after years of neglect. Her determination and innate connection with the farm have helped her overcome a steep learning curve. Marta's case highlights how, even with a lot of capital, a valuable and working farm and flock, and some knowledge of how to oversee them, it is still an enormous challenge to make the farm profitable over the long term. An important part of Marta's story is really her family's story, so I am fortunate to meet and interview Marta's mother, Carmen, who talks with us about being a wife and mother during the postwar years on the farm.

From Absentee Landowning to Learning the Land

The Visit, Part I: The City

A few days after my initial call to Marta, I meet her at her city home in a trendy area of old Seville near the fourteenth-century San Juan de la Palma's Church. Settled into the comfort of a large leather couch, Marta nostalgically recalls joining family, friends, and the farm's long-time resident Portuguese shepherd and his dogs for the twice-yearly short-distance transterminance. They moved herds thirty-three kilometers between the family's *dehesa* outside of Castillo de las Guardas (Seville) to their agricultural farm outside of Paterna del Campo (Huelva), where the grazing sheep would clean the fields in the winter. Setting out at dusk under a waxing or full moon, they would walk all night, arriving at dawn before the Andalusian summer heat hit forty degrees Celsius (one hundred degrees Fahrenheit). Marta shows me photographs of their treks and recollects celebrating upon arrival with a beer, bits of potato *tortilla* and cured serrano ham, and songs. At the same time, she recalls how fortunate they were to be able to afford a truck that carried supplies and provided a place for injured sheep and newborn lambs. The route was full of hazards: one farm had put up a fence and another had reduced the public right away to a funnel only a few meters wide by overplanting along its edges. Rocks hidden by the night caused people or animals to stumble. Once, a ewe went into labor. Even with all the obstacles, Marta declares "it's pure romanticism," and she confesses to being "addicted to transhumance and life in the country."

Her great-grandfather bought the farm sometime before 1920 and worked it and two other family farms with her father, who Marta fondly referred to as a postwar land boss (*"patrón-jefe de la posguerra"*). Before her father's passing, he held a lottery to distribute the farms to his children, and Marta inherited the nearly 1,000-hectare (almost four-square-mile) sheep farm of rolling *dehesa* mixed with areas classified as *monte mediterráneo*, as well as some ponds. Marta has retained a deep connection to her inheritance, both with the land and with the animals. There she raises a flock that fluctuates between four and seven hundred *Segureña* mixed with Merino sheep, along with some Inra 401 sheep—a newer "laboratory breed" developed in France. Marta may be a self-professed romantic, but she is also a foresighted businesswoman who hopes to make the farm profitable again. To this end, she is investing in raising Iberian pigs, establishing an ecological reserve, and selling hunting licenses for the property.

What began as occasional country outings to help move the flocks and vacation a few times a year at the farm Marta inherited has turned into the life of a farmer-owner. Once a high-powered event planner for an elite country club in Seville, she is learning the ropes of running a large *dehesa* and raising nearly a thousand sheep. Marta started out a decade ago with land that was in good shape, but she continues to climb a steep learning curve as she works to restore the farm completely.

Marta's experiences outside of Spain, where she lived and worked for many years, as well as her jobs running various hotels and a large country club, have broadened her perspective in valuable ways. Now that she has been called back to the land and traditions she grew up with, she understands, "if you're not on top of things 100% of the time, you pay a price." But the daily tasks and outcomes bring more satisfaction for her than working at a country club. She recognizes "I'm a woman of privilege," and feels fortunate to be able to work more closely "with what life has already given me."

The Visit, Part II: The Farm

After our meeting in Seville, Marta invites me out to see her work on the farm and witness the land, animals, and natural setting. So, on another early spring morning, my colleague Mar and I find ourselves turning down the old road leading out of Aznalcóllar, which suffered a disaster in 1998 when the dam holding toxic waste from a local mine poured into its waterways. The area has since been restored as a greenway, now filling with mountain bikers for a race. Locals warn us to not take the dangerous old road and to use the new road instead, but Marta's *finca* cannot be accessed by the new route. We must wind along an unbanked single-lane road (through a stomach-turning "140 sharp curves" as Marta says), at a speed not much faster than a donkey—the form of transportation here for centuries. I can't imagine anyone driving this road in the rain or fog. A few kilometers and forty minutes later, we reach a relatively flat plateau with a few gentle hills. In every direction, sheep graze. Around the next curve, the generations-old family sign — with its insignia for *ganadería*, warriors, and a cross — appears. When we stop to open the gate, a dozen sheep wander over to greet us. Driving down a gravel road, we come upon the landowner home estate, a large house which now belongs to the family who bought part of Marta's grandfather's original farm. We then pass a new white-washed duplex, built recently for the resident shepherd and his family. Finally, we arrive to the old farmhouse — the smallest of the three buildings — where Marta lives when she is working on the farm.

Marta greets us looking vastly different from when we first met in Seville, dressed in jeans with the classic sage green wool jersey preferred by shepherds. She invites us into the simple four-room working farmhouse. Two small bedrooms adjoin the front hall and heavy green curtains separate the main room with its low pine ceiling and a small wood-burning stove, the only source of heat for the rustic farmhouse. It is a chilly fifteen degrees Celsius (fifty-eight degrees Fahrenheit) inside this morning. With no central heat or air conditioning, the temperatures inside can range from freezing in winter to forty-four degrees Celsius in July (well over 110 degrees Fahrenheit). We peek into the small 10 × 12 foot kitchen that barely has room for a two-burner stove, a small sink, and a few open cupboards. The sparsely furnished main room includes a rustic dining nook, while two rocking chairs and a small, narrow sofa provide a sitting area. Marta seems to notice our surprise at the simplicity of the farmhouse and explains this is not a place to rest and relax. In fact, the sofa is a new addition; there never used to be one. As Marta says, "you don't sit down or lay around much here because there is always work to be done." The couch contrasts sharply with the deep, soft "L"-shaped leather couch in her Seville living room. The few adornments — including a set of traditional *cencerro* bells and an antique water bottle from the farm's past — further accentuate the farmhouse's function. On a shelf there are a few books about breeding, along with a copy of *Don Quijote* and of an Agatha Christie novel. Above it hangs a picture of a Swiss transhumance with cattle that Marta's father gave her, complete with an engraving of her father's motto: "The land's worth what a man's worth."

I soon learn that Marta's outlook on life and the farm is as informed by her parents' work ethic as her years abroad. Since her birth in 1968, Marta has been coming to this farmhouse and land. She fondly recalls summers here. She says she imperceptibly absorbed the work of traditional sheep husbandry from her childhood visits. As a young girl, eight years behind the next-youngest sibling, Marta spent a lot of time with the resident shepherd just playing on the farm. She recalls how the shepherd built a swing for her and shared his "magical cures and potions." Although Marta loved these years, she had more options at age nineteen than her mother's generation of women, and she wanted to gain experience in other European countries. Marta worked in France and later studied hotel management in Switzerland, becoming an expert in the event-planning industry. At age twenty-seven she returned home, where she met her husband, had two children, and launched a high-powered career in hotel management. She jokes that the hard-working character she inherited from her parents, not to mention her experience working abroad, made her "one hell of a wedding planner." Her years in Switzerland also taught her how the Swiss have a vastly different relationship to their land, animals, and cultural identity. Martha believes that the Swiss value a deep connection with their own pastoral traditions and that they know how to harness this connection for tourism and profit.

Today, Marta has left the sixty-hour-a-week job planning baptisms, first communions, confirmations, weddings, and funerals, for another sixty-hour-a-week job running her own farm. Although she still commutes several times each week between Seville and the farm, she acknowledges that, for the farm to run well, she needs to spend more time there and learn how to do the work herself. The daily physical labor is both a joy and a hardship:

> You have to be on top of things day in and day out, and you have to work with the shepherds.... Part of the money I earned at the club I lost on the *finca* when I wasn't there.... First are the hens; they're the queens. You've got to feed them. Then you feed the dogs; then you put feed in the troughs for the lambs that are in the feeding area and the ewes that are good for re-breeding. We leave everything ready for the next morning. You finish with the cattle and the pigs so that when you get back in the afternoon you've got less to do. We still haven't had the time change, and by 7:00 it's already night. It's a little bit of a pain in the ass. You've got to count them, feed them, and see that they've eaten.

At first, Marta was stunned by the twelve-hour days and the pain from the demanding physical labor:

> At 8:00, 8:30 we were in the fields until it was getting dark. Non-stop. By 2:00 I hurt everywhere. I said, "I'm gonna have to take drugs!" Something! An ibuprofen, some kind of ointment, a heating pad. I'm dying here. But it all turned out OK because we've learned a ton.

While she is a quick learner and in great shape now, Marta details other aspects of her new life. Like the physical labor, living in the countryside brings both comfort and challenges. While the isolation can offer a deep sense of peace, over time it can be hard. Marta jokes that for the last ten years they have at least had electricity. Still, she recognizes that few people want to live this far from town: "There's a silence and a darkness that make a lot of people afraid."

Walking the Farm: Livestock Cycles and New Initiatives for Land Use

Even in spring, the midday sun begins to burn early, so Marta quickly moves us toward the door for what becomes a four-hour walking tour of the *finca*. In each part of our tour, Marta explains the natural cycles we witness and how her recent investments have helped them thrive. As someone who both summered on the farm as a child and is now learning about the full seasonal cycle of the farm and animals, Marta is an ideal teacher for an outsider like myself.

Our first stop is where the traditional sheep-keeping takes place. Here, she carefully describes the cycle of care for, depending on the year, between four and seven hundred *Segureña*-Merino sheep, focusing on how they must be separated, fed, and moved around — all of which require daily vigilance. "I grew up around all of this," Marta explains as she points to sheep on both sides of the road, sheep in a separate field, and more sheep in a newly constructed barn. Her farm includes the "full cycle" of sheep being raised on extensive-grazing and fully organic principles. The first group of sheep Marta shows us are marked with an "X." At this point in spring, she explains, she and the shepherd-manager have selected the *recrías*, ewes who have given birth and have shown promise as good breeders. They look for a successful previous pregnancy, faces with good morphology, and strong teeth, among other health indicators. The selected sheep are then set out in a pasture at a ratio of about 30 ewes to one male sheep during the traditional breeding days associated with the ancient saints' feast days of San José (March 19) through to San Juan (June 24). With pride, Marta notes some ewes have had many birth cycles, yet "they still don't look old."

Another set of ewes in an adjacent field are marked with an "O," because they have not yet given birth. She refuses to give them melatonin, which some farms use to induce a stronger heat cycle and fertility. Smiling, Marta explains that this breeding process is "as much art as skill" and that the ewes do best "if they look for their own boyfriend." The newborn lambs are in yet another field or still in the birthing area along with their mothers, who are under closer supervision. She explains: "Sometimes the first-time mothers aren't that good, and they don't do very well." As we heard in our last chapter from Fortunato, new mothers are often tired and nervous.

Under the shade of intermittent holm oak trees across the gravel drive, a few dozen grazing sheep marked with an "M" (ready for market) have reached about sixteen kilograms, but several will be held back and allowed to reach about 23 kilos, the preferred weight for Arab markets. They will be taken for local processing by CorSevilla, a collective of about five thousand producers. Marta's sheep, she reports proudly, generally sell with "extra" rating, which signals high-quality flavor and texture due to her extensive grazing practices.

We now move from the pastures into a beautiful, new two-story barn as the morning sun streams in through the main nave. The sweet smell of fresh hay wafts over us, and we hear the weak bleating of a few new mothers and their lambs. Marta introduces us to her young water dog, who is being trained to master the important guard work of a sheepdog. Upon command, he eagerly jumps up to Marta's shoulder. He will guard the new mothers as they are being monitored to ensure good nursing habits get established. We see one mother continually butt her lamb, but Marta assures us that by putting the two of them in the pen barely large enough for both of them, they will soon figure it out. While just a few lambs and their mothers are in the barn now, it will fill later in the season when shearing season begins and inclement weather hits.

Before her father split the farm into three parts for his children to inherit, the land encompassed 2,500 hectares and supported at least 1,200 sheep. Today the flock has been reduced to between four and seven hundred. Marta ticks off the current challenges she and pastoralism in general face: decades of stagnant market value for lamb, generational turnover of shepherds, new animal diseases, and oppressive government restrictions. Regarding the first economic challenge, she repeats a story we have heard from all our interviewees: the price of lamb had stagnated at the 1980 price of about 40–50 euros, with farmers receiving just 5–8 euro per sheep. "Why bother?!" she exclaims. More recently, however, the repercussions of global-market changes have tipped the scales back to Spain. With the ripple effect of Brexit in 2021 on the Commonwealth states of Australia and New Zealand, Spain is once again the primary exporter of lamb to Europe. Lamb prices have doubled this year, but

Marta remarks that there is an ironic edge to this change: now there are very few shepherds to raise sheep.

As we have heard from Juan Vázquez (Chapter 1), Pepe Millán (Chapter 2), and Fortunato Guerrero Lara (Chapter 3), the generational turnover of shepherds is on everyone's mind. In Marta's case, the farm had a full-time shepherd for nearly twenty years, who Marta describes as "otherworldly." He was expert at mixing up remedies from local plants to cure sick sheep and would suddenly disappear and reappear as he stealthily checked on sheep when he heard a fox or wolf. He knew how to work "the lead sheep, that are fine-tuned when they are raised to help lead the rest, so they begin to follow the flock." He could imitate the sound of a whip to move the sheep and trained the shepherd dogs and the guardian mastiffs. Since his retirement, several shepherds have worked for them, but none have lasted: "The days of near-slavery are long gone — as it should be — people don't want to sleep under trees in rough conditions." Marta has already been through three sets of workers. The first left because of a severe drinking problem — alcoholism is not an uncommon problem in these rural, isolated places. Then, she hired recent immigrants from Romania who were delighted to have good living conditions in the new duplex built for farmhands, but they soon moved closer to a town because they had school-aged children. Next, she hired someone she calls a "new/old" shepherd, someone with traditional skills but newer ways of working together with owners. Once again, Marta reports, the situation did not work out: during the pandemic, when she and her family moved to the farmhouse fulltime to escape Seville's lockdown and contagion, the resident shepherd took a job at a nearby farm because he wanted more solitude and control. In another case, she realized that a skillful shepherd had set up an unauthorized side-business to rent use of the land to hunters — a potentially lucrative business but one that can also damage the ecosystem. Now, Marta is training a young couple with little experience but a strong desire to live the pastoral life. She understands the challenge of finding a balance between trustworthy, knowledgeable shepherds who work well with her and people who can tolerate a rural lifestyle.

Fig. 4.2 A local shepherd works for hire on Marta's *dehesa* (2018).

In addition to market prices and scarcity of shepherds, another hardship Marta describes is the devastation brought by diseases. Disease is an inevitable part of sheep-farming. She recalls how her father's pigs were stricken with the African swine fever (*PPA: Peste Porcina Africana*) in the 1970s and that he never recovered from the shock of having to slaughter so many animals. She herself has had to deal with an outbreak of Bluetongue, a viral disease affecting livestock throughout the area. Marta initially had to stop the biannual transhumance because movement of flocks through open lands was prohibited due to the likelihood of contagion. Later, when she tried to reinstate the practice, one of her ewes tested positive for the infection brucellosis: her whole flock was categorized as M3, which meant it had to be quarantined. Marta hopes to reinstate a small-scale transhumance (known technically as a transterminance) soon.

It's been eight years since the last transhumance. Normally we'd do it on foot, and it was 33 kilometers, but when there was an outbreak of Bluetongue, they kept us from moving the herd on foot because of the threat of a spread. And we had to move them by truck. So, the last transhumance we did by truck. And this year, when I talked to [a local landowner], who has a *finca* of 1000 hectares that's some five kilometers down this same road, she told me she's got a lot of pasture and not much livestock. So, last year she offered to take my sheep to her *finca* in the summer because they maintain her land quite well, and they don't do any harm. People really don't mind because they clear the land of brush and cut down on forest fires. So, this year, I'm going to see if I can get my M4 rating back and start the transhumance with the sheep again by foot. It wouldn't really be for transhumance, it would be for the benefit of the pastures. It would be what the Junta de Andalucía rates as a "pasture benefit." And I'd take them here, to our *finca* El Campillo, in the summer.

While the neighbor's land will tide her over and Marta's sheep will clear and fertilize it, she still hopes to resume the practice of a short transterminance. Extensive grazing, she acknowledges, "is complicated."

Marta, like other informants, also mentions an increase in government regulations, which can be just another hurdle to efficient pastoralism and profit. She cites the difficulty caused by the recent "tug of war and locking horns" of the political parties — one often undoing policies established by the other — as well as the enormous amount of paperwork that has made pastoralism nearly impossible for anyone who does not have the means, time, and training to work with lawyers and government officials. She has had to hire an engineer to map out land usage, then a lawyer to authorize the plan; this year, too, Marta must prepare a new action plan for the Junta de Andalucía (the executive branch of the provincial government). The plan reflects a series of recent regulations that must be observed, many of which come from the EU headquarters in Brussels. Marta, like other shepherd-farmers, complains that the EU does not understand the delicate ecosystems in Andalusia, such as the *dehesa*, and the sustainable-grazing traditions that have evolved over centuries.

> Let me give you some examples: let's say I want to add a parcel of land, well, I have to ask permission; I want to cut down a dried up live oak tree, well, I have to go to the Junta de Andalucía and ask permission; I want to move the herd from one pasture to another, well, I have to go to the office with the agrarian guide, which comes from the Junta de Andalucía, and ask permission. Another example: let's say a sheep dies, they want me to locate the dead animal by its ear tag, which is like its ID. Excuse me? I have a rather large range of land. They say, "No, it's not that, it's that in Brussels...." Sure, in Belgium, a tiny country with intensive grazing flocks where the guy who's setting the standards maybe doesn't understand just how large the expanse of our land is. He's using standards that put you on a farm where they've got 200 animals in a pen. That way they can control things easily, but here? Here it's a lot healthier and upkeep is

easier. I always feel like the Junta de Andalucía treats me like an accused criminal, like I always have to go around defending my innocence, proving that I haven't done anything that goes against their standards.

The government always wants to control everything, right? Don't they control every area of our lives? Don't they know that we're the ones who are the first to be concerned about preserving the environment? I'm the most concerned about my *finca*, and I want it to be perfect: the trees not dying, the herd in good health. The first person concerned about all of that is me.

Despite the government hurdles, Marta admits that the regulations have brought some benefit. Working on her plan has helped her consider new areas of revenue to make the farm profitable, given that sheep-raising alone is not sufficient. The government has helped by providing startup funds for some of the new projects. One of her newer ventures is raising Iberian pigs. As we walk further down the gravel road to visit this operation, we pass a springtime explosion of color. Marta explains that an unseasonable thirty-seven liters of rain fell during Holy Week. Now the pastures are unusually green and speckled with red poppies, lavender, daisies, and yellow rockrose. The sounds of bleating sheep fade, and grunts punctuated by intermittent squeals become louder. Under the dappled shade of an old holm oak and a handful of cork oaks, the classic long, dark shapes of Iberian pigs come into view. As the warm sun climbs higher, about a dozen huddle together either napping or rooting around to coat themselves in a cooling layer of dirt. Marta sees my surprise and observes that in a couple of months, when the temperatures can easily hover around 45°C for hours, the farm animals all find ways to keep cool. The sheep have their own technique: they circle around facing toward the center to cool themselves, moving the hot, still air with their collective breathing.

For this new porcine-related enterprise, Marta is able to utilize land not appropriate for grazing sheep. Since she only takes on part of the early life cycle of the pigs, the effort can be profitable. Marta raises around 500–700 Iberian pigs (*ibéricos*) bred with a white breed variety; about half are hers and the rest belong to a business partner. The piglets arrive in February to her farm, but because the *ibéricos* in particular require an enormous number of acorns to feed their huge appetites, her farm simply does not have enough acorn-producing holm oaks to support grown pigs. So, they stay until late summer, when they are moved to another farm with more acorns to finish the feeding process and to qualify as *"Ibérico de Bellota"* or *"Sánchez Romero Cinco Jotas"* pigs, the meat from which, after two or three years of curing, brings a premium price at popular Christmas markets in early December.

Fig. 4.3 Iberian pigs graze on Marta's *dehesa* for months each year (2018).

However, there are many pitfalls of the pig-raising enterprise, especially when it involves going into business with another investor. As we walk to a fenced-in muddy plot outside a long-arched metal barn, the calm scene under the oaks changes to a din of squealing as hundreds of pigs dart around, pressing against each other. For the first time, Marta bristles as she recalls how the partner, a former veterinarian, had assured her that their pigs would get along fine, despite being from different broods. "He deceived me!" she repeats several times. His pigs were wild and attacked her pigs, slept on top of them, and took most of the feed. Her own pigs suffered life-threatening stress, stopped eating, and became ill — some even had heart attacks. She had to invest in a large barn to separate the two broods; the solution was costly. Disgusted by the partner's lie, Marta observes that as a livestock professional, he surely was well aware of the problems that mixing the two broods might cause. "He took me for a fool just because I was a woman." The most difficult part of learning the trade and running a farm, she argues, is that she is at a deep disadvantage as a woman in a man's world.

After visiting the pigs, we head to the farm's reserve area. A peaceful stroll through rolling meadows alive with the spring songbirds and a couple of ponds takes us to a fenced-off area with young trees. Marta smiles broadly, explaining how the area serves as "a small ecological reserve" with habitat for black bass, ducks, grey herons, and a host of other animals and birds. The fenced area of fourteen hectares is dedicated to restoring the native holm oaks as part of a reforestation project sponsored by the European Union. No livestock is allowed in the area. Marta then relates a vivid example of the damage done to her farm and others nearby. After years of neglect, during which non-native eucalyptus trees were not thinned and the underbrush was left to grow unchecked, a forest fire broke out and raged through 29,000 hectares, including much of her farm. The fire lasted only forty-five minutes from start to finish, but, as one worker recalled, it was "like the fire was screaming, and it was horrific." For two years, the *finca* could not function, but Marta argues that they were also fortunate. Since the fire was so rapid and intense, it moved through the *finca* quickly and did not deeply damage the trees. Luckily, it bypassed the farmhouse, though by just fifteen meters. Her brother, who inherited a part of the farm where the sheep used to go, now helps her every year by sending one of his workers to cut a fire-prevention lane around the farm. More recently, Marta also has received a large grant from the EU to further replant the part of the ecologically valuable *dehesa*. She hopes this extensive work will revitalize the wooded areas of the farm. Increasingly, advocacy on behalf of the Andalusian *dehesa* has influenced EU funding and national regulations.

As we make our way up the final stretch back to the farmhouse and pass a tractor from 1941 (one of the first tractors in Andalusia), Marta repeats her motto: "It's complicated; you really have to be dedicated to your work." She summarizes the challenges of a sheep farmer-owner: stagnant market prices, shortages of shepherds, epidemics and diseases, and oppressive government regulations, not to mention the long days of hard work and semi-isolation. Although "some people look at you with envy, it can be a bitch of an inheritance." Marta jokes that the farm "is a pain in the ass, but I love it." When I ask what she likes best about being a farmer-owner, she doesn't skip a beat and lists three things: "The quality of life is better; at night there's a peace, and I sleep well; and I love the animals because they don't talk back." The "pure romanticism" of the biennial transhumance during her childhood and later vacations at the *finca* have now become more than nostalgia. Marta is an essential contributor to the work of this farm.

Fig. 4.4 Parcels of Marta's *dehesa* are dedicated bio-reserves for local flora and fauna (2018).

As our visit comes to an end, Marta offers us a local beer and whips up some rustic tapas from her pantry: a Spanish potato salad with fresh farm eggs, tuna, and red peppers, dressed with her own homemade vinegar. She observes that her life trajectory of leaving and coming back to Spain, inheriting the land, and then returning to it must include the story of her eighty-eight-year-old mother, Carmela, who lives in Seville and would certainly offer another perspective that should be recorded. Carmela was married to the "postwar land boss" and ran a large household on an isolated rural farm in the early years after the civil war. Her perspective foregrounds the huge changes in gender roles in just one generation — although with forty years difference in their ages.

Looking Back: A Postwar Wife of a Landowner, Carmela Espinosa Calero

Marta's mother, Carmela Espinosa Calero, spent a dozen years as a young postwar wife and mother living on one of the family *finca*s. Her story helps us to see more clearly how these Andalusian mother-daughter landowners have worked within a traditionally male world, pushing up against gender boundaries by managing a household and making a world for themselves in the field in the process.

A week after our visit to the farm, Marta and I meet at the Metropol Parasol, the famous modernist landmark in the heart of old Seville (popularly known as "Las Setas") built at the turn of the twenty-first century, after construction for a much-needed parking garage was halted by the discovery of an ancient Roman marketplace. We pass a Renaissance convent before arriving at her mother's apartment. Carmela, a petite, spry woman, greets us. As we step into her apartment, we seem to step back in time. Elaborate hand-carved antique settees, cabinets filled with figurines, and a formal dining table fill the room. Saints in oil paintings look on as Carmela proudly displays crocheted doilies and tablecloths from her 1940s bridal trousseau. Her live-in domestic helper from Colombia serves us a snack of *café con leche* with traditional almond cookies made by the nuns of the nearby convent.

Carmela now perches on the edge of a straight-backed chair, remarking that the key to good physical health is never slouching into an easy chair. I smile, recalling how the small, firm sofa at the farmhouse had been a very recent addition. Still energetic after walking to Seville's famous bullring La Maestranza to see the opening of the season, Carmela clearly still maintains the traditional activities of a woman of her class and generation. When I begin the interview with a question about living on the *finca*, Carmela's voice fills with excitement. She delights in having an audience as she paints a lively scene with vignettes polished through the lens of memory and a keen wit.

Fig. 4.5 Marta's mother, Carmela Espinosa Calero, in Seville (2019).

Born in what she calls a "small city town" in 1928, she met her future husband at a fair when she was just fourteen years old. He was eight years her senior. He was "the rich young man from the neighboring town," she reports, and, as the only son, he inherited the family's lands. At seventeen years old, he enlisted with the Nationalists when the civil war broke out and three years later returned home to manage the family's extensive land holdings. He met Carmela soon afterwards. The couple married in 1948 and began life on the farm in the province of Huelva, where they remained for almost twenty years.

Although managing rural life on her husband's *finca* in the postwar years and raising what would become a family of seven daughters and one son was clearly challenging, Carmela was clearly a strong-willed young wife who insisted on making the best out of rural life. Her anecdotes reveal the demands made on a young woman who had never lived on a farm. Their first-born child was deaf, and a son was stillborn.

It was five kilometers to the nearest village, Paterna del Campo, and the farmhouse had no electricity or running water. Carmela had to go into town for supplies by burro.

Despite these challenges, she was determined to bring joy to her isolated farm life. One year, during the height of the Francoism, she hitchhiked in full traditional dress to the renowned Seville Feria de Abril:

> I was probably thirty, something like that, still at a good age for having a good time. I got into a car with a man who, instead of going to the fair, could have taken me somewhere else, even to Constantina. Can you imagine? And I was not going to get home late, not on your life. So, I went up to a man who was starting his car, and I asked, "Sir, where are you going?" He said he was going to the fair. "Would you mind taking me? I need to be let off at the main entrance." I didn't want anyone I knew from the booths inside to see me get out of another man's car. I was always one who wasn't afraid to take a risk, as we say around here.

In another attempt to help enliven rural life, she had a rudimentary pool built to cool off in the scorching summer heat, but she broke both legs jumping into the shallow waters and had to endure the long and painful trip by burro to a town with a doctor. Though the hardship and loneliness of farm life seep through her story, it is clear that she fought to maintain her innate joy for life, even while living with her "hard-working, melancholy husband." Like many of her generation, she never mentions her husband's Nationalist wartime activities or why he left his high-ranking position under Franco's new regime to return to the *finca*s and rural life. Still, Carmela took on the duties of a wife without losing her sense of humor. With glee, she recounts being charged with packing his suitcase for the first time.

> The first time I packed his suitcase, I didn't know how to pack for a man. I wondered, "How do I fold his jackets?" He asked me: "With four brothers, you've never packed a suitcase?" I answered, "Why would I pack a suitcase for my brothers?" "Fine," he said: "I'll show you how just once, but the next time I tell you I want you to pack my suitcase, you're going to do it on your own." "Sure, yes, don't worry," I responded. Then he showed me how to pack his bag, and I learned. On our honeymoon he was in the shower, and there was no bathmat. He took off his underwear and stepped out on to them. He then says to me, "Carmela, bring me another pair, these are wet." I looked in the suitcase, and there were none.

> I went to my sister-in-law, who was younger, and I said, "I don't have any underwear for your brother. I forgot them." Surprised, she said: "Oh my, Carmela, what are you going to do when he finds out...?" "Look, I just forgot them, I didn't mean to," I told her. "Well," she said, "if it only happened once, then it will all be fine." He took it well, and it really made me laugh because, as they say, anything can happen in Castilla. Since his pants were made of fine wool, they itched him a bit. And I was like, "Ha, ha, ..., look at your brother, ha, ha, ha. He can't stop scratching." "Why are you laughing?" "I'm not laughing," I had fun with it. All the things he had to put up with. And he didn't get mad. He thought it was funny.

When I ask about her own education, Carmela smiles, but without a pause, answers: "I was a very good administrator." This was a key role for the proprietor's wife, but she adds impishly that she learned because, as she repeats several times, "every night I went to bed with a very clever man" who didn't let the farm go into debt. In between the lines, it is clear that, as a postwar woman married to a wealthy, land-owning husband, there was no opportunity for formal education. She learned how to run the household and family "on the job" — and stood by her savvy businessman husband.

> In the countryside it's like everywhere else, if you have money in your pocket, you're fine. What you can't do is go to the country owing money. That's the way I always thought about it, and so did he. You've got to buy and make it with your own money, not with any money that you've borrowed from the bank. The moment you have to pay high interest, all you earn goes back to the bank. I haven't studied this as a career or anything like it, but every night I went to bed with a very clever man.

A key part of Carmela's work of managing a large household of workers and children was the preparation of the abundant farm products. She fondly recalls her recipe for large pots of garbanzos and fresh roasted lamb. Even simple eggs could be turned into a delicious meal, but it was the traditional *matanza del cerdo* — the process of slaughtering a pig that often weighs around two hundred kilos and preparing all the different meats, oils, and soaps from a single animal — that most required her skill and time. I hear how important this skill is from many of my informants: to make the most of the animals you have raised. At the same time, I recall Fortunato describing how the latest government regulations prohibit livestock farmers from carrying out this tradition on their own farms (see Chapter 3). Carmela recounts that there often were as many as nine slaughters a year that would provide staple meats in many forms for many months and months.

> One year I killed nine pigs. In December, January, February, I did nine *matanzas del cerdo*. I had the maid who helped me and a woman from town who knew how to do it who came to teach me. But after that, I alone made the foie gras, the paté.

Although in those years she describes herself "like an earthquake" in the kitchen, she admits to not liking to cook now. Marta, who has been listening to her mother's stories as we talk, now speaks up for the first time, noting that her mother still has a bit of "trauma" after so many years of overseeing such a big operation.

The family grew, and times changed after two decades of living on the farm. By the 1960s, the five oldest children were attending boarding school in Seville. The cost of room and board for five school-age children was becoming exorbitant, and Carmela was tired of the isolated rural life. So, she traded the rural environment for a home back in the city. Yet this new situation, she recalls vividly, brought its own sense of isolation. While at first her husband joined them in Seville, he soon recognized that the *finca*s suffered from his absence. Even though these years coincided with Franco's push toward the modernization of roadways and public transportation to develop tourism in Andalusia's sun-drenched coasts and culturally exotic towns, commuting daily was still out of the question. So, he moved back to the *finca*. Carmela now enjoyed a dynamic urban environment, but, without her "rooster," she recalls, a new sense of loneliness crept in:

> I'd call him, and I'd say, "Pepe, I don't hear the hens clucking, and I'm very sad. Why don't you come get me?" I wanted to see him. "What's the matter Carmela? Tell me what's the problem. What's wrong?" I'd say, "I want to be with you. I don't hear the turkeys either. I don't want to stay here. I'm better off in the country." "Very well, I'll come for you this afternoon." And he'd come get me. I missed him very much.

Since leaving the *finca*, Carmela has only returned to it as a vacation pastime. She recalls her days on the *finca* with what seems to be a mixture of distaste and nostalgia — a pride in her ability to run a household with limited resources along with an acceptance of this sometimes-frustrating existence. Carmela surely has many more stories to offer to an interested listener like me, but when she hears the seven o'clock bells calling worshippers to San Pedro's Church, she abruptly changes gears, saying, "you have to live up to God's demands too." She hasn't been to Sunday Mass yet that day. We accompany her on the two-block walk to church and, with a few kisses on the cheek to say goodbye, she disappears inside.

Carmela understands that she has lived a privileged, traditional life. Coming from an aristocratic family that had once owned a large part of what is now Doñana Natural Park but lost everything when her thirty-year-old father became ill with Parkinson's, she married a prosperous, industrious man. But as she charmingly recalls the postwar years on the *finca* and the early years of modernization, Carmela also reveals the challenges even privileged women faced in a highly gendered society as they navigated customary responsibilities, all while trying to find a space for themselves as well. Traditional pastoralism established clear roles for property owners and shepherds, as well as for their families, which remained fairly static until the turn of the twenty-first century.

Conclusions and Update

Despite generational differences, both mother and daughter seem to approach their own lives in a similar way: Carmela by striving for independence and expression in the small ways that were acceptable at the time, and Marta by being a woman in charge in the countryside. Marta observes: "As far as generations go, women my age find ourselves closer, educationally speaking, to our mothers and even our grandmothers than to our daughters." Both mother and daughter understood that the health of the farm depends on the owner living on the farm at least part-time and staying involved in the daily decision-making, as well as on working closely with dedicated shepherds who tend to the animals. Marta is still learning what it takes to run a good farm and care for animals, but she is also taking measures to improve the quality of life for people who work her farm: she has provided new accommodations, a restructured pay scale, paid vacation, and makes efforts to consult regularly with her farm managers. She has even learned one of her mother's skills: the resident shepherd taught her how to perform the traditional slaughter, and they split the 220 kilos of meat they prepared; it will feed both their families for months.

When I check back in with Marta two years after the start of the COVID-19 pandemic, she sadly informs me that her mother has passed. Carmela could fight COVID-19 but not the new loneliness that came with lockdown. Marta also updates me on how much she has learned about how to manage her flock and to work to keep a shepherd. Moreover, she has a new business partner with a more comprehensive plan for raising pigs. He provides about six hundred pigs, while she provides land and labor for raising them. While Brexit doubled the price she got for lamb, her return on pork fell dramatically during the pandemic with the global lockdown. Seventy million tourists normally visit Spain every year, she explains, and many of them visit Andalusia for a taste of the famous cured serrano ham. Because of travel restrictions and health risks, however, this profitable trade collapsed. Most large celebratory events were cancelled, along with the orders for the *ibérico* ham that is traditional at these occasions. Marta had to sell many of her pigs at a loss, but the savvy businesswoman decided to keep some of them and began her own direct sales, offering package deals of sausages, ham, and pork loins.

By mid-summer 2022, tourism was mostly coming back, but Marta now struggles with a longer-term challenge that worsened for her during the pandemic. The post-pandemic job market and shortage of labor has wreaked havoc on finding a stable shepherd and set of farm laborers. This is when Marta told me about the difficulties relating to keeping her skilled shepherd. Like many landowners during the pandemic, Marta's whole family left Seville during the lockdown and moved to the farm, where they could be outdoors. But many shepherds and farmhands, she explains, enjoy solitude, and suddenly having a whole family around created a tense situation. When her neighbor offered the shepherd more money and space, he left, and it has been hard to replace him.

As the economy moves toward recovery, there have been many shifts in the labor market, so it continues to be difficult to hire people. Marta compares her attempts to find qualified workers who like living in the country and who are reliable to being in a soap opera. One man, for example, turned out to be involved in a drug operation. After firing him, Marta had to run the farm herself for nearly four months with only occasional help from friends and family. "If I don't have people working on the *finca*, everything falls back on me." Laughing, she recounts how one cold December night a neighbor called at 2:00 a.m. reporting that hundreds of Marta's sheep were wandering in the road. Dressed in pajamas, Marta single-handedly guided them all back to the farm.

Marta's and Carmela's stories help me to realize that the future of pastoralism depends on more than shepherds and grazing lands. Like Rafael Enríquez del Río and his work with Fortunato Guerrero Lara (see Chapter 3), Marta exemplifies a new spirit of collaboration. Farm owners like Rafael and Marta are a critical part of this traditional system, essential to moving it forward amidst new regulations and markets, as well as new threats to animals, land, and ecosystems. At the same time, landowners also need to offer better conditions and more equal relationships with their workers to attract and keep shepherds.

Through two distinct lenses — a mother's memory of rural life during the postwar and a daughter's present-day drive to return to the land — the vastly different worlds of two generations of land-owning women come alive. Both mother and daughter have sought to find their place in the world: Carmela went from the countryside to the city in middle age, and Marta has gone from the city to the country in the same period of her life. Carmela learned to survive and thrive in a rural world she knew nothing about — and indeed initially seems to have had little natural affinity for. She lived through the transition from postwar rural life to modernization and urban living in a world that increasingly connected social mobility to an urban lifestyle. Marta, born more than forty years later, found refuge in the farm during this new age. She watched older sisters come of age when democracy, and its resulting dramatic cultural changes and a gender revolution were in full force. Her life story, however, reveals another set of challenges. Marta wanted to return to the rural life and be the resident boss running the farm, but raising livestock is still largely a man's world. Choosing to follow in her father's footsteps in middle age, she is taking the reins as a good steward of the *finca*. Her mother has given her a legacy of sure-footedness when it comes to doing work that needs to be done in the campo. Marta hopes her inheritance will pay off economically, but more importantly, she values a newfound sense of balance between life in the city and on the farm that allows her to be proud of her contributions to the sustainability of pastoralism in her region.

Fig. 5.1 Dehesa San Francisco in Santa Olalla del Cala, Huelva (2017).

5. New Initiatives within Tradition: Ernestine Lüdeke and the Dehesa San Francisco and the "Fundación Monte Mediterráneo" (Santa Olalla del Cala [Huelva])

Every consumer, everyone who eats, needs to understand the cost to humanity of mass production of food sources at low costs and how they fail to support a viable future; society has to pay a lot to make up for the harmful effects to the environment.

The fragile, biodiverse *dehesa* is one of the last defenses Andalusia has in the face of the encroaching Sub-Saharan desert system, which is slowly but surely creeping north. It is up to us to be sure the younger generation understands and accepts this challenge.

I think the main problem in Andalusia is that the people who have owned land have never worked on the land.

Ernestine Lüdeke

Overview

From the first week of my research on transhumance and continuing through follow-up interviews five years later, people I met in Andalusia often brought up the name of Ernestine Lüdeke, the German woman" ("la Alemana"). Although she did not fit into my initial profile of traditional shepherds and their families, I soon discovered that many other Spaniards and foreigners alike are finding innovative ways to change and reinvest in traditional practices of pastoralism. In contrast to the generational knowledge that shepherds like Juan Vázquez (see Chapter 1), Fortunato

https://doi.org/10.11647/OBP.0387.05

Guerrero Lara (see Chapter 2), or Pepe Millán (see Chapter 3) inherited from their ancestral community, the story of Ernestine Lüdeke is that of an outsider who has become very much an insider in her efforts to conserve and revive pastoralism, as both extensive grazing and transhumance, and to promote the viability of western Andalusia's valuable natural resource, the *dehesa*. She works actively to integrate quality food production, biodiversity, and social change at local, regional, national, and trans-European levels.

Ernestine's story is rooted in her nature and character, but also on the *dehesa* she has spent much of her adult life cultivating. She raises Merino sheep on the Dehesa San Francisco that she and her husband Hans bought for farming. The sheep spend the winter in Andalusia and the summer in Northern Spain on both public and private lands controlled by the regional government of Castilla y León. During the five years that I have known Ernestine, she has worked tirelessly and collaboratively to find the best way to move thousands of sheep twice a year. The Dehesa also serves as the headquarters for their NGO, the "Fundación Monte Mediterráneo" (FMM), which focuses on moving food systems toward long-term sustainable models by supporting a wide range of biodiversity and sustainability initiatives all centered on pastoralism.

Ernestine's story is also about her neighbors, the people of Santa Olalla del Cala, a small town of 2,000 near her *dehesa*. While Ernestine's passion is driven by both ecological and practical considerations, she is also a strong advocate for the partners who live and work alongside her in rural Andalusia. All of her meat and dairy are made fresh, either on the farm or by friends and neighbors nearby. Ernestine employs many people in the town, a boon in rural Andalusia, where any industry is greatly valued. She also maintains connections with many small-scale rural entrepreneurs, such as the baker who makes the dark bread that she had little access to outside of Germany. Ernestine understands the need to develop rural life and how this need connects with farming. Not surprisingly, when we visit the town, many locals seemed to assume that we are German and greet us warmly, as if to say, "any friend of Ernestine's is a friend of mine."

Ernestine is equal parts teacher, organizer, farmer, cultural interpreter, environmentalist, and spokesperson. "I'm really a little bit of everything," she comments, "you need to be really flexible here!" She works with farmers to combine tradition with innovative ideas, and with government bodies and NGOs to help them understand farmers' issues. She also hosts camps and seminars to teach new generations about the countryside and food production. Her multifaceted approach has been featured in television shows, such as Canal Sur's *Tierra y Mar, Europeos, Destino Andalucía,* and *Europa Abierta,* as well as in newspaper articles and academic studies (e.g., Gordon and Holl, 2020). Her work models new ways to make the Andalusian *dehesa* sustainable. When Mar and I visit, we find that this mission to share her work with a broad audience includes keeping on hand a generous selection of coffee, wine, and beer. She has a deep desire to share not only her success but also her convictions. Toward the end of this chapter, in fact, we'll hear directly from her shepherd-manager, Daniel, who was trained in one of Ernestine's courses for new shepherds.

The Visit, the Farmhouse, and a Vision for the Future

When I first contact Ernestine, with no introduction other than her phone number from a journalist who had interviewed her, she immediately invites us out to see her farm. We set out the very next day from Seville. Following her directions to the Provincia de Huelva, we climb into the Sierra Morena, close to the Sierra de Aracena and los Picos de Aroche Natural Park, and wind past rolling hills, ravines, and *dehesa*s verdant with the onset of autumn rains after a scorching five months of record-breaking heat and drought. As another thirteenth-century frontier castle of Santa Olalla del Cala emerges on the horizon, we veer south before turning down a dirt road to the Dehesa San Francisco and drive through a trough that disinfects the tires; we continue four more kilometers through dry scrubland spotted with the characteristic oaks of the southwestern *dehesa*s. We continue along the bumpy terrain, past a giant oak on the left and forests of cork and holm oaks on either side. All along the side of the road, we see enclosures for a few cows and hundreds of sheep with mastiffs watching over them.

Entering the Dehesa, we first pass an old white farmhouse, called Vallebarco, which has been remodeled with the aid of EU funds for rural development to create a large educational center that can house twenty overnight guests. The road ends at a modern farmhouse that boasts elegant floor to ceiling windows and a swimming pool. When we get out of the car, a blond, blue-eyed German woman in her fifties energetically greets us (along with two somewhat suspicious guard dogs). Ernestine Lüdeke has just finished a day's work with a handful of shepherds involved in a local version of transhumance that she spearheaded. Inviting us into the large, modern living room while she prepares coffee and biscuits for us in the adjacent kitchen, Ernestine talks easily about her life and work. In any interview with Ernestine, the question about her origins and motivations soon comes up. Why Spain? Why pastoralism?

Fig. 5.2 Ernestine with a hawk on the *dehesa* (2021).

Born in Germany and trained as a teacher, Ernestine found the German educational system too rigid. She left her home country at age twenty-eight and took a teaching position in Spain. Instead of teaching as planned, however, the multilingual German was soon hired by the government of the Spanish Socialist party (PSOE) as part of the project to "modernize" Spain's image at home and abroad in the decade after the transition to democracy. The Ministry of Culture drew on Ernestine's knowledge of the European Union and appointed her as both a cultural interpreter and a public relations spokesperson for major concerts and theatrical productions in the capitol. By the early 1990s, the German Minister for Culture hired Ernestine to help create a pavilion for the recently unified Germany in time for the opening of the 1992 World's Fair in Seville. There she met her husband, German CEO Hans-Gerd Neglein. Together, they began to realize a shared vision, first by buying and restoring the Dehesa San Francisco as a working farm. Unlike Marta Moya, who inherited a successful *dehesa* from her parents (see Chapter 4), Ernestine and her husband bought their *dehesa* from a Sevillana family that had owned it since the early 1800s but who no longer kept it up.

During the first years on the *dehesa*, Ernestine secured funding for a handful of shepherds and flock owners to carry out transhumance by foot. A few years later, they hired trucks and have been practicing transhumance this way ever since — like Fortunato Guerrero Lara (see Chapter 3), taking advantage of being able to have extensive grazing year-round but avoiding the many difficulties of transhumance by foot. In fact, each year they have more sheep being transported back and forth, reaching 13,500 in November 2021. When it comes to shepherding, Ernestine is not driven by nostalgia. Her interest and commitment to transhumant shepherding is very practical: after carrying out an ecological and economical calculation, she saw the benefits of exporting the sheep for a season to summer grazing sites, as opposed to importing water and feed to semi-arid Andalusia. The traditional practices allow the *dehesa* to rest and regenerate and the mountain pasturelands up north to be put to use. The future of transhumance, she asserts, "must be practical, must be strategic, and we must choose our priorities."

Ernestine and her husband have also created the "Fundación Monte Mediterráneo" (FMM), housed in the Vallebarco farmhouse. The mission of the organization is to promote sustainable management of the *dehesa* ecosystem and to educate policy makers, farmers, shepherds, and even school-age children in its on-site educational center. Hans and Ernestine run the foundation as an NGO together, as President and Vice President, although they have distinct roles. While Hans contributes to the Fundación's longevity through funding, the day-to-day work is primarily in Ernestine's hands. She works hard, gets dirty, and is tireless with her chores and the care of their land. Ernestine takes little time for holidays or vacations but prioritizes her other passion outside her job by participating in spiritual retreats. What began as a love affair with her adopted country has turned into decades of work on multiple fronts to save Andalusian ecosystems, landscapes, and lifeways she is so passionate about.

As we share coffee and biscuits, Ernestine continues to talk about her life, the *dehesa*, and the work of the "Fundación Monte Mediterráneo", and it becomes clear to me that the very skill the Spanish and German governments found useful in the early 1990s — her ability to interpret rapidly changing nations and their places in the world and find innovative ways to educate the public — has been invaluable to her work at the FMM and the *dehesa*. When she and her husband bought the Dehesa San Francisco, it had been owned by the same family for over 200 years and had fallen into disrepair. The family lived in Seville and visited just a few times a year. "The last generation of brothers and cousins didn't have any idea about farming or animals," she remarks. "They couldn't care less." Only recently, and after twenty years of conservation work and repair, is the *dehesa* approaching its rich natural-life capacity. To accomplish this, Ernestine and Hans have re-introduced traditional farming methods for sustainable land management, including cork cultivation, extensive grazing, and even protection of animal species that had disappeared from the *dehesa* (primarily rabbits and vultures, along with certain amphibians). With the help of a manager, Ernestine oversees the daily operations of the *dehesa*, but she also works actively to integrate quality food production, biodiversity, and social change at local, regional, national, and trans-European levels.

Today, Dehesa San Francisco and the "Fundación Monte Mediterráneo" are a Spanish, and indeed European, reference point for educational programs and summits on biodiversity and the unique contribution that the *dehesa* system and extensive grazing practices can make to sustainable food practices in Andalusia. One example of this work is the day's work she has just finished with shepherds who are practicing transhumance with her. At the all-day meeting, she reports, they decided to pool resources to pay for grazing rights in public lands in Palencia, up north in Castilla y León, hire local shepherds there to tend the flocks, and rent a truck to transport their sheep in a modern-day transhumance. Ernestine observes that this system, while not ideal, still provides economic and environmental stability to both Northern and Southern Spain:

> We can neither be pure romantic ecologists and historians nor ignorant, stubborn farmers continuing five hundred years without change. We need to face the facts nowadays and find a way to reinstall transhumance in a new way as part of live organic husbandry. We need to get to a point where it can be part of a more global system.

When I ask Ernestine about transhumance in general and how this system looks moving forward, she recognizes that traditional practices (as well as public awareness about them) are always shifting but sees establishing good ecological and economic structures as key. Her deep commitment to transhumance and extensive grazing includes applying for funds to help offset costs, organizing farmers, negotiating stringent laws about licenses and blood tests for animals, and bidding at auctions to rent public-land pastures in the north. For this system to work, Ernestine explains, she must re-apply annually for transhumant funding to cover the difference between what farmers must pay (twelve euros/sheep) and the real cost. Sheep just don't bring enough at market to pay for this practice, but the benefits to the environment by far offset the costs, she explains. In addition to easing these costs, Ernestine has helped with logistical issues by successfully advocating for a change in testing laws. For example, transhumant livestock no longer need blood tests in the rockier pasturelands up north before returning to Andalusia. They are now quarantined and retested for diseases upon their return to the Sierra Morena each fall.

Ernestine shares a basic goal with Jesús Garzón — whom we met at the Festival of Transhumance in Madrid (see the introductory chapter) — to revitalize transhumance. He has worked to grow the total number of sheep that make the journey by foot along one of the main vías *pecuarias*. If at least 20,000 sheep do a biannual transhumance, he believes, it would reestablish a green corridor — clearing droving roads from encroaching vegetation and fostering biodiversity. The practice would then be sustainable, benefiting the animals, land, and local communities. As of 2021, Jesús Garzón and others he works with had thousands of sheep and hundreds of goats. On the other hand, Ernestine, like Fortunato Guerrero Lara (see Chapter 3), says that doing transhumance by foot is not viable because so many of the trails have been paved or grown over, and there is so little access to water and shelter along the way. She gives the example of doing transhumance by foot this year. When a retiring shepherd asked Ernestine for help to return one last time along a transhumance route he had done for decades but stopped about ten years ago, she agreed. It took thirty-four days, and they found there often was not sufficient access to trails or water. Yet, she argues, it is critical to keep transhumance going to ensure that sheep are not overusing land in the south but also helping to clear lands in the north. Every year, Ernestine continues working, despite the many "headaches and hassles", to increase the number of sheep involved in seasonal migration. She has succeeded by using new forms of transportation, which is the only way to ensure many of the benefits of transhumance to the environment and nearby communities.

For this work, the primary consideration right now, Ernestine believes, is to ensure that there are people who want to continue in the profession; the number of young people wanting to become shepherds has dropped dramatically since the turn of the twenty-first century. She observes:

> It doesn't make sense to fight for trails when we don't have shepherds to take care of the sheep. We need to be practical and first fight to attract young people to shepherding. We need scholarships for shepherds, training, a new management system. In twenty years, it will be too late.... Everything needs to come together. We don't want to fall back into this romantic view of walking with two or three thousand sheep with no telephone and no nothing. But it doesn't make sense either to say "well, it's not a good idea so we'll produce lambs in factories." We are trying to find a way to ... create a new consciousness for the real ecologic structure. Because a good ecological structure is a good economic structure. And a good economic structure is producing meat without any harm to society and creating biodiversity in the north and the south.

Besides offering scholarships, other practical, concrete aspects of creating a new management system are needed. Ernestine notes just a few. First, there need to be new labor conditions that provide quality-of-life guarantees and access to modern amenities now considered essential, such as access to Wi-Fi and a pool of substitute shepherds who travel to give people a day off each week. Second, there needs to be a center to organize logistics. According to her vision, there would be one center located in the north and another in the south that would help coordinate transport of livestock, ensure land access, and train shepherds for work in each of the regions.

The Dehesa San Francisco: Reestablishing a Sustainable System

After coffee, we leave the farmhouse, and Ernestine shows us around the *dehesa* itself, a multifunctional entity with traditional Merino sheep at the center but also includes other livestock, including cows, pigs, and goats. Traditional farming with sheep on Andalusian *dehesa*s needs to be understood as part of a larger system, she explains:

> Sheep are the perfect landscape architects in Southern and Northern Spain! And they need to be used in conjunction with a philosophy that each geographical area can make a contribution to a global system of food production and preserving ancient landscapes and biodiversity. We all know about how sheep and goats clean the fields, fertilize the soil, ensure reseeding of native flora, and keep brush from growing and causing vast forest fires. But it is the more global system and how different geographies work together with different roles in food production that needs to be recognized and instituted as well.

She drives us up dirt roads through oak, Portuguese holm, and cork trees, allowing us to view different pastures where the five hundred Merino sheep in her flock are separated according to life cycles and roles in maintaining the flock. Like the flocks of Fortunato Guerrero Lara (see Chapter 3) and Marta Moya (see Chapter 4), Ernestine's flock is separated into different groups with newborns kept close to the barns under the watchful eye of the mastiffs; the yearlings separated from their mothers now; the sheep selected for breeding another year; and others that are now ready for market. Although we are tempted to get close to a handsome two-year-old mastiff, Ernestine reminds us that these are not ordinary house dogs. The dedication of the "Fundación Monte Mediterráneo" to the ancient landscape and shepherding practices influenced their decision to raise only Merino sheep, the foundation of the medieval wool trade. She has deliberately selected the prized Merino breed to raise because of its good quality meat and wool (which is now experiencing a revival due to its soft texture and warmth with artisanal co-ops, as well as global market changes that have benefited the price of Spanish sheep products).

The farm itself is not economically self-sustaining, Ernestine allows, but she and her husband Hans have a vision for the *dehesa* that is expansive and just part of a larger rural-development plan. Besides the Merino sheep, they also raise some cattle, Iberian pigs, chickens, donkeys, and horses; they also harvest cork and grow a variety of garden vegetables. As we drive through a grove of *alcornoque* (cork) trees, Ernestine points out that the harvest, always tricky, has been especially slight this year. The bark from cork trees can only be cut every nine years, and because of climate change and extreme temperatures, a new fungus (*Phytophthora cinnamomi*) has begun to grow on some of the trees and create a dry rot, making it impossible to harvest the bark. If not checked soon, the trees will most likely die. This would not only affect the cork harvest but also the entire ecosystem of the *dehesa* since the trees also provide much-needed shade for livestock. Rather than dwelling on this challenge, though, Ernestine points with delight to a couple of rabbits running toward a ravine in the rolling hills of the *dehesa*. The property, she explains, had been overhunted, and there were no rabbits left by the time they bought the place. Since purchasing the property, they have successfully reintroduced rabbits, among many other animals.

The cultural geography of the *dehesa* makes it an ideal place to combine Ernestine's vision of sustainable food production and land management with hands-on experience and educational-outreach efforts. Traditional land-use and animal-production practices must be integrated with innovative structural changes. Producing meat on the land, for example, is not only viable but an essential part of a healthy ecosystem. It should be done in rural areas with agroecosystems that cannot produce anything but meat and milk, like they do in the Swiss mountains, she argues. Lower elevations should be reserved for appropriate crops like cereals and vegetables.

> It's crazy to occupy these lower areas for industrialized meat production; it should be done in areas not as well adapted for agriculture, in areas where grazing would help fire prevention, biodiversity. This arrangement might make meat more expensive, but at least it won't have a negative effect on us. Society has to pay a lot of money to make up for the harm of these industrialized companies and their meat production.

As we continue touring the land, Ernestine tells us about the collective "Ceribeco" that she and others founded to process and market meats and organic lamb. The collective markets their own brand of pork, cold meats, and other meats, providing the support for direct sales and a system for ensuring the shelf life of products that Fortunato Guerrero Lara had earlier talked to us about (see Chapter 3). As she talks, I begin to appreciate the breadth of her understanding, vision, and energetic involvement in all the moving parts that must work together to bring about rural development and sustainable food systems. She and Hans have invested their life savings to revitalize a property, raise livestock through extensive grazing and transhumant practices, process the meat they raise, and finally market it through a local collective they helped to establish. For Ernestine, this is true rural development: a practical way to reverse trends that have caused such harm to ecosystems and led to the countryside becoming depopulated.

From her life experience, Ernestine has gained an exceptional understanding of global systems. She clearly sees the roadblocks to developing opportunities for different regions in Spain to work together within European Union guidelines. Besides the challenges of grazing itself, there are many deeply ingrained structural impediments, including historical systems of ownership, social attitudes about modernity, and demands for lower food costs, and the more general lack of knowledge about the special conditions of the Andalusian *dehesa*.

First, and surely the most difficult to overcome, is a system of land-animal ownership-caretaking that goes back to Christian reoccupation of Muslim lands. Nobles received enormous tracts of land as spoils of war during the reconquest, and these became the foundation for large estates and farms whose legacies still shape the region today. In fact, the origin of the word "*dehesa*" comes from "defensa."

> I think the unfairness, the real socially very cruel system starts after the Muslim occupation. Christians split up community land, and of course the people who received the most land often weren't those who loved the countryside but greedy people who wanted to get out as much as they could from it. That's where I think this kind of insane relationship to the countryside starts. People who live on the countryside and work on the countryside are poor and have miserable living and working conditions. The people who own the land couldn't care less about it or the workers. They probably visit once, twice, or three times a year.

Local farmers still generally do not own land, and, as Juan Vázquez already pointed out (see Chapter 1), shepherds are not allowed to own more than four or five sheep or goats for their family if they do not have land to graze them on. Most of the owners live in the city and simply draw on the rents of the farm. As we saw with Marta Moya (see Chapter 4), some farm owners are trying to change this pattern of absentee landownership, but it is hard to do. A look at the genealogy of the ownership of Dehesa San Francisco itself reflects the ancient land-ownership system of large, landed estates specializing in agricultural exports. Originally established during Roman times, this land-use pattern persisted in Andalusia at least through the nineteenth century. In the case of Dehesa San Francisco, a single family owned more than a half-dozen farms in the area, which were then passed down to two sisters. One of the sisters built the first farmhouse on the Dehesa San Francisco and owned several other farms. A descendent, who wrote a history of the family's farms, comments on the dismal living conditions for laborers:

> Life in rural areas was awfully hard until the seventies. But in the seventies, farm laborers began to have a chance to buy a house in town and live there. But before and right after the Civil War, they didn't have any other options except to live wherever they could: in some farm outbuilding on the land, like area barns or pigpens that were scattered around the *finca*s. The luckiest got to stay in guard houses in Nava, San Francisco, and Pan de Pobres, or in the bigger houses of El Risco of El Cuervo or Vallebarco. (Manuel Duque Álvarez, *Historia de la Finca*, Fundación Monte Mediterráneo, (n. d.), https://www.fundacionmontemediterraneo.com/img/upload/files/historia.pdf)

Centuries of sharp division between those who own the land and those who work it have maintained an enduring gap. Many owners do not understand — and sometimes do not even care — about the welfare of their land, animals, or workers. The workers, in turn, may not be invested in making good decisions about land use and animal production they do not own. Ernestine describes in more systemic terms how the historical land-work division has contributed to widespread rural poverty in Andalusia.

> The lack of respect for rural knowledge and rural structures and rural possibilities ... is also why in Andalusia the rural population lives extremely poorly and extremely badly. So, it wasn't really an asset to live on the countryside. Unlike other areas in Europe and often in the United States, the owner of the farm does not work on the farm; in Andalusia the owner of a farm lived in Seville or in Córdoba. The person who worked on the farm never owned anything, and if you are working constantly on something which is not yours, it's very difficult to feel identified with the needs of an agroecosystem ... you're being badly paid, badly treated, exploited and whatever. Or, if you have a nice income, you don't have to really be aware of the negative aspects of it, or even live them, so why should you?

As Ernestine talks, I reflect on the irony behind stories I have heard from Juan Vázquez (see Chapter 1), Pepe Millán (see Chapter 2), and Fortunato Guerrero Lara (see Chapter 3). As far back as Cervantes, the shepherd has been idealized by urban elites as an exemplar of the balance between nature and human emotion. And yet, shepherds have been denigrated as ignorant and uncultured, presumed to be living in filth with animals. The class and land struggle over the centuries has only been exacerbated by recent cultural ideals of modernity as urban, mechanical, and technologically driven. Ernestine gives a compelling modern-day example. Sheep have recently been used as "firefighters" to clean under powerlines for the utility companies, but because of a whole modern infrastructure created to maintain these areas with machines, there are people with strong interests in ensuring that the mechanized process continues. Furthermore, workers would often rather use a machine and gas than walk around with sheep. She observes:

> The social status of working with machines is much higher than working with animals. The people working with machines don't use their knowledge, or the knowledge of farmers and shepherds, because cleaning the brush under powerlines with nice machines and using petrol for this work is viewed socially as much better than walking around with two thousand sheep to do the same work.

Ernestine talks about the contrast between how shepherds were viewed in the Middle Ages and the social stigma they fight today:

> The people who traveled with sheep, the sheep keepers who would walk up and down the droving roads, were people with a very high cultural standard. They would bring different fruit from the north to the south, they would tell stories and they would bring information. They were considered culturally educated and trained because they would travel to places where most people couldn't because they would just stay in their village. Nowadays anybody who works with sheep is considered the last idiot from the village.

As a self-proclaimed insider-outsider, Ernestine looks back a bit nostalgically to a time she views as the golden years, when the prestigious medieval organization La Mesta protected shepherds' rights (see the introductory chapter). She also looks toward a future with new pathways to food production, biodiversity, and sustainability. Just as La Mesta had core values with integrated structures and widespread societal respect, she believes that increased public awareness together with the development of an equal exchange between practicing shepherds, farmers, and government officials can lead to new structural models that could not only revive pastoralism but also launch it into being more central to Andalusia. However, Ernestine argues, there needs to be much more support and encouragement for a dialogue between farmers, shepherds, landowners, and the government. These entities cannot remain in different camps, and they must work together to create an infrastructure and train the work force needed to save the *dehesa* and mountain pasturelands from further economic and ecological damage.

> It's very nice to have organic farms, and it's very important to have organic farms. But if we just talk about here an organic farm and there an organic farm, we won't make it. We need a more global system. We need something like La Mesta. We need people to understand that we must get back to structures. We need to help people in the south and in the north match their interests. We need people who breed dogs, people who have sheep, people who produce certain products that we need for the dogs. We need architects who can construct simple housing in the north where people can stay. And we need modern people to tell us how, with solar panels, we can make warm water and have cell phones work. We need a structure for all this stuff.

Training the Future: The "Fundación Monte Mediterráneo" Educational Center

After our tour of the farm, Ernestine invites us into the educational center she and her husband have built over the old farmhouse of Vallebarco. In harmony with local building traditions, it is tastefully finished with white-washed walls and terracotta floors. The ground level has several seminar rooms with tables long enough for about twenty people. Upstairs, there are dorm-like rooms with communal bathrooms for overnight stays that are often occupied with guests living there for days or weeks at a time. Taking a seat at the table, Ernestine offers us coffee and a delightful collection of local pastries. Without much prompting, she continues to describe an impressive range of initiatives and activities the center offers: education of trainees from the European Union, a base for researchers carrying out ecology studies on the *dehesa*, organic food-production seminars, workshops for shepherds, and, recently, a gathering place to establish a national association to advocate for a new status for the *dehesa* within the Spanish and EU landscape.

Fig. 5.3 Olive trees, cork trees, and Merino sheep are the key to a healthy dehesa and, in the distance, the conference space for the "Fundación Monte Mediterráneo" (2017).

Ernestine explains that every year the center offers a variety of programs to encourage people to make food choices that help biodiversity and social development. In addition, they host programs that research, implement, and put into motion additional biodiversity initiatives. She gives the example of a recent FMM offering: a "bioblitz," funded by a Swiss foundation. Around 120 volunteers identified over 750 species of flora and fauna on the *dehesa* in a single weekend. They presented the results to the EU and the Junta de Andalucía as further evidence in their petition to make the *dehesa* ecosystem a special category within shepherding regulations. The FMM also sponsors programs that focus on social development and the role food production can play. Working with a Catholic social-services organization in Seville and a six-acre plot, they hosted a three-month program for at-risk young adults. After completing classes in organic farming and marketing techniques at the organization's center, the group spent nine months working the gardens in Seville. Seven of the original ten participants, Ernestine reports, are now employed in related fields. Next, there are knowledge share and training programs. FMM has applied for LEADER funds from the European Union to enable candidates from six countries to learn about the traditional shepherding practices, foods, and culture that Andalusian systems offer.

In yet another key initiative, the FMM addresses the critical shortage of shepherds. Ernestine created her own shepherd school when she found it difficult to get interns from Andalusia's *Escuela de Pastores*. Securing funds from the Swiss government, she trained four aspiring shepherds in the first year and has had great success in placing them: while she hired one as her new farm manager, two others participated in the transhumance to Palencia, and a fourth secured funds for her own *explotación* (large herd) of goats and now grazes them on public lands outside of Madrid. Ernestine seems to take in stride that this 100% successful outcome should be the norm for shepherd schools.

Wanting to understand better the current crisis in finding skilled, dedicated *ganadero*s and shepherds, I asked to interview Ernestine's shepherd-manager, Daniel, who trained recently at her own school for shepherds. He replied via email, and his story provides a glimpse of a new generation that did not grow up around livestock — or even in the countryside. Daniel's response was written as a single document with its own narrative cohesion. Although it is a contrast to the "walking around" farm interviews we have heard, his story illustrates well a promise for the future. Daniel articulates the attraction, hardship, and value of his new vocation — and he gives us hope that others will follow:

> My uncle, who passed away earlier this year, took care of goats when he was young. Although he had to stop, he always felt as if he were a shepherd, and he would have liked to have kept on doing it. I think about him a lot, and it motivates me to live out his dream.
>
> Shepherding is very special because it has gone from being a rather common profession in earlier times to the way it is today, with less people wanting to dedicate themselves to it and its tradition of preserving a part of our history and customs. Also, it demands you understand the animals, in this case the sheep, and the great psychological commitment it takes to spend hours alone, exposed to the weather. But it also has great value, for the way it cares for nature and the environment: taking care of a flock of sheep and moving them around the mountain lands benefits and regulates the growth of vegetation, soil preparation, and seed planting. Besides, the concept of a shepherd is one of a person who perfectly understands nature and its cycles. In many cases there's a

knowledge that you can't find in books. You can only acquire it through spending many hours in the mountains with the animals. It also has the value of freedom, of being away from all the everyday "pleasures" that can distract you.

The truth is I am lucky that my family has always supported me. They are really happy I'm doing what I like and what makes me feel good, which is how I feel when I'm living as a shepherd. They consider it a good and necessary job. As far as my friends are concerned, the truth is that many of them admire me for what I am doing. I talk to them or send them pictures, and many of them say: "I wish I could change jobs with you and live where you are." However, it's also true that other people, not so much my friends, but people I know, have asked me if it wouldn't be better to find something more related to what I studied and with better work conditions.

As to the future of farming, the forecast is not very good, due to the politics around agriculture and the lack of generational legacies in this sector. But yes, it's true that this new generation might produce some people who'll try it, and it could create a good base to preserve these professions. Things are going to have to change for people who work in agriculture as well as for the shepherds.

Daniel outlines for us the support he feels from family and his desire to leave the city to find meaningful work as a *ganadero*-shepherd, a profession crucial to a sustainable future, as we will see in the Conclusion to our book. He later underscores that while much more must be done to make it a viable, sustainable profession, the FMM has been a good place to start.

Ernestine is never idle. Increasingly frustrated by working with government agencies and programs sensitive to highly volatile politics of regional and national elections, she is also applying for EU funds under its climate-change initiative to establish her own program of firefighting sheep (see Chapter 6) while also working to develop nature tourism. She notes that, in Andalusia, after decades of Socialist government, a recent shift in political parties included a radical change: the *Ministerio de Medio Ambiente* (Ministry of the Environment) was merged into a much larger ministry, now called the *Ministerio de Agricultura, Ganadería, Pesca y Desarrollo Sostenible* (Ministry of Agriculture, Livestock, Fisheries, and Sustainable Development), where the focus on environment has been sandwiched in between other areas. With so much political reorganization, regional and national governments have not been able to sustain initiatives for rural development and the protection of fragile cultural and economic agrosystems.

Although Ernestine's confidence in government at all levels, including the European Union, has waned in recent years, she believes there is still hope in engaging the private sector and encouraging consumers to make sustainable choices. One example she cites is local agrotourism, which she sees as critical for Andalusia. The coast is dangerously over-developed, but the interior holds great potential. Developing tourism here would go hand-in-hand with conservation of natural ecosystems and even the reintroduction of traditional natural zones and practices, such as working farms, transhumance and transterminance, artisanal cheesemaking, local food preparation, and weaving. As she talks about her vision, I recall Patricio Vázquez's new venture to establish a working goat farm and hotel outside of Constantina (see Chapter 1).

At the core of all Ernestine's initiatives is her belief that all citizens need to be educated on these issues, from the European Union officials in Brussels to the children who will be making decisions about where their food comes from in the future. To this end, every summer, Ernestine offers internships on the farm in organic food services, as well as youth camps. Offering instruction in the English language (which is seen as "modern") is a draw for the camp, where participants end up living, working, and eating as people traditionally have done in the countryside. Along with language skills, they learn that sustainability does not have to be a chore. All the food served is certified organic, and much of it locally produced. Many children leave the camp with a new-found appreciation for healthy organic food and sustainable lifestyles. Ernestine hopes they will return home to influence their families and remember this experience when they become consumers. She remarks: "Every consumer, everyone who eats, needs to understand the cost to humanity of mass production of food sources at low costs and how they fail to support a viable future; society has to pay a lot to make up for the harmful effects to the environment." On a personal note, my own research assistant Lara Hamburger, who is an American living in Madrid, met Ernestine and was quickly recruited as an English-speaking camp counselor one summer. She recalls that, on the first day, children grimaced over the sheep-milk yogurt, but, by the end of camp, they were fighting over the strawberry flavor, agreeing that it was the best yogurt they had ever eaten!

Beyond training a new generation of shepherds and children, Ernestine also works to modify EU guidelines that fail to take into account Andalusia's unique landscape and the advantages of ancient methods of extensive grazing. European Union requirements present so many practical challenges that many farmers cannot meet them. As we talk today, she is outraged by a recent policy established by CAP: the European Union's agricultural-subsidy program for *dehesa*s like hers will now prorate/adjust subsidy amounts based on aerial photos that determine the percentage of the total acreage of pasturelands that is not in shade. "That is pure craziness," she exclaims. Sheep and goats depend on the light shade provided by *dehesa* trees, especially the cork, holm oak, and olive trees. These trees allow vegetation to grow and are part of a staple diet for small livestock. The sheep graze around these trees and help prevent forest fires by reducing undergrowth, so the animals and trees depend on each other for balance. Fueled by objections to this policy change, Ernestine and others are working with an Association established in 2014 to defend and advocate for the *dehesa* system, FEDEHESA (http://fedehesa.org/).

We must wrap up the interview because the camp parents are coming. Parents of children who will be spending part of their summer at the *dehesa* have been invited out to the farm today to have a look around and ask questions. "The fragile, biodiverse *dehesa* is one of the last defenses Andalusia has in the face of the encroaching Sub-Saharan desert system, which is slowly but surely creeping north. It is up to us to be sure the younger generation understands and accepts this challenge," she remarks as we leave. As it turns out, the famous sustainable-systems activist who introduced me to Fortunato Guerrero Lara (see Chapter 3), Paco Casero, has a granddaughter attending the camp. Both he and Ernestine give us the same warning: if nothing is done to stem industrial agriculture and meat production, much of Andalusia will be a desert in fifty years. When I talk with Paco, he has a personal perspective: "I want my great grandkids to know what it is like to have green landscapes in their lives."

Knowing our time is short as we say goodbye, I ask Ernestine for a thumbnail summary of what is needed for the future she envisions, and she lays these needs out once more: steady work in rural areas, new innovations linked with traditional knowledge, more investment from the private sector (governments are too mercurial), more attractive conditions for a new generation of *ganadero*s, and the reintroduction of transhumance both to develop the rural interior and to support tourism. But the fundamental building block for all of this is a broader change in consumer preferences. Ernestine concludes, "there isn't much time left; this way of life, this natural world is disappearing fast.... I want to believe ... step by step people will change."

Walking back to our car to head into town, Ernestine makes us promise to return soon for a social dinner to taste the farm's products, but for now she suggests we go to the town restaurant for a local Sunday meal. We are not disappointed. The owner spots us from the doorway into the kitchen and sends out a few local olives and acorn-fed *ibérico* ham to tide us over while we wait for a table to open. The place buzzes with local diners and people having an *aperitivo* at the bar. Once seated, we savor tender grilled lamb with rosemary and a vegetable soup made with the early spring harvest. Ernestine's farm is not only reviving the traditional *dehesa* and transhumance while training local, national, and European Union youth, farmers, activists, scholars, and government officials; it is also a catalyst for rural re-development in Santa Olalla. I can easily envision this area, with its proximity to Seville and beautiful landscapes, as a base for Ernestine's vision of rural tourism that includes farm and pastoral activities.

The long-term contribution of Ernestine and the "Fundación Monte Mediterráneo" on the local and national level is hard to quantify or project, but their work has already contributed to the changing of laws, developed funding opportunities, and supported practices related to traditional grazing in Andalusia. Perhaps most importantly, it has changed minds. Ernestine has turned her one-time status as an "outsider" to tradition and place to her advantage. She has a unique experience with global systems, as well as an understanding of smaller-scale social development possibilities. From school-age children to EU officials, she — along with many collaborators — is making an impact as a conscientious farmer-landowner, educator, and a visionary. As we return to Seville, winding back through *dehesa*s, mountainous pasturelands, and rural villages, we carry with us the hope that Ernestine's vision of slow but steady change throughout society (one she shares with Juan Vázquez (see Chapter 1), Pepe Millán (Chapter 2), Fortunato Guerrero Lara (see Chapter 3) and Marta Moya Espinosa (Chapter 4)) is possible — and that it will happen before it is too late.

Conclusions and Update

When I check back in with Ernestine in Fall 2021, her practical ideas and extensive collaborative efforts remain strong despite the deep financial losses of the Educational Center after a year and a half of pandemic-enforced inactivity. At the forefront of her work today is the culmination of a three-year project with Goovinnova (www.goovinnova.org), a collective that is working to make transhumance viable, as well as with the European Union group "LIFELiveAdapt", devoted to making extensive grazing sustainable throughout Southern Europe. The final meeting with the latter group just took place in Córdoba, bringing *ganadero*s together with other specialists and officials. As Ernestine describes the meeting, I soon realize how interrelated the world of pastoralism in Andalusia has become: when Fortunato Guerrero Lara (see Chapter 3) could not take my phone call earlier, it was because he was at this very meeting providing his valuable experience as a *ganadero*.

Along with other projects, Ernestine has once again prioritized training new shepherds and helping to establish new norms for their living and working conditions. "Once we have enough shepherds wanting to be in the profession, enough workers for the sheep and goats, and living conditions to keep them in the profession, then we can focus on trails," she argues. She nevertheless remains grateful to Jesús Garzón and all he has done for transhumance (see the introductory chapter), stating emphatically: "If it weren't for Jesús, we wouldn't even be talking about transhumance today!" In fact, Ernestine argues, transhumance can grow. In 2022, her collective once again sent over 10,000 sheep up north, and the move ended up being vital for the well-being of both the *dehesa* and her animals. As one of the hottest, driest summers on record, water became a problem for many people working with livestock in Andalusia. Now people are inquiring about joining her collective transhumance next summer. She explains:

> The problem is: people now understand and appreciate the service pastoralism performs for the eco-system, but the practice is still not fully remunerated. The government only pays two-thirds of the cost for transhumance because the government is afraid farmers will take advantage of subsidies, but there is no way to cheat! Each animal has a tag or a chip, is registered in a database, and must have a transport certificate. It is easy to track the animals and make sure they exist and are moved from south to north and back again. *Ganadero*s don't have time

to find funding every year for the other third of the costs, and the final market price for the meat does not cover it.

If *ganadero*s received full support for transhumance, she argues, many more would do it and thus benefit more ecosystems and produce higher nutritional value in foods purchased by consumers.

While Ernestine sees great strides in a growing awareness of the importance of pastoralism to Spain's future, she says there have also been huge setbacks at the level of government — namely, the Junta de Andalucía's closure of its separate ministry devoted to the environment. In addition, the European Union's new draft of CAP funding for 2023, with its recalculation of subsidies for pastoral practices, will most likely hurt the very people, the *ganadero*s, that make it all possible.

Ernestine's case illustrates how practitioners and supporters of traditional pastoralism face both the complexity of the system and the many unresolved threats to it in the twenty-first century. Yet her story also highlights how small, collective initiatives are seeking to reestablish extensive grazing and transhumance in a modern setting with stronger support networks. Ernestine herself combines the role of landowner, *ganadera*, and leader who is helping to create the scaffolding for pastoralism in Andalusia and beyond.

6. The Scaffolding for the Future of Pastoralism: Collectives and Training

Will the next generation know what a green Andalusia looks like? Will they know how important it is for people who live in the cities to support sustainability? Or will our grandchildren inherit the beginning of a new Sahara Desert?

Paco Casero

We need society and people living in cities to understand what shepherds do today. They manage environmentally high-value lands. They care for these high-value biodiverse spaces.

Maricarmen García

While carrying out the interviews for the life stories we have just heard, I quickly discovered that the story of pastoralism in Spain today involves more than just shepherds, *ganaderos*, and their flocks. I was struck by the impressive number of people and organizations that repeatedly came up in my conversations. We have just seen (Chapter 5) how Ernestine Lüdeke's organization works on many fronts to fortify extensive grazing. We also heard how Fortunato Guerrero Lara worked as president of a land reform collective (Chapter 3), and how Pepe Millán mentors shepherds-in-training with the Junta de Andalucía (Chapter 2). A variety of governmental programs, NGOs, and social movements often collectively referred to as *"plataformas"* provide an essential scaffolding underneath the individual family stories we have heard. While our informants often discuss the importance of outside factors, such as market forces, climate change, and politics, they also weigh how networks, policies, and organizations can help or hinder how well they can navigate complex and time-consuming socio-political,

https://doi.org/10.11647/OBP.0387.06

economic, and agrarian structures. In fact, nearly everyone I interviewed was involved with at least one governmental organization, educational project, public research institute, or local organization that advocating for or otherwise supporting extensive grazing practices. These *plataformas* often receive government subsidies and work with research programs throughout Andalusia. Many of them are integrated into national and even international organizations.

In this chapter, I include a brief sample of my interviews with dozens of people who work in predominantly Andalusia-based organizations and initiatives, in three general areas: collective associations, university- or government-sponsored professional programs, and direct shepherd- training programs. These areas often overlap, bringing together traditional shepherds, university-trained specialists, and activists working for pastoralism and environmental sustainability. Unlike the more detailed case studies of the families that work directly with animals, this chapter offers thumbnail sketches of some of the many actors involved in ensuring the success — and even the survival — of sustainable pastoralism. Here, we outline the work of scholars, activists, and NGOs and provide bibliography and links in footnotes for readers who would like to explore these areas further.

Collective Organizations, or "*Plataformas*"

Although it was an outsider's fascination with shepherds and their livestock that first captured my interest in pastoralism, I now realize that the work of Jesús "Suso" Garzón Heydt and his collaborators ensured that my interest would grow. As we saw in the introduction to *A Country of Shepherds*, Suso has had an outsized impact on the preservation of modern transhumance in Spain, successfully amplifying over decades his work on conservation, ecosystems, and sustainable practices.[1] As

---

1   Suso's name features in many of the recent news articles, events, and relevant organizations, especially dealing with extensive grazing and transhumance. See, for example, interviews with him (all in Spanish): 'Jesus Garzón Heydt' (Vimeo, 10 November 2010, https://vimeo.com/16715640), 'Jesús Garzón: la trashumancia y la red Natura 2000, en perfecta armonía' (YouTube, 26 November 2014, https://www. youtube.com/watch?v=aGHoztdRNAY), 'Trashumancia: "Andando y sembrando" un futuro sostenible' (YouTube, 16 October 2020, https://www.youtube.com/ watch?v=vygf3u3HCzE), and 'Los beneficios de la actividad ganadera' (Radio

Ernestine Lüdeke notes (see Chapter 5), Suso is probably the reason so many people continue to talk about transhumance. Since the early 1990s, he has led political and social movements to protect and promote pastoralism, including the founding of the highly visible national collective, the "Asociación Trashumancia y Naturaleza" (ATN).[2] When I interview Suso at the Festival of Transhumance in Madrid in 2017, the energetic activist is still practicing transhumance on foot with his own flock of about 1,000 sheep and several hundred goats. He recalls helping found ATN after participating in the UN's "Earth Summit" in 1992. He explains that the collective focuses on transhumance as a means to an end: a more sustainably managed Iberian Peninsula with protected natural areas. At the same time, Suso underscores the even broader focus of the ATN to raise awareness of how "the gains in Spain can help the rest of Europe's work on sustainable systems like transhumance." ATN helps to organize the Festival of Transhumance; makes the *vías pecuarias* more accessible by providing watering troughs and maps, as well as sponsoring conservation and clean-up projects; and offers experienced trekkers to aid shepherds in navigating the challenges of a modern transhumance. The group also advocates for policy changes and protective laws, such as Law 3/1995 protecting the *vías pecuarias*, or the 2017 declaration of transhumance as immaterial cultural heritage in Spain. Their work, along with that of other national collectives and hundreds of volunteers and staff, ensures a widespread awareness of transhumance as valuable living heritage and key for achieving environmental sustainability. As this book went to press, Suso had also broadcast a program on how transhumance could help stem the July 2022 crisis with wildfires breaking out in over fifty sites across Spain.

In October 2022, ATN joined forces with a handful of collectives, including the influential "Plataforma Ganadería Extensiva y Pastoralismo" (GEyP), which was launched in 2013 with the help of the activist organization "Entretantos".[3] In collaboration with the Spanish

---

Televisión Española, 5 February 2022, https://www.rtve.es/play/videos/para-todos-la-2/los-beneficios-de-la-actividad-ganadera/6342201).

2   Asociación Trashumancia y Naturaleza, 2021, (in Spanish:) https://www.pastos.es and https://www.facebook.com/TrashumanciayN/?locale=es_LA

3   Plataforma por la Ganadería Extensiva y el Pastoralismo, 2014, (in Spanish:) http://www.ganaderiaextensiva.org; Fundación Entretantos, 2012, (in Spanish:) https://www.entretantos.org.

government (always referred to as *la Administración*), these organizations helped to draw up the first-ever strategic plan for extensive grazing in Spain. At 150 pages, the *Propuesta de bases técnicas para una estrategia estatal de la ganadería extensiva* (Proposal for Specialized Strategic Governmental Support of Extensive Grazing) diagnoses the current state of extensive grazing, outlines specific objectives, and proposes a series of actions to support pastoralism more widely.[4] Among these is the need to understand and support extensive-grazing practices and how they provide a unique set of benefits on multiple levels. A better understanding of these practices will help create policy that supports good land use and socio-economic sustainability.

Many of the researchers I interviewed are active in the GEyP and contribute to their broad-reaching work. Their website highlights this work and even includes an informative, accessible publication on extensive grazing. For example, it offers succinct explanations of the vital, multifaceted role of pastoralism: "This activity is essential for the land and for society because it not only produces quality products, but it also shapes the landscape, helps control forest fires, regulates water cycles and soil quality, helps to strengthen biodiversity and to preserve cultural heritage and territorial identity" (*Propuesta* 12). It also reminds readers that pastoralism supports the "Sustainable Development of the Rural Environment" ("*Desarrollo sostenible del medio rural*") law (Ley 45/2007), which mandates the need to "preserve and restore the heritage of the rural environment as well as its natural and cultural resources" (Art. 2.1). The publication puts forth four general areas that need to be addressed. These include the need to highlight the benefits that extensive grazing for the environment and rural development, especially in contrast to intensive grazing; this differentiation would help government officials create policies to support pastoralism. Another key area it identifies is the need to work on developing sustainable,

---

4   The actions outlined include the following: the "definition and distinctions of extensive grazing"; the "betterment of governance related to extensive grazing"; the "betterment of socioeconomic sustainability for extensive grazing"; "optimization of the relationship between extensive grazing and the land"; and the "promotion of research, training, innovation and information sharing about extensive grazing". See Silvia Zabalza et al., *Propuesta de bases técnicas para una estrategia estatal de la ganadería extensiva* (2021), WWF España and Transhumancia y Naturaleza, pp. 50–110, https://www.wwf.es/nuestro_trabajo/alimentos/estrategia_estatal_para_la_ganaderia_extensiva/

high-quality, and distinct products for the market and to strengthen the social, political, and collective connections that allow these products to do well on the market (*Propuesta* 24).

Another individual working closely with these initiatives in the extensive grazing movement is the man who introduced me to Fortunato Guerrero Lara (see Chapter 3), Francisco (Paco) Casero Rodríguez, a life-long advocate for Andalusian agrarian reform and collective action. My neighbor in Seville had suggested that I contact Paco, and, to my surprise, Paco was eager to meet with me. Considered a national hero by many, Paco has been an environmental activist as far back as the Franco regime, organizing day laborers and leading regular hunger strikes to protest environmental degradation and human-rights abuses. He was a founder of the "Sindicato Obreros del Campo", created the "Confederación Ecológica Pacifista Andaluza", and has authored dozens of essays and several books. His recent work focuses on ecological challenges facing southern Spain, including topics such as the role of the *dehesa* system and the need for a more inclusive CAP to protect traditional, sustainable practices and rural livelihoods.[5]

When I call Paco, he invites me to the headquarters for the NGOs he founded, "Fundación Savia" and "Ecovalia",[6] which promote the value of natural systems at local and national levels. Although it is Holy Week and most of Seville is on holiday, the office buzzes with dozens of young volunteers. As we talk, he points to his active postings on social media[7] and passionately demands that we consider what legacy we are leaving for our descendants: "Will the next generation know what a green Andalusia looks like? Will they know how important it is for people who live in the cities to support sustainability? Or will our grandchildren inherit the beginning of a new Sahara Desert?"[8] As we saw earlier, Paco is a man who practices his own principles: he sent his grandchildren

---

5   Francisco Casero, 'La ganadería extensiva seguirá siendo víctima con la nueva PAC', Portal de Andalucía, 15 December 2020, (in Spanish:) https://portaldeAndalucía. org/opinion/la-ganadería-extensiva-seguira-siendo-victima-con-la-nueva-pac/

6   Fundación Savia, 2018, (in Spanish:) https://www.fundacionsavia.org; Ecovalia, 2013, (in Spanish:) https://www.ecovalia.org/

7   @paco_casero on X (formerly Twitter).

8   See also, Paco Casero, '¿Qué pensarán de nosotros nuestros nietos cuando vean lo que les hemos dejado?', *El diario de Jerez*, 30 November 2020, (in Spanish:) https:// www.diariodejerez.es/jerez/Paco-Casero-Fundacion-Savia-nietos_0_1523247952. html

to Ernestine Lüdeke's rural summer camp (see Chapter 5). Paco urges me to help get the word out and even sends me home with a T-shirt and book bag to help advertise the movement for a green Andalusia, suggesting that my daughter might want to wear it to school.

By fall 2022, Paco's activism on behalf of extensive grazing and its land-use systems had culminated with a well-informed, passionate brief about the urgent need to intervene in the restructuring of the new European Union's CAP that will affect subsidies through 2027. Writing to the Spanish Minister of Agriculture, Luis Planas, Paco underscores the Spanish government's historical record of failing to understand, recognize, and fight for the fundamental role of extensive grazing in Spain: "There is no extensive grazing without pastures, and no pastures without extensive grazing... 65% of Spanish land can't be cultivated, but you can use it for grazing... [but] 70% of Spanish pastures are excluded from the CAP." In theory, the CAP's restructuring of the "Ecoesquema" ("Ecoscheme") is going to save pastoralism from near extinction, but in fact, Paco argues, it only "masks" a new system that will penalize further these land-use systems. He points out that the *"pago básico"* (basic unit of subsidy from the CAP) is unfair. One only has to look at other Mediterranean countries to see this. In Spain the *pago básico* is 60 euros/hectare, but in Italy it is 229 euros/hectare, and in Greece it is 258 euros/hectares. The *pago básico* in Spain needs to at least be doubled in order to make pastoralism viable. Paco suggests restructuring the way extensive grazing, pasturelands, and the *dehesa* have been defined and categorized, which would affect 40% of the land in Spain.

One of the most influential collectives in Andalusia — a group that shepherds like Pepe Millán (see Chapter 2) belong to — is "Asociación de Pastores por el Monte Mediterráneo" (APMM).[9] Currently led by Rogelio Jiménez Piano, the APMM was founded in 2009 and promotes pastoralism and its benefits to the agricultural ecosystems of Southern Spain. The organization publishes maps and guides, offers opportunities for knowledge-sharing between professional specialties, facilitates networking between shepherds, and aids in the production and sales of products. One of their most widely publicized programs, the fire-prevention program "Red de Áreas Pasto-Cortafuegos", popularly

---

9   Asociación de Pastores por el Monte Mediterráneo, 2010, (in Spanish:) http://pastoresmonte.org, and on *Facebook*.

known as the "sheep as firefighters" (*ovejas bomberos*) mentioned by Ernestine in Chapter 5, teams up with shepherds, the Junta de Andalucía, and a research group at CSIC-Granada ("Pastos y Sistemas Silvopastorales Mediterráneos", see below).

Pressed for time between his own work in shepherding, the collective, and his government position, Rogelio suggests we meet up during the 2016 inaugural round table, "Retos sobre el pastoralismo del siglo XXI", ("Twenty-First-Century Challenges for Pastoralism"), at the *Escuela de Pastores* (Shepherd School). Wearing an "Asociación de Pastores por el Monte Mediterreáneo" t-shirt and talking in a booming voice, Rogelio makes clear that he dislikes "the whole picturesque notion that society has about our profession". He is much more interested in the reality of the challenges that student-shepherds see ahead of them. Rogelio addresses their concerns about access to pastureland, licenses, and funding, and about how to run a cheese-making business before moving on to a lengthy discussion about a far less-common topic: the importance of knowing which breeds have been developed over many centuries to flourish in specific microclimates and topographies. He asks each student: "What breed will you raise? Why?" As Rogelio speaks, I recall Fortunato Guerrero Lara (see Chapter 3) and Pepe Millán (Chapter 2) emphasizing how the native breeds they raise, adapted to local conditions, are essential to success in their profession.

Ever practical, Rogelio moves on to two other cornerstones of success that often are not publicized. Future shepherds and *ganaderos* need to know that, as markets change, more profit comes from quality than from quantity. He predicts that Spaniards, as they increasingly embrace responsible consumerism, will demand high-quality products and develop a loyalty to their producers. The final cornerstone is also essential: these aspiring *ganaderos* need to start building support networks now. Collectives, government agencies, mentors, and colleagues will be critical to successful outcomes — not to mention in gaining competency in traditional practices, new technology, and knowledge of the vast bureaucracy that increasingly governs pastoralism. "We don't have to follow the sixteenth-century model", he jokes. "We have GPS, cars, WhatsApp. Will drones be next?!"

These collectives and their leaders highlighted here all help to bridge the gap between *ganaderos*/shepherds, markets, researchers, government agencies, and the public. As we have seen, they offer support for transhumance, apply for subsidies, create networks among shepherds, and advocate for extensive grazing as part of a holistic vision to ensure the sustainability of delicate ecosystems within the modern marketplace. Their work is also vital to the promotion and the valuing of extensive-grazing practices and pasturelands at the level of European Union policies. As of 2022, all of the aforementioned *plataformas* are involved in advocating for better CAP subsidies for the type of pastoralism practiced in southern Spain.

Each of these *plataformas* also has a highly public-facing mission and employs social media — primarily X (formerly Twitter), Instagram, and Facebook — to promote pastoralism. The national "Asociación Trashumancia y Naturaleza", for example, has over 12,000 Facebook followers, while the regional "Asociación de Pastores por el Monte Mediterráneo" has about 1,700. Social media are particularly useful for sharing key information about recent policy developments with an engaged public.[10] Whether supporting an NGO, government-funded group or grassroots collective, social media inform a diverse audience about sustainable shepherding and amplify their voices to thousands of followers.

University-based Training, Research, and Projects

As we have seen in our snapshots of collectives like the "Asociación Pastores por el Monte Mediterreáno", publicly funded universities and government research agencies play an important role in the scaffolding of pastoralism. Some of the most active research groups are based at the Universities of Seville and Córdoba and the Consejo Superior de Investigaciones Científicas (CSIC-Granada). Two of the most widely publicized projects, the *ovejas bomberos* and the *Escuela de Pastores*

---

10   In March 2021, for example, ATN posted a wide range of news articles and blogs about issues related to rural life and shepherding, an invitation for an academic conference, an online event for women in farming, an update about animals and shepherds the organization is collaborating with, a workshop for people working with livestock, a post about Earth Day, and a few re-posts from partner organizations. Some individual shepherds even track their own flocks or transhumance on social media to share with curious public. See for example, bordamatiasfarm on Instagram and @felipemolina73 on X (formerly Twitter).

(discussed below), come out of this collaboration, so I decided to interview several of the university-trained people involved.

When I interview the CISC-Granada researcher Dr. Ana Belén Robles Cruz,[11] who led the 2003 working group "Pastos y Sistemas Silvopastorales Mediterráneos" (Mediterranean Pasture and Silvopasture Systems) that developed the fire-prevention program "Red de Áreas Pasto-Cortafuegos de Andalucía" (Andalusia Pasture-Firelane Network Area),[12] she talks in practical terms about the popular *"ovejas bomberos"* (sheep as firefighters) program she helped to develop. The benefit of grazing animals in different sites, she explains, is that it provides a source of income for shepherds and, simultaneously, serves as a cost-effective tool for maintaining public lands. Ana draws on her scientific botanical training — in particular, her studies of the impact of sustainable shepherding on the soil, plants, and vegetation in southeastern Andalusia, one of the driest regions in Europe. Her group obtains funds from the Junta de Andalucía and works directly with shepherds from collectives like the "Asociación Pastores por el Monte Mediterráneo".

Notably, Ana's group was also instrumental in revitalizing the *Escuela de Pastores* (School for Shepherds) to refocus it after the initial years and provide more practical applications for the aspiring *ganadero*s. She hopes that this support and activity will spur more young people into wanting to work with livestock but admits that, despite her team's success in modernizing some extensive-grazing practices, she has not yet seen a corresponding increase in the practice of shepherding: "The future is not good. Despite the fact that there are more *plataformas*, scholars, and aid, it is still a very demanding job, and there aren't many young shepherds." Nonetheless, Ana and her collaborator, Dr. María Eugenia Ramos Font,[13] emphasize that giving *ganadero*s more agency and tools is

---

11 *ResearchGate*, 'Ana Belén Robles', https://www.researchgate.net/profile/Ana-Robles-4. See also her research group's page: Pastos y Sistemas Silvopastorales Mediterraneos, 2014, (in Spanish:) https://www.eez.csic.es/evaluacion-restauracion-y-proteccion-de-agrosistemas-mediterraneos-serpam

12 Junta de Andalucía, Consejería de Medio Ambiente y Ordenación del Territorio, Proyecto RAPCA, 2015, (in Spanish:) https://www.juntadeandalucia.es/medioambiente/portal/documents/20151/591684/6_triptico_rapca_con_sangria.pdf/e8b9d60b-f81a-cb3b-41f7-5e8c80affca8?t=1655287442732.

13 Google Scholar, 'María Eugenia Ramos Font', https://scholar.google.es/citations?user=yQG681gAAAAJ&hl=es

still the key to the future of pastoralism. Ana insists, "you have to spend time with the people: the *ganadero*s and the shepherds. You have to give them the attention they deserve, talk to them, get close to them and involve them in research and practice. You have to restore their worth and their role." Ana and her team continue to work alongside local and regional government to organize shepherds and give them a voice in the management of their affairs. Many of their initiatives — including fire control, working with native breeds, and interviewing practitioners to brainstorm new solutions — are part of their collaboration with the collective research group "Open2Preserve".[14]

As I finish my interview with Ana, another of her collaborators, Fidel Delgado Ferrer,[15] joins us with an important comparative perspective on how to develop more markets and roles for shepherds. He, like others we have heard from, is interested in the ways France is moving toward a national commitment to its ecosystems and biodiversity. Fidel mentions that a new law has been proposed there that would require all state-funded institutions to use a percentage of locally sourced food.[16] In addition, France offers a system of professionals to care for livestock so that *ganadero*s and shepherds can take some time off. Fidel notes with irony that Spain sells much of its sheep and goat milk to France, which then produces and sells its internationally famous French cheeses. Echoing the complaints of shepherds and *ganadero*s we have interviewed, he notes that Spain's often restrictive laws have inhibited the development of a vital cheesemaking industry and closed off a potential avenue of revenue. Spain, Fidel argues, needs to invest in measures like France does, "so that there's a better quality of life for the *ganadero*; you have to recognize that extensive grazing produces more than just food... and recognize its benefit for society."

---

14   Open2Preserve, 2018, https://open2preserve.eu/en/
15   See also Alto Minho FIRECAMP, 'Fidel Delgado Ferrer – AMAYA/Junta de Andalucia', YouTube, 8 January 2018, (in Spanish:) https://www.youtube.com/watch?v=Ep8KBVISE5k
16   France's parliament has passed a law requiring all of the nation's "collective restaurants" (school cafeterias, hospital cafeterias, senior living communities, prisons and other state institutions) to source at least 40% of their food locally. The proposal will need to be approved by the French Senate before it becomes law. See (in French:) https://www.assemblee-nationale.fr/14/propositions/pion3280.asp

Another highly influential researcher, Dr. Yolanda Mena Guerrero,[17] multitasks by working actively with goat farmer Pepe Millán to teach a new generation of university-trained professionals how to collaborate with each other and with those who care for livestock, as well as by helping to draft new agro-pastoral policies. Based at the University of Seville, she has published widely on extensive-grazing systems and sustainable goat-milk production. When we meet at a small office in the Center for Agroforestry (*Ciencias Agroforestales*), she is surrounded by team members working on a grant that is due within days. She suggests that we sit outside for the interview so she can enjoy the spring day. As Yolanda begins, she admits to being stretched thin by the number of research projects she works on and by the urgency of the situation for Andalusia's extensive grazing. Trained as a veterinarian, she collaborated with Pepe Millán on the documentary *La buena leche* in the hopes of promoting goat ranching, the outstanding nutritional value of goat milk, and the usefulness of goats for land management in mountainous regions (see Chapter 2). "There is little recognition of this pastoral tradition", she explains. "Most people focus on the more picturesque sheep." Yolanda has deep respect for Pepe, insisting that she learns far more from him than he does from her. Her role, she clarifies, is to be a catalyst connecting a whole gamut of people and agencies with those who keep Andalusia's pastoral traditions alive — the shepherds themselves. She facilitates "communication among all actors, among *ganadero*s, researchers, specialists and the government in order to sensitize and raise public awareness". Yolanda believes that talking directly with the *ganadero*s "helps sell you on sustainable pastoralism and allows you to step away from large *supermercados* (supermarkets) filled with intensive farming products. It also improves the quality of the food you eat and the environment." One of her newer initiatives is the creation of "a collective brand, a brand-name quality seal" to help consumers easily identify the products the *ganadero*s produce.[18] In a recent project, Yolanda teamed up with Ernestine Lüdeke and the "Fundación Monte Mediterráneo" (see Chapter 5) to work with "AgriTrain"—an organization training

---

17 Prisma, 'Yolanda Mena Guerrero', https://bibliometria.us.es/prisma/investigador/2657

18 Federación Andaluza de Asociaciones de Caprino de Raza Pura "CABRANDALUCÍA", 2005, (in Spanish:) https://www.cabrandalucía.com/

teachers to educate students about sustainable pastoralism.[19] She is also an active member of "Entretantos/Plataforma de Ganadería Extensiva y Pastoralismo", where she contributes to the new strategic guidelines for national policy regarding pastoralism.

Just as nearly everyone mentions Suso Garzón when talking about transhumance in Spain, nearly everyone also mentioned the Andalusian veterinarian, María del Carmen García Moreno.[20] While Yolanda and Ana lead university-based projects and training, Maricarmen highlights the significant role trained professionals can play in promoting pastoralism in their daily practices and beyond. In 2020, she became director of the Sierra de Castril Natural Park in Granada, but, when I interview her, she is still working for Oficina Comarcal Agraria ("Agrarian District Office") and as a veterinarian while also traveling throughout Andalusia and Extremadura to document traditional transhumance, photographing and gathering information about this fast-disappearing practice. When I first call her she is on the trail in Extremadura helping Suso and others with a spring transhumance. She invited me to join them, but instead we met in Seville a week later where she was delivering a talk on transhumance as cultural patrimony. Soft-spoken and highly focused, Maricarmen explains that she is in a race against time to document "every transhumance, every native breed, and every transhumant shepherd and his traditions. Photography helps transmit the emotional part, the human side of transhumance." She remarks (only half-jokingly): "See this gray streak in my hair? It's been a difficult year!" Her traveling photography exhibitions, recorded interviews, and videos are reaching a broad public. Yet this may not be enough to make significant changes, she says, tearing up with emotion.[21] "We're losing our heritage. I'm pretty

19   AgriTrain, 2016, https://www.agri-train.eu/?lang=en
20   Gescan, 'María del Carmen García Moreno, veterinaria, fotógrafa y directora de un Parque Natural', 12 March 2020, https://gescansl.com/maria-del-carmen-garcia-moreno-veterinaria-fotografa-y-directora-de-un-parque-natura
21   Her story and message have been broadcast on popular TV shows, such as *Tierra y Mar* (Tierra y Mar & Espacio Protegido Canal Sur, 'María del Carmen García Moreno, veterinaria, fotógrafa y directora de un Parque Natural', YouTube, 9 March 2020, (in Spanish:) https://www.youtube.com/watch?v=OstSaUzOa-o) and through her traveling photography project (Turismo Caravaca, 'La visión de la trashumancia a través de los ojos de la fotógrafa Mari Carmen García Moreno', 5 June 2018, http://www.turismocaravaca.com/blog/

pessimistic about the future of transhumance, but with photography, we document the tradition, and that's enough to give me some inner peace." Still, Maricarmen continues to fight for the future and has even begun work in a new area — organizing *ganaderas*, the women who work in this traditionally male profession.[22]

Fig. 6.1 Veterinarian María del Carmen García presents information on the benefits of transhumance to students at the *Escuela de Pastores*, Andalucía (2016).

When I attend the *Escuela de Pastores* the following year, I am not surprised to see Maricarmen there delivering material to students and fielding emergency veterinary calls on her cellphone at the same time. Somehow, she manages to provide a comprehensive presentation on the history, practice, and benefits of transhumance and pastoralism while simultaneously texting with a *ganadero* who is birthing a ewe. In her closing remarks, the vet urges her young audience to consider the benefits of transhumance and to stick with their desire to be shepherds. "Come join in on the transhumance this spring and find out how it works", Maricarmen encourages. "Hands-on training and good comradery come with it!" Later, she summarizes her views: "We need society and people living in cities to understand what shepherds do

la-vision-de-la-trashumancia-a-traves-de-los-ojos-de-la-fotografa-mari-carmen-garcia-moreno/).

22 Ganaderas en Red, 2016, (in Spanish:) http://www.ganaderasenred.org/

today. They manage environmentally high-value lands. They care for these high-value biodiverse spaces."[23]

This preservation activity among professionally trained university researchers and other specialists — and their increasing insistence that work must be done in close connection with the *ganaderos* themselves — has been one of the biggest changes in pastoralism in the last decade or two. The results include a recent improvement in the social status for shepherds, the emergence of new researchers who focus on practical solutions, and increased national attention on the benefits of pastoralism. And yet, despite this newfound appreciation and activity, each of the people I interview notes that there remains a long road ahead before these initiatives make a significant impact on the ability of shepherding as a profession to attract a new generation. It is this bottom-line reality that ultimately led me to the *Escuela de Pastores*. I wanted to interview students and teachers and see the impact this training outside of traditional knowledge handed down from one generation to the next might be having in filling the widening gap in the profession as long-time shepherds retire without replacements.

Shepherd School for a New Generation

Sooner or later, every person I interview over the course of a year mentions the *Escuela de Pastores* as a point of reference for their own ideas about the future of pastoralism. While *dehesa* owner Ernestine Lüdeke (Chapter 5) tried without success to sponsor an *Escuela* intern, Marta Moya (Chapter 4) hopes to contact the school, and goat farmer Pepe Millán (Chapter 2) mentors several students every year. Transhumant shepherd Fortunato Guerrero Lara (Chapter 3) still participates in some of their educational projects, despite some skepticism.

The idea of a dedicated school for shepherding began in the Basque Country, but now at least six provinces, including Andalusia, have their own programs.[24] This *Escuela de Pastores* is sponsored by two arms of

---

23   Tierra y Mar & Espacio Protegido Canal Sur, 'María del Carmen García Moreno, veterinaria, fotógrafa y directora de un Parque Natural', YouTube, 9 March 2020, (in Spanish:) https://www.youtube.com/watch?v=OstSaUzOa-o

24   Plataforma Ganadería Extensiva y Pastoralismo, 'Las escuelas de pastoreo en España', 25 July 2019, (in Spanish:) https://www.ganaderiaextensiva.org/

the regional Andalusian government — the Junta de Andalucía and the "Instituto Andaluz de Investigación y Formación Agraria" (IFAPA) — but it also benefits from the participation of collectives, research centers, and members of the shepherding community. Each spring, the *Escuela de Pastores* sets up in a new location in Andalusia, hoping to reach the broadest number of candidates. The year we visit (2016), the initial events are taking place at the "Estación Experimental del Zaidín", a research center in Granada.[25] As my colleague, María del Mar, and I turn down a small lane to the agricultural campus, the Sierra Nevada sparkles in the distance as the early-morning sun illuminates its highest peaks. When we enter the building, the on-site coordinator, Yolanda Mena's former student Dr. Francisco (Paco) de Asís Ruiz Morales,[26] extends a warm welcome. Dressed in jeans and a sweatshirt, he will oversee twenty students who will live, study, and work together for a month at the center before heading to their practicums all over Andalusia. Paco, like his mentor, believes in bridging the academic and real worlds. He blends hands-on work with *ganadero*s, such as helping to establish a local cheese shop, with research projects. And, rather than teach behind closed doors, he makes an effort to include the public. Today he has invited scholars, journalists, leaders of associations, and government officials to join the students. Indeed, it was at his urging that I attend these opening days.

For the next three months, students will split their time between the classroom and the fields, learning an impressive range of skills that highlights the complex nature of the profession, including knowledge needed to care for livestock from birth, selection of appropriate breeds for their specific geographical areas, animal nutrition, grazing practices and land use, and veterinary care. They will also learn the importance of navigating local, regional, and European Union regulations; obtaining funding for biodiversity initiatives; and successfully marketing their

---

escuelas-de-pastoreo/; Escuela de Pastores de Andalucía, X Escuela 2021, (in Spanish:) https://escueladepastoresdeandalucia.es/es/x-escuela2021

25 Estación Experimental del Zaidín (2014, https://www.eez.csic.es/) in Granada, is a branch of the Consejo Superior de Investigaciones Científicas (CSIC-Granada) funded by the Spanish government and part of a larger organization: Pastos y Sistemas Silvopastorales Mediterráneos.

26 *ResearchGate*, 'Francisco de Asís Ruiz Morales ', https://www.researchgate.net/ profile/Francisco-De-Asis-Morales; ORCID, 'Francisco de Asís Ruiz Morales ', https://orcid.org/0000-0002-0905-4481

products. After weeks of classroom sessions, internships will provide hands-on experience with different breeds, farm practices, and diverse geographies. Just as importantly, as we heard the APMM president Rogelio Jiménez note, their experiences here will help students establish networks for the future.

Twenty students — twelve men and eight women — selected from a pool of forty applicants come from all over Andalusia: Tarifa, Alpujarras, Almejar, Cádiz, Málaga, Córdoba, Sierra Norte, and Huelva — as well as from a variety of backgrounds. As one student, Sergio, explains, although he has no background in shepherding, he is eager to go back to the land. He has worked all over Spain but, after helping a friend with his *explotación* (large flock), wants to join the *neo-rurales* even as he wonders if the idea is crazy because he is not sure if he can adapt to the lifestyle it requires. In fact, one of the Junta de Andalucía officials who helps with the program later explains to me that this year there are fewer students like Sergio who do not already have a connection to pastoralism because it is hard, otherwise, for them to access land and obtain a license for owning a flock. With each passing year, the school has enrolled more students who grew up around livestock and attend because they want to master new skills — both bureaucratic and practical — to secure their own *explotación* and learn new ways to make it economically sustainable.

A half-dozen students gather around me, enthusiastic to talk about the new venture they are embarking upon, and eagerly share their individual goals and concerns. María's family in Tarija has a pair of goats now but wants to establish a full herd. Belén will inherit her grandfather's flocks, but she is concerned about the effects of climate change and decreased access to pasturelands. Paula works with her grandfather's livestock but wants to learn how to establish a cheese shop with the goat milk to make it more profitable. Sonia, having first studied law, now wants to return to her family farm and the *Malagueña* sheep they raise. She is eager to learn the economics of the business and how to access government subsidies so they can make a living. Sonia comments: "This is a traditional way of life; however, it can only be viable — maintained and transformed — if the government supports us." Her comment sparks a heated debate among the students as they discuss new regional restrictions and CAP requirements. Sonia clearly has struck a chord: in the end, if they are to be successful, each of them must be able to make extensive grazing cost-effective. Still, in the damp morning chill, their energy fills the room and fills observers like me with optimism for the future.

Fig. 6.2 Francisco Bueno Mesa, *ganadero* and student at the *Escuela de Pastores*, Andalusia (2016).

An older student about to turn thirty, Francisco Bueno Mesa, brings an experienced point of view to the discussion, noting how access to pastureland is increasingly difficult as intensive agriculture has grown exponentially in Southern Andalusia. After graduating from school and working in the tourist industry for nearly ten years, he is returning to his family tradition as a goat farmer. He reports that, growing up on a goat farm outside of Málaga, he personally experienced the feeling of marginalization many shepherds speak about: "It used to be that the shepherd was the lowest of the low. An illiterate. He didn't know how to read or write. Only in the country was he worth something, and then it was only for farming, for raising livestock and things of that sort. Only that." After ten years in the booming tourist industry, however, Francisco returned to shepherding, even though, like Fortunato's son Javier (see Chapter 3), he felt pressured by society to use his education for a different vocation:

> It seems like people expect something different from those of us who have completed some schooling. For example, I did my college prep *bachillerato* and all of that. I studied a lot. I like to read; I love to read. But some say I can't, or I shouldn't, be a shepherd. They say I have to be something more than that.

Nonetheless, Francisco chose to return to the family shepherding tradition:

> I want to continue down this road to being a shepherd, a goat farmer. Everybody in my family, my granddad, my great granddad, has raised livestock. They raised goats, and we've always made a living from all this. We've been able to eat thanks to farming.... I realized that I really like taking care of animals, and I want to follow in my dad's footsteps.

Besides learning about new funding and support systems at the *Escuela de Pastores*, Francisco has acquired a new understanding of the importance of shepherding and the value of his own contribution to the future:

> I'm learning the benefits of raising livestock. It's good for the forests and for biodiversity. Because of what we're doing, you can now go out in the countryside and see that there's vegetation, seeds are being replanted.... People still say that shepherds or *ganaderos* are the lowest of the low, but people are finally realizing that a lot of people live and a lot of natural diversity thrives because of *ganaderos* and what we do.

Several weeks later, I contact some graduates of the school and begin to glimpse the immense challenges, even after extensive training, that face young people who chose a pastoral profession. One, Paqui Ruiz

Escudero, explains that the inability to obtain pastureland, start-up funds, and a license to own livestock together acted as a barrier blocking her from taking up a full-time profession as a shepherd. Before enrolling, Paqui had already completed a thesis related to new pastoralism and worked with sheep in France. She explains that Spain should learn from French practices: "There's a vision. They value your identity as a shepherd in France. There's a culture that values local products over and above big business and the supermarkets." As part of a new generation, Paqui believes that new models for shepherding need to include the creation of more collectives among multiple family and friend groups who share the daily care of animals and marketing their products: "Society has changed, and you have to recognize new paradigms in shepherding; there aren't a lot of farming families who can do it on their own." Despite this vision, Paqui admits that her own experience in teaming up with a traditional shepherd ended in a misunderstanding exacerbated by gender bias against female shepherds.

Another graduate of the *Escuela de Pastores*, Mamen Cuéllar, echoes these observations. Like Paqui, she had first teamed up with shepherds in a rural area, where she was promised access to pastureland and support. However, her "outsiderness" along with traditional gender bias made collaboration impossible. "Male shepherds of a certain age", she notes sadly, "keep the male tradition of staying all alone with their animals, even though they continue to suffer from so much solitude. They are uncomfortable talking to a woman shepherd. If you don't have a man by your side, your hands are tied." Nonetheless, Mamen believes this attitude will change with more women going into the profession: "We women like being part of a community. We need collectives and a lot of creativity and energy."

Five years had passed since Mamen's experience. By the time we spoke in 2018, she was working at the University of Córdoba, but she was still keeping a hand in the trade, raising a half dozen animals on a small parcel of land. By 2018, Paqui had also given up shepherding as a full-time activity and begun to work at a research center for pastoralism in northern Spain. While both women benefited from the knowledge they acquired at the *Escuela*, officials have registered the frustration of *neo-rurales* like Mamen and Paqui. This is part of the reason that, as of 2022, the shepherd school has changed its focus to people who already have access to pastures and now, also, provides students who complete the whole course with a license and start-up funding from the Junta.

While attending the opening sessions of the 2016 *Escuela*, I also interview several of the Junta de Andalucía officials there. A middle-aged man dressed in a traditional green woolen shepherd sweater, Luis Jiménez García (coordinator of the *Consejería de la Agricultura, Pesca, y el Desarrollo Rural* (Ministry of Agriculture, Water and Rural Development)), tells me that he interviewed and selected each of the twenty students enrolled this year. He chooses, as he says, not to be a "protagonist" in this narrative and urges me to focus on the students instead. Later, when I watch him in action, I see he has the gift of a natural teacher. As the group gathers around him after a session, Luis gently challenges them: "Are you ready for this training, all this information, and learning the logic of so much bureaucracy?" After outlining new laws and penalties for the care and movement of livestock, he jokes about the importance of following guidelines: "We're not going to take the rogue's road. Your fame depends on your future." Luis concludes by connecting the pastoral movement with a broader social context: "We've got to spread the good news about what we do and about responsible consumerism. Don't be pessimists: You can do this!" As Luis finishes, the president of an association that focuses on specific breeds, Juan Antonio Mena, chimes in with a precept passed down from his grandfather, who was also a shepherd: "First you have to dream, and then fight for it." After more than fifty years as a shepherd, he understands that learning often comes through trial and error, part of the necessary "marriage" between dreams and hard work: "Combine all your dreams together with hard work but seek the support of the people around you. You'll go farther together, not alone."

This keen focus on galvanizing the next generation of shepherds for the task at hand is reinforced by José Ramón Guzmán Álvarez (Junta de Andalucía, *Dirección General de Gestión Medioambiental en la Consejería de Medio Ambiente*).[27] Instead of agreeing to an interview with me, José

---

27   This is the arm of the regional government that in controversial political move just a few years later was absorbed into the broader department that also includes intensive

Ramón invites me to attend his presentation. A man who appreciates poetry and culture, he artfully narrates the story of pastoralism. Both humorous and provocative, his presentation weaves together cultural references, history, anecdotes, and visual imagery, including a quote from *Don Quijote* and paintings by Murillo. He evokes both Spain's past "Golden Age" and present reality, observing: "It's one of the oldest professions in the world... there are no master's degrees or doctorates in shepherding, just 10,000 years of experience and tradition." Yet, he continues, "shepherding has changed, and you have to take advantage of the other experts, aid, and information." He offers the students a new narrative, an updated story of a country of shepherds who are neither Biblical holy men nor the "village idiot" but rather essential workers who will play a critical role in the sustainability of pastoralism — both in terms of its environmental impact and its cultural significance for Spain. He leaves no doubt in anyone's mind of the cultural and economic importance of their undertaking in the *Escuela de Pastores*.

The growth of shepherd schools has certainly caught the public eye: these *escuelas* have been featured on the front pages of *El País* and *The New York Times*, as the lead segment on the national RTVE news, and in regional programs on television Canal Sur.[28] This media attention taps into a revival of interest in shepherding not only as a symbol of Spanish identity but also as an important contributor to biodiversity. All this promotion helps, but, as nearly everyone I interview says, the greatest need is for young people who are willing to become shepherds, governments that can work rapidly to find effective solutions to the many hurdles they face, and a society that will support them with their purchasing power.

---

agriculture, the Ministry of Agricultura, Ganadería, Pesca y Desarrollo Sostenible. For an example of his recent work on policy, see José Muñoz-Rojas, José Ramón Guzmán-Álvarez, and Isabel Loupa Ramos, 'The complexity of public policies in Iberian *montados* and *dehesas*', in Teresa Pinto-Correia et al. (eds.), *Governance for Mediterranean Silvopastoral Systems* (2021), London: Routledge, pp. 169–88, http://dx.doi.org/10.4324/9781003028437-10

28 Lucía López Marco, 'Entrevista a Francisco de Asís Ruiz, coordinador de la Escuela de Pastores de Andalucía', Mallata.com, 27 March 2018, https://mallata.com/entrevista-a-francisco-de-asis-ruiz-coordinador-de-la-escuela-de-pastores-de-Andalucía/

Resiliency, Outreach, and a Changing Cultural Narrative

As we have seen, advocacy and information-sharing also contribute to (re-)building the cultural narrative about how the life path of a shepherd working in extensive grazing is interwoven with Spanish history and identity. In Spain, the narrative of pastoralism as cultural patrimony is now widespread. Every year, hundreds of videographers produce short-form documentaries about pastoralism and transhumance. These documentaries feature long shots of pastures or mountains, traditional music, interviews with shepherds, and close-ups of everyone's favorite subjects: lambs, goats, and cheese. As Ana Belén Robles notes, "initially many of these videos actually hurt the pastoral movement because they presented practices as an irreversibly dying process, and shepherds as 'non-modern'. However, more recent videos tend to emphasize the adaptability and relevance of these traditional ways in the twenty-first century." Many productions adopt an approach of social commentary and even include a call to action by drawing viewers' attention to the perils of climate change, economic upheaval, and the social marginalization of farmers. In January 2021, for example, the popular show *Tierra y Mar* took on the topic of the new CAP proposal and how it would affect *ganaderos*.[29] While the *plataformas* themselves rarely produce videos, their members are commonly featured. Indeed, many of the people I interviewed appear in these short documentaries (see individual chapters) — among them shepherds Fortunato Guerrero Lara and Pepe Millán, *dehesa* owner and foundation president Ernestine Lüdeke, veterinarian and transhumance advocate Maricarmen García, the *"ovejas bomberos"* program, Yolanda Mena, and Paco Ruiz. Jesús Garzón, the president of "Asociación Trashumancia y Naturaleza", shows up in more than a few!

Another popular development in the process of rewriting the traditional narrative of Spanish pastoralism are the more than twenty museums and traveling exhibitions focused on the history

---

29   Canal Sur, 'Tierra y Mar: La nueva PAC y la labor de los ganaderos en la *dehesa*', YouTube, 30 January 2021, (in Spanish:) https://www.youtube.com/watch?v=AXphDIBbP3A

of shepherding, transhumance, *vías pecuarias* (droving routes), and sustainable livestock practices across Spain. These museums are designed to educate both locals and tourists, but, perhaps more significantly, they contribute to the continuation and innovation of the local/national identity story and promote the role of pastoralism and associated cultural geographies as sites of memory: sites around which people develop a sense of a shared national history. Perhaps the best known is Guadalaviar's Transhumance Museum in Teruel.[30] It offers a public-education program and encourages tourism, but it also plays an active role by partnering with organizations to sponsor research projects and hosting meetings for shepherds.

Another popular cultural development includes local celebrations of shepherding that have been revived as part of regional fairs, which were historically linked to livestock sales and the marketing of shepherds' products. Attracting thousands of visitors, they showcase the renewal and repurposing of traditional events. Even more to the point, with widespread access to social media, some shepherds have taken into their own hands the narration of their lives, their experiences with transhumance, and work. More than a few have posted directly on social media, sharing their profession with each other and an interested public.

European and International Support

Although our focus has been on Andalusia, Spain, I cannot leave this chapter without mentioning a few projects and organizations at the European and international levels that some of our informants have cited as being key to our more regional organizations discussed earlier. In Europe, the conversation focuses on the role of pastoralism in big-picture climate-change mitigation and how a practical pan-European approach might support traditional and sustainable livelihoods. There is a vast array of traditional pastoral practices across Europe, each specific to climate and geography, most notably in Italy, the Alps, the Balkans, and across the Pyrenees between Spain and France. Several organizations

---

30 Museo de la Trashumancia, 2015, (in Spanish:) https://museodelatrashumancia. com/

advocate for sustainable pastoralism across Europe, such as the "European Forum on Nature Conservation and Pastoralism" (EFNCP), which focuses on policy that affects common lands and extensive grazing. Others, such as the European Union-sponsored project "LIFE LiveAdapt", collaborate with people like Ernestine Lüdeke and Yolanda Mena Guerrero, scholars at the University of Córdoba, and collectives like Entretantos, FEDEHESA and Goovinnova to study climate change and solutions based on extensive grazing in Southern Europe (France, Spain, and Italy).[31] Another international organization some Andalusian researchers are connected with is "Pastres",[32] which studies how we can learn from the global challenges that pastoral systems present and facilitates dialogue among stakeholders in government policy, markets, and environment-resource allocation.

International projects supporting pastoralism in general are widespread, but to name a few: the "International Union for the Conservation of Nature" (IUCN), the "Food Crisis Prevention Network", and the "Food and Agriculture Organization" (part of the United Nations) have all highlighted pastoralism as a key element in systems of sustainable food production and land conservation.[33] It is this connection to sustainability that gives the story of Spanish pastoralism such a strong presence on the international stage. Ernestine's farm and foundation often collaborate with groups abroad to protect the *dehesa* and to find funding for transhumance, training, and even to develop markets for local, sustainable products that can appeal to consumers both in Andalusia and abroad. The "Fundación Monte Mediterráneo" (see Chapter 5) is just one example of how regional initiatives to protect ecological systems are part of a global effort — including widely separated communities on the Asian and African continents — struggling with the same challenges with transhumance, marketing pastoralism, and the threat of desertification

---

31 Grupo Operativo Ovinnova, 2020, (in Spanish:) https://goovinnova.org/
32 Pastres focuses primarily on China, Kenya, and Italy as test cases in three continents (Pastres: Pastoralism, Uncertainty, Resilience, 2017, https://pastres.org/)
33 UN Environmental Program and International Union for Conservation of Nature (IUCN), 'Sustainable Pastoralism and the Post 2015 Agenda', 2015, https://sustainabledevelopment.un.org/content/documents/3777unep.pdf; IUCN and UNEP, 'Pastoralism and the Green Economy – a natural nexus?', 2014, https://portals.iucn.org/library/sites/library/files/documents/2014-034.pdf.

facing whole regions. A more local initiative with international impact is the Festival of Transhumance in Guadalaviar, which invites an international cohort of transhumant shepherds from places like Kenya and Tanzania to share their own local traditions with the wider community of pastoralists.

Highly visible international initiatives like the prestigious (and money-making) UNESCO designation of Intangible Cultural Heritage bring global recognition to transhumance as both a sustainable environmental practice and its cultural heritage. Spain received this designation for transhumance in 2023.[34] In addition, the United Nations has announced another way to highlight pastoralism: it has declared 2026 the International Year of Rangelands and Pastoralists.

Extensive livestock practices are, by nature, local. Traditions and practices are intimately connected to the land on which animals are born, raised, and prepared for market, but, in our globalized society, local practices can have a universal impact. The struggles in one society often mirror the struggles in another. It is no coincidence that stories of transhumance have been picked up by *The New York Times*, the BBC, and other organizations across the world; nor is it strange that they highlight the threat of climate change to livelihoods and ecosystems. The information about *plataformas* in this chapter has provided us with a broader view of the myriad researchers, activists, organizers, and bureaucrats who dedicate their lives (in some cases, all their available weekends) to extensive grazing. They help us to appreciate the highly interdependent nature of structures, laws, and trends that will allow shepherding to adapt, or allow it to fade away as a relic. They make clear that we all, as citizens and consumers, have a role in the survival — or demise — of sustainable pastoralism. The question remains: can the work of dedicated researchers, practitioners, and *plataformas*, together with the intense international interest generated in local approaches to sustainable agriculture and ranching, lead to real long-term change in habits of consumption and lifestyle that will protect traditional pastoral practices from further decline? While we cannot predict the future, some conclusions may be drawn, as we outline below.

---

34   UNESCO, 'Transhumance, the seasonal droving of livestock',
     Inscription 18.COM 8.b.14, https://ich.unesco.org/en/RL/
     transhumance-the-seasonal-droving-of-livestock-01964

Conclusions:
Challenges and Opportunities

Society has changed, and you have to recognize new paradigms in shepherding.

Paqui Ruiz

We must be practical, we must be strategic, we must choose our priorities.

Ernestine Lüdeke

I wish there were more people like you; that there was a voice that would speak for us. We're not heard. We need to recognize that the world needs all of us, each and every one.

Fortunato Guerrero Lara

A Country of Shepherds: Stories of a Changing Mediterranean Landscape has taken shape around the case studies of a few shepherds and *ganadero*s based in southern Spain and the regional organizations that offer them support. As we have seen, each of the individuals named here is part of a wider network of family, friends, and collaborators. Our project quickly revealed a snapshot of a larger agricultural system that spreads not only geographically — across Andalusia, Spain, the European Union, and the world — but temporally, across generations of family and cultural inheritance. We have heard a common story among the shepherds of their marginal social and institutional position in the modern world. And yet, the ancient practice of transhumance itself proves to be one of the best examples of the interrelated nature of agricultural systems in a globalized world. We have seen how it has evolved from a practice strictly associated with caring for livestock in the country to a sector that cares for environmental sustainability, animal welfare, and cultural heritage while also maintaining sound ecological land practices.

 https://doi.org/10.11647/OBP.0387.07

We conclude here with a brief overview of common points raised by the shepherds, resident landowners, and activists whom we have met in *A Country of Shepherds*. Putting these distinct voices in conversation with one another, we gain a wider view of the practices of transhumant shepherding and extensive grazing, as well as the collective efforts keeping them alive. I will summarize obstacles our informants point out and how they relate to larger systemic issues. Then, I will discuss the resilience of this tradition and new paths forward that foster hope for the future of pastoralism in Andalusia.

Systemic Challenges

A common observation from many of our informants is the marginalization of pastoralism. As we heard from Pepe Millán (Chapter 2), despite advocacy through documentaries and national television programs, people involved in the care of livestock in extensive grazing systems report a continuing social stigma surrounding the profession. He notes his own efforts at training the very people who interview him to speak respectfully, "you have to treat each other equally, with respect." More widely, Pepe points to an increasing reliance upon supermarkets in even the most remote of urban centers, which has contributed to a general lack of knowledge surrounding food systems, even among young adults. Modern consumer preferences for the standardization, lower costs, and "cleanliness" of supermarkets often ignore the importance of local diversity and do not recognize the environmental value-added of extensive grazing.

This has led to another challenge. The increased separation of the spheres of production and of consumption exacerbates an old trend in Spain and elsewhere: the urban-rural divide. Consumers are more physically alienated than ever from the lands where their food is produced. Traditional transhumant practices had already decreased with the introduction of railroads. Today, ever-increasing regulatory burdens imposed internationally, along with rising fees and falling sales, have forced many shepherds to abandon the transhumant, overland routes in favor of truck transport. With this precipitous drop in foot traffic by shepherds and the brush-clearing activities of the animals, these routes have become so unkempt they are often unusable even as hiking trails. While this loss of public land is difficult to quantify, it certainly makes less visible the work that goes into raising these animals and, thus, the products that come of them. In a country like Spain, where an urban-rural divide has taken such dramatic hold over the past century, consumers are more physically alienated than ever from the lands where their food is produced.

As more consumers choose mass-produced supermarket meats, farmers turn to cheesemaking and other strategies, hoping to enter a market with longer-lasting and more-profitable products. And yet, the often-stringent government quality regulations on these secondary products at times has driven this promising source of supplemental (or, in some cases, survival) income to a standstill. The journalist Marta Fernández sums up the future situation: "From a holistic point of view, the social and environmental benefits from shepherding are clear. But in terms of sustainability, one pillar is lacking: the economic one. Therefore, if we wonder if there is a future in this activity, the professionals say it is clear: yes, but there must be supplemental income" (Fernández 6).[1] Here, it is important to consider the role of CAP payments in supplementing incomes (so support can come from markets and/or from policy programs). In plain, direct language, Ernestine Lüdeke (see Chapter 5) gives us the bottom line: "Every consumer, everyone who eats, needs to understand the cost to humanity of mass production of food sources at low costs and how they fail to support a viable future. Society has to pay a lot to make up for the harmful effects to the environment."

This leads us to a third systemic challenge, that of the burdensome regulation imposed at all levels, from the regional to the national and pan-European communities. Shepherds, landowners, and activists all emphasize the oppressive nature of successive layers of bureaucratic obligation. Regulations often impose barriers to *ganaderos* and shepherds who must pay additional duties, adhere to quality assurance and hygiene standards, and navigate a mounting culture of bureaucratic red tape. Shepherds Juan Vázquez (Chapter 1), Pepe Millán (Chapter 2), and Fortunato Guerrero Lara (Chapter 3) all note the lack of help in applying for funding when they are in the field all day and complain of new policies

---

1   She continues to comment that society "is increasingly aware of environmental sustainability and animal welfare. At the same time, society increasingly distances itself from the impact that the biased interpretation of sustainability really has on the rural environment and its inhabitants who amass a valuable demographic, sociological, territorial, economic, and environmental heritage through the care of their animals" (Fernández 9).

that threaten their livelihoods, such as the new definition of pasturelands on which subsidies are based. Even the resident landowners, like Marta Moya (Chapter 4) and Ernestine Lüdeke (Chapter 5), observe about how time-consuming it is to follow the constantly shifting laws and requirements. For example, the European Union calculates pasturelands without an understanding of how the delicate Mediterranean *dehesa* functions. However, there has been growing awareness of this gap in policy, and new eco-schemes and greening strategies are attempting to take into account a broader definition of regional methods of sustainable farm and land management that are aimed at maintaining public goods.[2]

These problems have been exacerbated by the 2020 elections that overturned decades of Socialist rule in the Junta de Andalucía. The new government "cancelled" the department dedicated to the environment where José Ramón Gutiérrez Álvarez (see Chapter 6) worked (*Consejería de Medio Ambiente*); it is now part of the unwieldy department that also oversees the competing interests of intensive agriculture (*Consejería de Agricultura, Ganadería, Pesca y Desarrollo Rural*). The question today is whether the Junta's significant contribution up to now can continue to be effective with no office dedicated specifically to sustainability and the environment.

When I interview José Ramón about the changes in government, he observes: "We're not very agile. We can't move things along very quickly," and other interest groups, including animal-rights activists, bring "new contradictions that put into question extensive-grazing practices. Now there are barriers to everything we used to do naturally." Others, like Ernestine, argue that not only are there barriers, but that there is a lack of sufficient economic support on the part of the government at the regional, national, and European level for the environmental and territorial services that shepherding provides — services that benefit everyone. Increasing administrative costs and extensive paperwork draw attention, time, and resources away from the primary work of shepherding, which has itself had to struggle in a world characterized by constant technological innovation. Overwhelmed and worn out, Fortunato exclaims, "it's impossible. There's no time. New things are always coming out, and more paperwork. It's all a huge mistake forced on us by the politicians."

---

2   https://ec.europa.eu/eurostat/statistics-explained/index.php?title=Glossary:Eco-schemes

At the European Union level, the CAP legislation often has not been responsive to local and regional needs in member countries, such as in the case of Andalusia. The draft of the proposed new laws, slated to go into effect in 2023, has shaken every individual I checked back with in 2022. As Yolanda Mena mentions in our last chapter, the proposal is for a "green CAP", (now in force 2023–2027) but, in the way it is being configured currently, "the *ganaderos* doing extensive grazing have very little weight. It's becoming more and more complicated." As activist Paco Casero told us earlier (see Chapter 6), many people lay the blame at the feet of the Spanish government, saying officials have long ignored the value of extensive grazing for its role in maintaining rural environments; providing high-quality, sustainable food sources; and even preserving the natural and cultural patrimony. Most advocates are proposing structural changes that would redefine the unique, multivalent contribution of the extensive-grazing system. Key to this restructuring would be establishing more equitable distribution of the European Union's CAP subsidies, which the new 2023–2027 version has attempted to address.

A fourth systemic hurdle, and one with deep historical roots, is what many see as the stubborn resistance of many traditional landowners to adopt techniques of sustainable pastoralism. In contrast to trends of modernization over the last half-century, it can be difficult to re-adopt traditional, sustainable practice. In our interviews, we heard from landowners who decided to become more permanent or semi-permanent residents on their farms and to work directly with their managers. Marta Moya (see Chapter 4) even calculated how much she lost before she began living at least part-time on her land and got to know how to run a sheep farm and shore up its traditional sustainable practices. Looking back in 2022, she observes that "I lost part of the money I earned working at the club in Seville when I wasn't on the *finca*. I still hadn't learned how to properly run the *finca*." Another resident farm owner, Ernestine points out that the lack of understanding and respect follows the lines of rural-urban divide that we have been tracing. Much like Fortunato, she expresses a frustration with those landowners who refuse to listen to the expertise and long-term vision of those who live in closest connection with the land, and who are often interested only in the increasing rent they can charge for land use. As we heard earlier (see Chapter 5), she sums it up, saying "it's very difficult to feel identified with the needs of an agroecosystem if it's not yours, you're being badly paid, badly treated, exploited. Conversely, if you have a nice income from your farm, you don't have to really be aware of the negative aspects of it, or even live them."

To change this lack of mutual respect and the urban-rural divide, as Fortunato notes, requires both landowners and consumers to better understand the interlocking nature of production, exchange, and consumption that supports all local, national, and global food systems — not just transhumant shepherding. Fortunato describes for us the compatible nature of sustainable farming and maintaining olive groves. But the first step must be for "people to be more aware of what's going on" — by "people", he refers to everyone from consumers to landowners and government officials.

A fifth challenge, surely the most well-discussed in the news, is the impact of global-market forces, over which local producers have no control. Markets are governed as much by real shifts in climate and political upheaval (one of the hottest summers on record and the war in Ukraine are the most recent examples in 2023) as they are by speculative investments. Looking at the last couple years alone, we see how a global pandemic spread fear of disease and affected shepherds as much as anyone. Shepherds rely on a functioning economy and the ability to move their flocks between spaces.[3] If their animals become ill, they lose business. And, while on the move, their access to veterinarians is limited. Yet, because people who work with livestock are considered essential workers, they were exempted from the harshest restrictions of the lockdown in spring 2020.

In this same period, climate-related catastrophes hit hard. For example, a wildfire broke out in the area where the family farms of the *Escuela de Pastores* student Francisco Bueno Mesa (see Chapter 6) are located, near Sierra Bermeja, Málaga. In just the first five days, more

---

3   While some transhumance was altered and both the Festival of Transhumance and the *Escuela de Pastores* were suspended in 2020, they resumed in 2021. P. O., 'El coronavirus deja este año a Madrid sin ovejas', *Telemadrid*, 16 October 2020, (in Spanish:) https://www.telemadrid.es/coronavirus-covid-19/Madrid-ovejas-trashumancia-coronavirus-0-2277972206--20201016070152.html; Javier López, 'Plan B de la trashumancia para evitar al coronavirus', *ABC de Andalucía*, 22 June 2020, (in Spanish:) https://sevilla.abc.es/andalucia/sevi-plan-trashumancia-para-evitar-coronavirus-202006220740_noticia.html?ref=https:%2F%2Fwww.google.com%2F; Sara Batres, 'Trashumancia en tiempos de coronavirus', *RTVE*, 18 November 2020, (in Spanish:) https://www.rtve.es/noticias/20201118/trashumancia-coronavirus/2057446.shtml

than 19,000 acres burned, and 2,500 people had to evacuate as 650 firefighters and hundreds of emergency military personnel fought the flames (Aritz Parra, AP 9/15/21). Marta Moya also recalled for us the fire that spread through her *dehesa* and rendered it useless for several years. A decrease in extensive-grazing practices means that large areas of highly flammable undergrowth are no longer cleared. Just days before the fire outside of Málaga erupted, the World Bank predicted massive population migrations due to climate change by 2050.[4] The most vulnerable region will be Sub-Saharan Africa because of its "desertification, fragile coastline, and dependence on agriculture", but the environment in southern Spain is also at high risk. Ernestine, once again, puts it plainly:

> The fragile, biodiverse *dehesa* is one of the last defenses Andalusia has in the face of the encroaching Sub-Saharan desert system, which is slowly but surely creeping north. It is up to us to be sure the younger generation understands and accepts this challenge.

She and Paco Casero believe there is still time (though as Ernestine states, "not very much") to ensure regions of Andalusia do not become just another extension of the Sahara.

In addition to climate change and a pandemic, we have also heard how politics can radically shift market trends in a short time. As Fortunato explained in fall of 2021, the reduction in lamb export products from the UK to the European Union due to Brexit actually increased demand and prices for Spanish lamb production for the first time in decades. However, speculative markets can also inject uncertainty for producers: the stock trading on commodities necessary for the raising of livestock, such as animal feed, adds even more variables to an already volatile market for the high-quality, labor-intensive meats raised by Fortunato and shepherds like him. He reminds us again that developing widespread awareness is the key:

> The whole market thing is very complicated.... When you produce a fresh product, you have less margin for maneuverability. And then there are the speculators who are in the mix who say: "I buy, I owe, I have my

---

4   It is estimated that between 44 and 250 million people will have to migrate (published the Groundswell report (13 September 2021) and Renato Brito AP 9/14/21).

grain seller, I sell it just a certain way...." People need to be more aware of what's going on.

Even with the large gain in lamb prices from Brexit, however, speculative markets reacting to the extreme drought in spring 2022 and forecasts for the months ahead fueled a crisis. According to Yolanda Mena, it is the worst disaster she has witnessed in more than thirty years working in sustainable pastoralism. She is alarmed at what is happening:

> In 2021–22 there was a brutal increase in the cost of production — up to seventy to eighty percent in feed costs for livestock. Between the drought and speculation, no grains have been produced and costs have gone up. For example, in November, forage fodder — essential fiber for grazing animals — was planted, but instead of cutting it for hay, driven by speculation caused by the drought, it was harvested for grain, and now there's not enough hay. The crisis that the people who do extensive grazing are facing is the worst I've seen in my lifetime, worse than the recession of 2008.

Perhaps the most critical challenge to the whole system of sustainable pastoralism, however, is the problem of the generational renewal: the number of shepherds retiring without replacements. Many shepherds recognize this as a problem of inheritance. The struggle to pass onto subsequent generations a practice that often offers fewer and fewer gains — not to mention more and more roadblocks — characterizes the lives of many shepherds today. In the absence of these future stewards of the lands, transhumance will evaporate in obsolescence. Fortunato observes:

> In just twenty years, livestock on this land, our land, has disappeared. Just twenty years; I'm not exaggerating. I've worked at it for a long time. What's happened is that the *ganadero*s who have stayed, we've stayed because it's what we love. You've been raised around this, it's what you love, and the truth is it takes a lot out of you. It's no longer about what you earn or don't earn. We make the sacrifice, and sure, we live with the costs of the sacrifice we're making.

Many working conditions would need to change to help keep and attract new shepherds and *ganadero*s to the profession. The city dweller Daniel (see Chapter 5) who left to work as a shepherd-manager at Ernestine's farm summarizes:

> There are a lot of situations where working conditions for contracted shepherds are not the best for a job that's so demanding of self-sacrifice. They have to work too many hours and are probably poorly compensated as to living facilities and days off. In many cases, their monetary compensation is way below what it should be.

Even the efforts of many *ganaderos* (such as Fortunato and Pepe) and some landowners (such as Ernestine) to organize collectively as part of a growing mass of advocacy platforms — not to mention those of regional governments (such as the Junta de Andalucía) to help fund pastoralism and to teach classes on the practice — are not enough to guarantee its permanence. The shortage of workers has worsened, at least temporarily, due to new labor shifts since the pandemic, says Marta Moya. When the lockdown took place in Andalusia, many farm owners who lived in the cities moved to their farms, sharing lodging and routines with resident laborers and shepherds. She says: "This mixing of people did not go well. Often the people who work the farms are there because they not only like nature, but they like the solitude and independence of working primarily on their own without the landowner and their families there 24/7." In the aftermath of those four or six months of the lockdown, "there was a lot of movement all around." Many shepherds quit their positions. In Marta's case, she has had to manage the farm and animals on her own with sporadic help from family for nearly a year as a range of workers have come and gone — most of whom have little experience. Now, because of her own experience with the challenges of shepherding, like having to rescue her flock from a country road at midnight, Marta has a personal understanding of the demands of the work. As we heard earlier, she emphasizes: "If you weren't invested in the welfare of the sheep, would you go out in the freezing cold?"

A Path Forward

Despite these and other systemic challenges, the individuals we have heard from all recognize a path forward based on the environmental benefits these traditional practices offer, and they express hope that a cultural renewal in the public sphere will create stronger markets and policies to sustain pastoralism. First, many agree that the tide is turning as the public and governments become increasingly aware of the critical role for pastoralism in environmental and rural sustainability. In the five years between my first and final interviews, the conversation changed. During the first months of the pandemic, because people who work with livestock were considered essential workers, they were exempted from the harshest restrictions of the lockdown in spring 2020. By 2022, shepherds, resident landowners, and advocates all commented on a shift in public awareness about pastoralism as sustainable-ranching practices and transhumance. *Ganadero*s are as important to ecosystems as bees, according to student-*ganadero* Francisco Bueno:

> They say that if there weren't any bees the world would cease to exist because bees give us pollen. It's not the same relatively speaking, but it is true: if there weren't sheep, goats, and this type of livestock, we would probably not have the diversity that we have right now. They no longer say that the shepherd or the *ganadero* is the lowest of the low. People are finally realizing that a lot of people live and a lot of natural diversity thrives because of *ganadero*s and what we do. We have to realize this; we have to make sure that others realize this.

Despite the persistence of urban-rural and production-consumption divides, more people understand the benefits of buying local, sustainably produced food and products if they can afford them. People working within the *plataforma* system note progress in marketing high-quality woolen and food products to select markets that have expanded due to public awareness.[5] The government official José Ramón Gutiérrez smiles, saying, "After ten to fifteen years of public campaigning, society is recognizing that we're at a crucial moment for extensive grazing. As the saying goes, 'better late than never'." Yolanda Mena at the University of Seville also sees a corresponding shift:

> What I've perceived in the last few years is a greater sensitivity for the extensive grazing type of pastoralism and *plataformas* that support communication between all actors — *ganadero*s as well as researchers. They're all coming together.

Secondly, as more consumers and government officials understand the contribution made to the environment and society by the production of local artisanal goods, there are more opportunities for direct marketing. Small producers like Juan (Chapter 1), as well as Pepe's daughter Rita,

---

5   See, for example, the group Govinnova (www.goovinnova.org), in which Ernestine Lüdeke is an active member.

have been able to capture a part of this market. In fact, Juan turned the catastrophe of the pandemic to his advantage: when he contracted COVID-19 and his buyer halted all purchases from him for six months, he was forced to seek other solutions. Motivated by the Junta de Andalucía's loosening of restrictions, Juan and his wife Manoli are able to sell their cheeses directly to established customers. When I last saw Juan, he could not linger to talk long because he was busy delivering their hand-crafted cheeses. As Rita Millán (see Chapter 2) explains:

> It's up to all of us to change how we do things; to get rid of the middlemen and make direct sales to the consumer. So yes, then you can make a profit. If not, it's very, very, very hard. It depends on feed prices if you have a good year. It depends on many, many things, and then, on what they want to pay you.

Part of the project to help with direct sales is better marketing, which includes creating easily identifiable brands and, as Rita notes, using the internet to reach a broader clientele. As the president of the collective "Asociación Pastores por el Monte Mediterráneo" noted, "responsible consumerism needs to continue developing and grow deeper roots in society, and *ganaderos* need to know this loyal consumer market will demand high quality products." Indeed, Yolanda Mena's working group at the University of Seville has launched "a collective brand, a brand-name quality seal" to help consumers easily identify high-quality local products.

Thirdly, as current labor opportunities continue to be inadequate to meet the needs of many people, pastoralism offers an alternative to the modern urban lifestyles in which some people feel cut off or alienated from nature, community, and tradition. When I first began this project in 2015, the impact of the 2008 global recession was still being felt in Andalusia, especially by young people who were often unemployed or underemployed. Teaching English at the University of Seville at that time, I was shocked to find that 80% of the students taking my course saw only two options to make a living: either to work in the tourist industry or emigrate to another part of the European Union. English was the passport to both. Since then, unemployment has decreased, but many young people still have not found much stability. Since the advent of the global pandemic in 2020, which hit urban Spain particularly hard, COVID-19 became a catalyst for people to escape congested urban areas — at least for now. A man in his early thirties at the *Escuela de Pastores*, who wants to become a shepherd, says: "I don't like working in the city, but I do like working with animals. Besides, there's an urgent need for more shepherds." People like him express interest in living more closely to nature, having a personal connection to their work, making a contribution to the environment, and finding a livelihood that can sustain them. As we heard from the shepherd-manager Daniel:

> When I would run into people that had found shepherding, I was always attracted to the work they were doing, the way they lived, the way they acted. It was something that just drew me in. In these last few years, after doing a round of training in forest management, I came to the conclusion that I needed to experience the essence of shepherding. I felt the need to get out of the city, the fast-paced rhythm of today's society and everything that has to do with urban life.

Fortunato's son, Javier, also noted for us that, in 2016, the conditions of economic crisis over the previous five years had pushed some young university-educated Spaniards back to their hometowns and to the countryside more generally, where many of them ultimately would find work in professions, such as shepherding, for which they were not originally trained. Around this migration has sprung up a neo-ruralist movement, in which both people from small towns and from large cities have come to find new meaning in their lives through their adoption of those traditions that they had previously disavowed or never known. As we heard, Javier believes there is a role for everyone and every profession, but that food production is key: "In life it takes all kinds: construction workers, engineers, shepherds. And *ganadería* is at the base of it all. If that goes away, then everything goes away."

Fortunato comments that "the best inheritance I can leave him [Javier] is his career," and other shepherds speak in similar terms of inheritance. Even Juan — who asked us rhetorically, "Who wants to do this on a Saturday night?" — finds himself taken aback by the eagerness of some members of the younger generation, including his own nephew, to take up shepherding. Even then, as the perspective of Javier already suggests, this is not the same specialized career for which the youth have been university trained, reminding us: "You have to live it. And besides, you have to pass it on from generation to generation. You can't learn it from a book." Pepe Millán also told us how he learned without a father or schooling but through his keen sense of observation: "You have to watch nature.... You can study all you want, but you have to watch and learn."

A fourth aspect of this shift in pastoralism, then, is the shift in education and training for labor opportunities in the profession. While "the book" that Javier and Pepe refer to above may be a stand-in for contemporary educational and labor models, study is becoming more common in order to sustain pastoralism. The newer generation, like Pepe's daughter Rita, studied the administrative hoops to handle multiple sets of regulations and paperwork. Besides the traditional walking stick to herd their flocks, they need internet access and knowledge of how to work with government policies and funding. This is why the Junta de Andalucía now guarantees graduates of the *Escuela de Pastores* help in attaining licenses for land and flocks. They also learn more about the environmental and cultural benefits their work provides. While many long-time shepherds are amused at the thought of shepherd school, there are growing numbers of graduates from these shepherd-training institutions. Recent graduates of the *Escuela de Pastores*, as well as a fourth-generation shepherd like Francisco Bueno, increasingly understand the larger environmental, economic, and cultural value of the work they do: "Thanks to us, a lot of people live from livestock, but it also benefits the environment." *Neo-rurales* that we heard from, like Daniel who trained at Ernestine's educational center, see their role and the skill it requires:

> Shepherding is very special because it has gone from being a rather common profession in earlier times to the way it is today, with fewer people wanting to dedicate themselves to it and its tradition of preserving a part of our history and customs. Also, it demands you understand the animals, in this case the sheep, and the great psychological commitment it takes to spend hours alone, exposed to the weather.

As we saw in Chapters 5 and 6, these shepherd-training programs provide students with a vast range of information and practical skills; once completed, they now also increasingly come with a near-guarantee of work. In addition to addressing the need for a higher standard of living, the schools are now training their students on how to market their products. The director of the *Escuela de Pastores*, Paco Ruiz, for example, teaches a course on how to establish cheese shops.

Ownership and fair pay are a critical fifth area for nurturing a path forward. Every informant, whether shepherd, landowner, or university researcher mentions the importance of improving these aspects. Since generational inheritance poses a daily concern for shepherds today, the recent ability of shepherds to apply for funding to own their own *explotación* (large flock) and to assist with costly access to land, as well as the *plataformas* that help them access these funds, are critical to being able to set up their own practice. In *A Country of Shepherds*, we have heard from three families of shepherds that have developed their own businesses, as well as shepherd-managers who are finally being given better working conditions. Both are relatively new situations and give workers more of a stake in the outcomes of their labor. Owning their own businesses, however, has come at a steep cost in terms of time, money, and stress. While these *ganadero*s see it as the only way forward to live better and, perhaps, to have interested family members take over, they also note that the responsibilities of ownership, too, are not sustainable in their current form. Fortunato's family, for example, now owns all of their flocks, but they cannot continue to work at the current level; the need to move beyond subsistence living cannot be at the cost of no time off. As Fortunato ironically jokes: "The only good thing, and the reason we keep going at it, is because the *ganadero* works so much that he doesn't spend anything. He doesn't have time to spend." For her part, *Escuela de Pastores* graduate Paqui Ruiz argues that new collectives of shepherds are the key to moving forward. "There aren't a lot of farming families who can do it on their own." They need better working hours and vacations for a better quality of life. All three of the landowners we interviewed also recognized this need for both ownership and better working conditions for their shepherd-managers. As Marta stated, "The days of near-slavery are long gone." "We need to be practical," argues Ernestine, "and first fight to attract young people to shepherding ... we need a new management system. In twenty years, it will be too late!"

To reach this goal, there needs to be more focus on a sixth area, changes in government policies. We have seen some concrete beneficial changes in local, regional, and European Union regulations to support pastoralism. The subsidies offered for an *explotación* have been the catalyst for several of the families we interviewed to expand their work. They have also been a catalyst for the family of Vanesa Pablo Fernández (see Chapter 1) to work toward having their own business while the local town supported them by offering temporary grazing land. As Vanesa explained earlier, in three years they have gone from three goats to nearly two hundred and can now apply for government subsidies. She jokes about how she has gotten into great shape, but she also gets to the heart of what needs to happen in the profession: "It has to be your project," your own business. Fortunato suggests there needs to be much more support:

> Everything can always get better in life.... For the government's part... if they could compensate public *fincas* without charging us for the pastureland, giving us a little assistance, it would help out a lot because this sector is now on the edge of disappearing.

But, as Paco Casero and others note, the Spanish government often has not fought hard enough for pastoralism within the European Union CAP system, nor has it fairly distributed funds from it. Both Vanesa and Rita Millán conclude that the only way to help close this gap without more subsidies is to "sell directly to the consumer" to avoid middlemen taking a big cut of any profits made.

The regional government's loosening of restrictions on the sales of locally produced cheeses saved Juan's family during COVID-19, and now every graduate of the *Escuela de Pastores* receives a license for their own flock. Positive change in government practices around pastoralism does make a difference. When I catch up with José Ramón Gutiérrez in 2022, he proudly notes that the *Escuela de Pastores* is thriving. It had sixty applicants for twenty-five places this year, and completion of the program now "fulfills requirements that make you eligible for government subsidies". José Ramón is preparing his notes for the closing session, a round table that includes collectives and shepherds as they discuss: "What does extensive grazing need to learn in the twenty-first century?" His basic philosophy motivates his work:

> Shepherds need the ability to communicate — to communicate what they do; what they need. They are no longer those solitary figures who have very little to do with the town they come down to visit every once and a while. Today they share the same rural environment and the perception of the world — just like any young person.

The researcher working with Ana Belén Robles's group at CSIC, María Eugenia Ramos Font (see Chapter 6), is part of this emerging generation living in a highly digital, connected world. She believes that "young people have to step up; young people have the power" to make positive change and make these demands. She smiles, saying she knows they are out there already making connections, sharing knowledge: "I follow a WhatsApp group that has 143 members. They're always sharing things, tricks, what they like, how many births they've had." These connections could be harnessed and become powerful forces for change. According to journalist Marta Fernández, "social networking can be the megaphone for them to be the 'influencers' for this sector" (8). This new movement, however, must be accompanied by political support, as shepherd-manager Daniel notes:

> As far as the *ganadero*s are concerned, especially small-time *ganadero*s, certain governmental policies must change to allow for profitability from these *explotaciones* without affecting the quality of the *explotación* or the labor conditions of the workers.

Other administrative decisions made by the Junta de Andalucía, such as the selection of directors of public lands, can also ensure long-term sustainability. Directors need to understand how the viability of public land often depends on integrating pastoral practices with land-management plans. The photographer-vet-activist we interviewed in Chapter 6, Maricarmen García, for example, was named Director of the Parque Natural del Castoril in 2020. Her vision of the close relationship between land management and extensive grazing will help ensure biodiversity and combat the negative effects of intensive agriculture in southern Spain. The key, as we heard from Maricarmen above, is that "we need society and people living in cities to understand what shepherds do today. They manage environmentally high-value lands. They care for these high-value biodiverse spaces."

Finally, shepherds and others working in programs related to land use and pastoralism also continue to strengthen the scaffolding on a wide range of issues to make it more profitable. Besides help with transhumance and knowledge sharing, one of the biggest focal points among shepherds has been advocacy for reform in agricultural and livestock policies. We saw in Chapter 6 how many *plataformas* have joined efforts to change proposed new CAP guidelines that undermine the strides made in sustainable pastoralism. Yolanda Mena describes how the European Union proposal restructures CAP subsidies into a two-part subsidy system, with one part directed to practitioners but with a new set of requirements that would make it "increasingly more complicated for the *ganadero*s who practice extensive grazing and have very little weight to make changes to the strategic plan". She also lists a whole series of activists, organizations, and conferences working to change the proposal before it's too late. Many of the *plataformas* we mentioned above — such as "Asociación Pastores por el Monte Mediterráneo", "Asociación

Trashumancia y Naturaleza", "Fundación Savia", and la "Plataforma por la Ganadería Extensiva y el Pastoralismo" — were developing collective campaigns when I last interviewed them. They were hoping to help focus policy on transhumance and extensive grazing that was going to be included in the CAP "eco-scheme" that was rolled out in 2023. They set out to demonstrate these systems' ecological benefit.[6] These organizations amplify the voices of shepherds and *ganaderos*, who are faced with bureaucratic changes that threaten the viability of their work.

This extensive government activity and programming, however, is overwhelming for most *ganaderos* and shepherds who must dedicate full-time to the care of the flocks, as Pepe noted. In response to this dilemma, Ana Belén Robles's group is developing a concrete solution, a central office dedicated to assisting *ganaderos* with bureaucratic red tape, helping smaller-scale agriculture workers navigate the increasing regulation of pastoralism. She explains that bureaucratic changes like the ones proposed in the new CAP wreak havoc on people who work with livestock: "They need to dedicate time to their animals. They don't have time to do paperwork or do the work to rent pasturelands. They need someone else to do it, and many times it's left up to their wives who are the administrators for the family." If we expect a new generation of young people to take up the profession, she maintains, we must acknowledge that they will demand a certain lifestyle like their peers that includes free time, having an internet connection, and a decent income. We need offices to help them secure funding, access to pasturelands, and support for a good quality of life. Echoing Fortunato Guerrero Lara's observation, Ana sees how otherwise young people "look for other ways out. Or they look for extra work or an alternative so they can still be close to the land."

While each of these initiatives will strengthen the future of pastoralism, people like Ernestine Lüdeke caution that these partial models are often not enough to sustain transhumant shepherding. Larger structures are needed, she insists. People with any investment in it at all must "get to a point where it can be part of a more global system" that prioritizes a very practical strategy, matching the interests of everyone involved:

> We need people who breed dogs, people who have sheep, people who produce certain products that we need for the dogs. We need architects

---

6   See, for example, Por otra PAC, 2019, (in Spanish:) https://porotrapac.org/

who can construct simple housing in the north where people can stay. And we need modern people to tell us how, with solar panels, we can make warm water and have cell phones work.

As a transhumant shepherd himself, Fortunato points out, "Transhumance has always happened, but now it could easily fail because there isn't a population who gets their products from transhumant livestock." Employing some of the very infrastructures she outlines, last year (2022), Ernestine's collective of transhumant sheep reached nearly 14,000, and Jesús Garzón's nearly 20,000. There is reason for hope, but there is also a clear call to action on all our parts.

Evidence of this increased awareness of the need for a unified approach at the level of the national government is the recent publication, *Propuesta de bases técnicas para una estrategia estatal de la ganadería extensiva* (October 2022), which, as we saw in Chapter 6, is the result of a collaborative process with some of the most influential collectives in Spain. The document outlines a whole range of concrete actions for the Ministry of Agriculture to approve. To name just a few of those actions that dovetail with what we have heard: creating a centralized bureaucracy for paperwork; establishing educational banks of information; restructuring CAP subsidies; legislating fiscal incentives for extensive grazing over intensive agriculture; requiring purchase of extensive grazing products for state functions; assuring access to pasturelands; helping generate public-private initiatives; incorporating more women; connecting young shepherds with those who are retiring; and initiating public campaigns on the nutritional and climate benefits of extensive grazing (*Propuesta* 101–24). The action list is impressive, and the hope, given the current crisis in pastoralism, is that it will move forward in a timely manner. If the action plan can be implemented soon — and if we as consumers can make sustainable choices — then positive change is on the horizon.

In our case studies of transhumant shepherding and extensive grazing in Andalusia, we have heard about many factors that are not under the control of individuals. From changes in local and regional government, market demands, and access to pasturelands and droving roads, to climate change and the global economy, the speed of change has accelerated and manifested itself in both changing consumption habits and the destruction of traditional habitats. In our chapter on the plataformas, we discussed scaffolding as the structures and support that surround extensive grazing, yet as we have seen in *A Country of Shepherds*, this infrastructure relies on multiple layers and interconnecting roles in society to ensure resiliency and sustain the practice. Moving forward, we can visualize it as interlocking system of public policy, professional organizations, and community networks, as well as of individuals like us who can change our patterns of consumption to support more local products for a larger net benefit: sustainable ecosystems, cultural traditions, and rural development. Landowner Rafael Enríquez del Río (see Chapter 3) noted, in his efforts to bring on a number of family businesses to help manage his farm, the problem of rural depopulation: "A fundamental building block are the people who live in the country. When people leave the rural areas, what happens? You lose your culture." More importantly, this sustainable, multifunctional farming, he argued, is our only path forward, "especially if we want to live in a world that's not so cruel".

Recent changes to this way of life are partly balanced by new opportunities: modern innovations in communication have allowed the traditionally marginalized shepherds to stay connected to family, collaborators, and markets more than any time in history. A new cultural interest and respect for time-honored traditions has resulted in an explosion of cultural production and renewed public interest, especially among young people who represent the future of these practices. Consumer preferences are changing worldwide. The scaffolding support offered by the *plataformas* has continued to mature. Finally, the reality of global climate change has galvanized public and government attention to environmental issues.

All these developments offer hope to the people we interviewed, and courage to keep going. We have to admire a businessman who would endure the loss of 60% of his stock and still plan to rebuild, a shepherd nearing retirement who retools his family business to meet the emerging demands of a new economy, and a landowner who works alongside her manager doing the hard work of farming and to see first-hand the changes that need to be made. Now it is up to the larger community of consumers, leaders, and politicians to show the resiliency these traditional practitioners already possess. As Ernestine points out so clearly: "There isn't much time left; this way of life, this natural world is disappearing fast. I want to believe … step by step, people will change." The practitioners of transhumance, like those of all subsistence livelihoods, have always been grounded in true resilience. Shepherds like Pepe Millán possess a keen power of scientific observation that have helped them adapt over millennia — from seasonal changes to climate challenges, drought, pestilence, crop failures, livestock disease, and countless other challenges — by constantly changing their practices. For them, resiliency isn't an academic term: it has always been a way of life, a matter of survival, not of choice.

We have heard a common story among shepherds, landowners, and their advocates. Each group points to the ancient practice of pastoralism as a way forward, as the practice proves to be one of the best examples of the interrelated nature of agricultural systems in the globalized world. The long-standing cultural narrative of Spanish shepherds as symbols of humble Christian virtue, integral to Spanish identity, or more recently, as eco-heroes, is not enough to keep this tradition alive and protect the valuable cultural landscapes and eco-systems threatened by extinction. We all have a part in how this story will unfold globally over the next couple decades. As citizens — and consumers — we will have powerful input into its outcome.

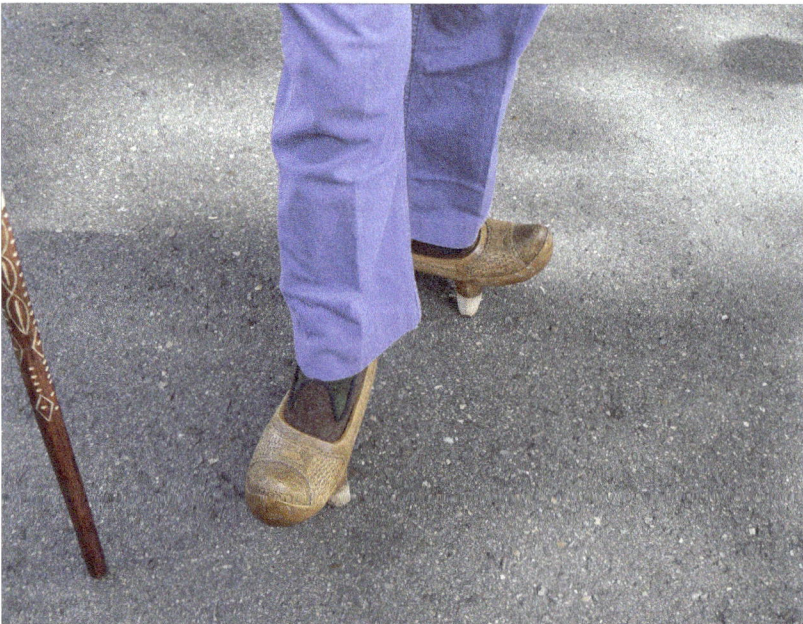

Fig. 7.1 *Zapatos tradicionales del pastoreo* [traditional shepherds' shoes] (2017).

Selected Bibliography

Abellán García, A. Antonio and A. Olivera Poll, 'La trashumancia por ferrocarril en España', *Estudios Geográficos* (1979), vol. 40, n. 156–57, pp. 385–413.

Acuña Delgado, A. and D. Ranocchiari, 'Pastoreo trashumante. Práctica ecológica y patrimonio cultura, un estudio de caso', *Gazeta de Antropología* (2012), n. 28 (2).

Aguirre-García, J., J. M. Edeso-Fito, A. Lopetegi-Galarraga, A. Moraza-Barea, M. Ruiz-Alonso, S. Pérez-Díaz, T. Fernández-Crespo et al, '"Seasonal shepherds"' settlements in mountain areas from Neolithic to present, Aralar–Gipuzkoa (Basque country, Spain)', *Quaternary International* (2018), vol. 484, pp. 44–59.

Aitken, R., 'Rutas de trashumancia en la meseta castellana', *Estudios Geográficos* (1947), vol. 8, n. 26, pp. 185–99.

Alenza García, J. F., 'Vías *pecuaria*s: un milagroso patrimonio en espera de una gestión sostenible', *Ambianta* (2013), n. 104, pp. 74–89.

Amat-Montesinos, X., 'Landscape and heritage of the transhumance in Spain. Challenges for a sustainable and responsible tourism' (2017), IPAC's international conference 'Innovations sociales en patrimoine, en tourisme et dans les musées: savoirs canadiens, espagnols et d'ailleurs', 11–12 May 2017, Quebec. Congress Proceedings available at the Repositorio Institucional de la Universidad de Alicante, https://rua.ua.es/dspace/bitstream/10045/66107/1/AMAT-2017_transhumance_landscape_heritage_spain.pdf

Antón Burgos, F. J., 'La trashumancia en España, hoy', in J. L. Castán and C. Serrano (eds.), *La trashumancia en la España mediterránea: historia, antropología, medio natural, desarrollo rural* (2004), Zaragoza: Rolde de estudios aragoneses, pp. 481–94.

Antón Burgos, F. J., 'Nomadismo *ganadero* y trashumancia: balance de una cultura basada en su compatibilidad con el medio ambiente', *Anales de Geografía de la Universidad Complutense* (2000), n. 20, pp. 23–31.

Antón Burgos, F. J., 'Trashumancia y turismo en España', *Cuadernos de Turismo* (2007), n. 20, pp. 27–54.

Antón Burgos, F. J. and P. Vidal González, Pablo (eds.), *Trashumancia de los pastores turolenses a la Sierra de Espadán, Castellón* (2006), Universidad Católica de Valencia y Universidad Complutense de Madrid.

Beckmann, Hubert B. and J. Garzón Heydt, 'Transhumance as Tool of Species Conservation in Times of Climate Change', *Genesis* (2009), vol. 1, n. 27.

Belosillo, M, *Castilla merinera: las cañadas reales a través de su toponimia* (1988), Madrid: Colegio de Caminos, Canales y Puertos.

Biskho, C. J., 'Sesenta años después. La Mesta de Julius Klein a la luz de la investigación subsiguiente', *Historia, Instituciones, Documentos* (1982), n. 8, pp. 9–57.

Boerma, D. and P. Koohafkan, 'Pastoral systems as cultural landscapes : lessons from FAO's Globally Important Agricultural Heritage Systems (GIAHS) Initiative', in *Pastoralisme méditerranéen: patrimoine culturel et paysager et développement durable* (2010). F. Lerin (ed.), Montpellier, pp. 17–24.

Bunce, R. G. H., M. Pérez-Soba, R. H. G., Jongman, A. Gómez Sal, F. Herzog, and I. Austad (eds.), *Transhumance and Biodiversity in European Mountains* (2004). Report of the EU-FP5 project TRANSHUMOUNT (EVK2-CT-2002-80017). IALE publication series, n. 1, pp. 321.

Cabo Alonso, A. 'Algo más sobre la trashumancia en la Meseta', in *Aportación en homenaje al profesor Luis Miguel Albentosa* (1993), Tarragona: Universidad de Tarragona, pp. 393–411.

Cabo Alonso, A., 'Funciones no *ganaderas* de las viejas *vías pecuarias*', in *Historia, clima y paisaje. Estudios geográficos en memoria del profesor Antonio López Gómez* (2004), Universidades de Valencia, Alicante y Autónoma de Madrid, pp. 99–110.

Carrera Díaz, G., *Territorio, Industrias y élites locales. Propuesta metodológica para una carta etnográfica de Constantina* (2009), Seville: Junta de Andalucía, Consejería de Cultura.

Casas, J. M., 'The National Network of Transhumance Routes in the Kingdom of Spain', in R. G. H. Bunce, M. Pérez-Soba, R. H. G. Jongman, A. Gómez Sal, F. Herzog, and I. Austad (eds.), *Transhumance and Biodiversity in European Mountains* (2004), pp. 249–54.

Castán, J. L. and C. Serrano (eds..), *La trashumancia en la España mediterránea: historia, antropología, medio natural, desarrollo rural* (2004), Huesca: Centro de Estudios sobre la Despoblación y Desarrollo de Áreas Rurales.

Castel Genís, J. M. and Y. Mena Guerrero, 'El sector caprino y su contribución al desarrollo rural', in *Agricultura familiar en España* (2007).

Córdoba, M. M. Valera, *et al.*, 'Pasatiempos educativos como estrategia de aprendizaje activo en Producción Animal', in *Recursos educativos innovadores en el contexto iberoamericano* (2015), Alcalá: Universidad de Alcalá.

Cruz Sánchez, P. J. and C. Escribano Velasco, *Patrimonio material e inmaterial de las vías pecuarias en el entorno de la Cañada de la Plata. Una mirada a las manifestaciones culturales de la trashumancia tradicional* (2013), Valladolid: Junta de Castilla y León.

CUADERNOS DE LA TRASHUMANCIA. [http://www.magrama.gob.es/ es/biodiversidad/temas/ecosistemas-y-conectividad/vias-*pecuarias*/ num_1al12_vias_*pecuarias*.aspx#para0] nº 00–24.

De Miguel, J. M. and A. Gómez Sal, 'Los paisajes de la *dehesa* y su papel en el comportamiento del ganado extensivo', *Quercus*, (1992), n. 81, pp. 16–22.

Delgado, Á. A. and D. Ranocchiari., 'Pastoreo trashumante. Práctica ecológica y patrimonio cultural, un estudio de caso', *Gazeta de Antropología* (2012), vol. 28 (2).

Del Molino, S, *Contra la España vacía* (2021), Madrid: Alfaguara.

Diago Hernando, M., *Mesta y trashumancia en Castilla: (siglos XIII al XIX)* (2002), Madrid: Arco Libros.

Domínguez, F. J., *Dehesas y trashumancia en el Sur, las fronteras de Andalucía* (2008), Córdoba: Asociación ADROCHES para el Desarrollo Rural de la Comarca de Los Pedroches.

Elías Pastor, L. V. and J. Grande Ibarra (eds.), *Sobre cultura pastoril. Actas de las IV Jornadas de Etnología, El Molino de Solórzano, La Rioja, mato de 1990* (1991), Instituto de Conservación y Restauración de Bienes Culturales.

Fernández Álvarez, F. *et al.*, *Trashumancia: paisajes, vivencias y sensaciones* (2006), Madrid: Ministerio de Medio Ambiente, Medio Rural y Marino.

Fernández, E. F., 'La trashumancia en Sierra Nevada y su patrimonio cultural inmaterial', Manuel Titos Martínez, Teodoro Luque Martínez and José Manuel Navarro Llena (eds.), *Actas Del I Congreso Internacional de Las Montañas. Sierra Nevada 2018, 8–11 de marzo de 2018* (2019). Granada: Universidad de Granada, pp. 321–35.

Fernández, E. F, 'Prácticas productivas tradicionales y diversidad biocultural', in Carmen Castilla Vázquez and Óscar Salguero (eds.), *La etnografía como forma de vida: un homenaje al profesor Rafael Briones Gómez* (2020), Granada: Seminario Permanente de Estudio de las Religiones (SPER) de la Universidad de Granada, pp. 255–80.

Fernández, M, 'La cara B del pastoreo: mucho más que medioambiente', *Ganadería* (2022), pp. 6–9.

Fernández-Giménez, M E., 'A shepherd has to invent': Poetic analysis of social-ecological change in the cultural landscape of the central Spanish Pyrenees', *Egology and Society* (2015), vol. 29, n. 20.

Fernández-Giménez, M E. and F. Fillat Estaque, 'Pyrenean Pastoralists' Observations of Environmental Change: An Exploratory Study in Los

Valles Occidentales of Aragón', *Pirineos. Revista Ecología de Montaña* (2012), n. 167, pp. 145–65.

Fernández-Giménez, M E. and F. Fillat Estaque, 'Pyrenean Pastoralists' Ecological Knowledge: Documentation and Application to Natural Resource Management and Adaptation', in *Human Ecology. An Interdisciplinary Journal* (2012), vol. 2, n. 40, pp. 287–300, http://dx.doi.org/10.1007/s10745-012-9463-x

Fernández-Giménez, M. E., E. Oteros-Rozas and F. Ravera, 'Spanish women pastoralists into livestock management: Motivations, challenges and learning', *Journal of Rural Studies* (2021), n. 87, pp. 1–11, http://dx.doi.org/10.1016/j.jrurstud.2021.08.019

Fernández-Giménez, María E., F. Ravera, and E. Oteros-Rozas, 'The invisible thread: women as tradition keepers and chenge agents in Spanish pastoral social-ecological systems', *Ecology and Society* (2022), vol. 4, n. 27, http://dx.doi.org/10.5751/ES-12794-270204

Flores Del Manzano, F., 'Acercamiento antropológico al mundo trashumante', *Revista de Extremadura* (1995), n. 16, pp. 3–16.

Gaona, C. D., M. S. Rodríguez, G. G. Castro, and V. R. Estévez, 'La *ganadería* ecológica en la gestión de los espacios naturales protegidos: Andalucía como modelo', *Archivos de Zootecnia* (2014), vol. 63, n. 241, pp. 25–54.

García Martín, P. (ed.), *Por los caminos de la trashumancia* (1994), Valladolid: Junta de Castilla y León.

García Martín, P. and J. M. Sánchez Benito (eds.), *Contribución a la historia de la trashumancia en España* (1986), Madrid: Secretaría General Técnica, Ministerio de Agricultura, Pesca y Alimentación.

García Martín, P., *Cañadas, cordeles y veredas* (1991), Valladolid: Junta de Castilla y León.

García Martín, P., *La Mesta* (1990), Madrid: Historia 16.

García Martín, P., *El patrimonio cultural de las cañadas reales* (1990), Madrid: Ministerio de Agricultura.

Garzón Heydt, J., 'La trashumancia como reliquia del Paleolítico', in *Simposio Trashumancia y cultura pastoril en Extremadura* (1994), Seville, 28–30 September, 1992, Asamblea de Extremadura, pp. 27–36.

Garzón Heydt, J., 'La trashumancia con razas de ayer para recuperar el patrimonio del futuro', *Naturzale* (2004), n. 18, pp. 77–97.

Garzón Heydt, J., 'Importancia ecológica de las cañadas, cordeles y veredas en España', in *III Congreso virtual sobre Historia de las Vías de Comunicación* (2015), Asociación Orden de la Caminería.

Gerbet, M. C., *La ganadería medieval en la Península Ibérica* (2003), Barcelona: Crítica.

Giralt Y Raventós, E., 'Los estudios de historia agraria de España desde 1940 a 1961', *Índice Histórico Español* (1959), vol. 24, n. 5, pp. IX–LXXIX.

Gómez-Pantoja Fernández-Salguero, J., *Los rebaños de Gerión: pastores y trashumancia en Iberia antigua y medieval. Seminario celebrado en la Casa de Velázquez* (15–16 January, 1996) (2001), Madrid: Casa de Velázquez.

Gómez-Sal, A., 'Fundamentos ecológicos y la importancia del medio natural en los sistemas de *ganadería* extensiva de la Península Ibérica', in *Medidas agroambientales y sistemas ganaderos en Europa: su contribución a la conservación de los paisajes culturales* (2004), Seville: Consejería de Agricultura y Pesca, Junta de Andalucía.

González Ramiro, A., 'Ordenación territorial, puesta en valor y aprovechamiento paisajístico de las *vías pecuarias* desde una perspectiva de gestión multifuncional y polivalente. Aplicación al caso particular de Extremadura' (2017).

González Pérez, V., 'Uso de las *vías pecuarias* y roturaciones: una conflictividad histórica entre *ganadero*s y labradores', *Investigaciones Geográficas* (2011), n. 54, pp. 101–32.

Gordon, Philip, and Kate Holl, 'Three-dimensional farming: agroforestry in Spain and its relevance to Scotland', *Scottish Forestry* (2020), vol. 74, n.1, pp. 43–46.

Grande, J., 'Tradiciones en el camino', in *Caminos naturales de España* (2011), Madrid: Ministerio de Medio Ambiente y Medio Rural y Marino, pp. 100–05.

Ibáñez Verdú, I. and J. Molero Cortés, 'La trashumancia en Andalucía' (2009), Proyecto piloto Desarrollo Sostenible Mediante La Trashumancia Tradicional (ARM/1288/2009).

Irigoyen-García, J., *The Spanish Arcadia: sheep herding, pastoral discourse, and ethnicity in early Modern Spain* (2013), Toronto: University of Toronto Press.

Klein, J., *La Mesta, Estudio de la historia económica española:1273–1836* (1981), Madrid: Alianza.

La trashumancia en España. Libro Blanco (2013). Madrid: Ministerio de Agricultura, Alimentación y Medio Ambiente.

La trashumancia en la Cañada Real Conquense: valores ecológicos, sociales y económicos asociados a una práctica ganadera tradicional. Informe de síntesis para responsables de políticas. Madrid: Universidad Autónoma de Madrid. (2012).

Las vías pecuarias en Andalucía: oportunidades de tratamiento a nivel territorial. Seville: Junta de Andalucía, Consejería de Obras Públicas y Transportes (1991).

Lazo, A., 'El ganado como herramienta de conservación de espacios naturales', *Quercus* (1995), n. 116, pp. 31–33.

Llamazares, J., 'Por el Oeste español. Los caminos de la trashumancia', in *Caminos naturales de España* (2011), Madrid: Ministerio de Medio Ambiente y Medio Rural y Marino, pp. 88–93.

López Marín, M., *Tiempo de Trashumancia* (2012), Editorial Cumio.

López Ontiveros, A. and J. Naranjo Ramírez, 'El nomadismo y la trashumancia en Sierra Nevada, según Juan Carandell y Max Sorre', *Cuadernos Geográficos de la Universidad de Granada* (2000), n. 30, pp. 431–43.

López Sáez, J. A., L. López Merino, F. Alba Sánchez, and S. Pérez Díaz, 'Contribución paleoambiental al estudio de la trashumancia en el sector abulense de la Sierra de Gredos', *Hispania* (2009), vol. 231, n. 69, pp. 9–38.

López Sáez, J. A., F. Alba Sánchez, S. Robles-López, S. Pérez-Díaz, D. Abel-Schaad, S. Sabariego-Ruiz, and A. Glais, 'Exploring seven hundred years of transhumance, climate dynamic, fire and human activity through a historical mountain pass in central Spain', *Journal of Mountain Science* (2016), vol. 7, n. 13, pp. 1139–1153.

López-Salazar Pérez, J. and P. Sanz Camañes (eds.), *Mesta y mundo pecuario en la Península Ibérica durante los tiempos modernos* (2011), Cuenca: Universidad de Castilla-La Mancha.

Malalana Ureña, A., 'La transhumancia medieval castellana: aproximación historiográfica', *Hispania* (1990), n. 175, pp. 779–91.

Mangas Navas, J. M., 'Recovery of the national network of transhumance routes: the programme of the Ministry of the Environment', in R. G. H. Bunce, M. Pérez-Soba, R. H. G. Jongman, A. Gómez Sal, F. Herzog and I. Austad (eds.), *Transhumance and Biodiversity in European Mountains* (2004), pp. 265–69.

Mangas Navas, J. M, 'Cañadas de paso y pasto. Senderos de paso y posta', in *Caminos naturales de España* (2011), Madrid: Ministerio de Medio Ambiente y Medio Rural y Marino, pp. 106–11.

Manzano Baena, P. and R. Casas, 'Past, present and future of Trashumancia in Spain: nomadism in a developed country', *Pastoralism* (2010), vol. 1, n. 1, pp. 72–90.

Manzano, P., N. Ng'eny, and J. Davies, 'La Iniciativa Mundial por un Pastoralismo Sostenible (IMPS) y la importancia económica, social y ambiental de los pastores a nivel global', in *II Congreso Nacional de Vías Pecuarias* (2010), Cáceres: Junta de Extremadura, pp. 336–43.

Manzano, P., 'Trashumancia y vías pecuarias. Ganaderos, ecologistas, científicos y políticos debaten sobre su futuro', *El Ecologista* (2006), n. 48, pp. 38–39.

Marín Barriguete, F., 'La defensa de las cañadas reales en el reinado de los Reyes Católicos', *En la España Medieval* (1996), n. 19, pp. 239–73.

Marín Barriguete, F., 'Mesta y vida pastoril', in *Revista de Historia Moderna* (1992), n. 11, pp. 127–42.

Márquez Fernández, D. and A. M. García López, 'Las vías pecuarias como patrimonio rural en su adaptación hacia nuevas funcionalidades del territorio', in José María Gómez Espín y Ramón Martínez Medina (eds.): *Los espacios rurales españoles en el nuevo siglo. Actas XIV Coloquio de Geografía Rural* (2008), Murcia: Universidad de Murcia, pp. 57–68.

Martín Casas, J. (ed.), *Las vías pecuarias del Reino de España: patrimonio natural y cultural europeo* (2003), Madrid: Organismo Autónomo Parques Nacionales.

Mateu, J. F., 'Huella de la trashumancia en los paisajes mediterráneos', in P. Vidal and J. L. Castán (eds.), *Trashumancia en el Mediterráneo* (2010), Huesca: Centro de Estudios sobre la Despoblación y Desarrollo de Áreas Rurales, pp. 193–228.

Medidas agroambientales y sistemas ganaderos en Europa: su contribución a la conservación de los paisajes culturales. Seville: Consejería de Agricultura y Pesca, Junta de Andalucía (2004).

Melón Jiménez, M. A. and A. Rodríguez Grajera, 'Aportaciones al estudio de la *ganadería* trashumante: el puerto real de Perosín (siglos XVII y XVIII)', *Norba* (1983), n. 4, pp. 337–49.

Mena Guerrero, Y., A. Benhamou Prat, J. M. Mancilla Leytón, E. Morales Jerret, and D. Martin Collado, 'Factores que determinan la resiliencia del sector caprino andaluz: una visión desde los actores locales', *Tierras. Caprino* (2022), n. 39, pp. 46–50.

Mena Guerrero, Y., and J. M. Mancilla Leytón, 'La *ganadería* caprina en el *monte mediterráneo*', *AE. Revista Agroecológica de Divulgación* (2017), n. 27, pp. 28–29.

Merino García, J, and J. L. Alier Gándaras, 'La multifuncionalidad de las *vías pecuarias* españolas en el marco del desarrollo rural', *Tecnología y Desarrollo, Revista de Ciencia, Tecnología y Medio Ambiente* (2004), n. 2, pp. 3–26.

Mercadal, D. and Unidad de Documentación e Información del Centro Internacional de Estudios de Derecho Ambiental (CIEDA-CIEMAT) (2022), 'Propuesta de bases técnicas para una Estrategia Estatal de Ganadería Extensiva', *Plataforma por la Ganadería Extensiva y el Pastoralismo.*

Moneo, J, and F. Nebrada, 'Vocabulario de la Mesta', *Revista de Extremadura* (1995), no. 16, pp. 65–68.

Moreno Fernández, J. R., 'La *ganadería* trashumante en la Rioja (1752–1865). Una revisión bibliográfica y cuantitativa', *Brocar* (1996), n. 20, pp. 277–302.

Moreno, M. G., E. R. Serrano and A. G. Martínez, 'La trashumancia actual en la provincia de Jaén: Su contribución a la conservación del patrimonio natural y cultural', in *I Congreso Internacional 'El patrimonio cultural y natural como motor de desarrollo: investigación e innovación'* (2012), Seville: Universidad Internacional de Andalucía, pp. 1319–1324.

Nori, M., *Transhumances, mobility and migrations in Mediterranean pastoralism* in: 'Crises and resilience in the Mediterranean. Agriculture, natural resources and food' (2017), Bibliothèque de l'iReMMO (Institut de Recherche et d'Etudes Méditerranée Moyen-Orient), Paris, https://iremmo.org/

Nori, M., 'Migrant Shepherds: Opportunities and Challenges for Mediterranean Pastoralism,' *Journal of Alpine Research* (2017), pp. 105–4, https://doi.org/10.4000/rga.3554

Nori, S. and M. Gemini, 'The Common Agricultural Policy vis-à-vis European pastoralists: principles and practices', *Pastoralism: Research, Policy and Practice* (2011), vol. 27, n. 1, http://dx.doi.org/10.1186/2041-7136-1-27

Olea, P. P. and P. Mateo-Tomás, 'The role of traditional farming practices in ecosystem conservation: the case of transhumance and vultures', *Biological conservation* (2009), vol. 8 n. 142, pp. 1844–1853, http://dx.doi.org/10.1016/j.biocon.2009.03.024

Otero-Rozas, E., F. Ravera, and M. García-Llorente, 'How Does Agroecology Contribute to the Transitions towards Social-Ecological Sustainability?' *Sustainability* (2019), vol. 1, n. 16, pp. 4372, https://doi.org/10.3390/su11164372

Prieto Guijarro, A., 'Gestión económica y técnica del ganado bovino en régimen extensivo: *dehesas*', *Agricultura y Sociedad* (1994), n. 73, pp. 295–314.

Ravera, F., E. Otero-Rozas, and M. Fernández-Giménez, 'Embodied Perceptions, Everydayness, and Simultaneity in Climate Governance by Spanish Women Pastoralists', in Amber J. Fletcher and Maureen G. Reed (eds.), *Gender and the Social Dimensions of Climate Change* (2022), New York: Routledge, pp. 119–44.

Rebanks, J., *The Shepherd's Life: Modern Dispatches from an Ancient Landscape* (2015), New York: Flatiron Books.

Riesco Chueca, P., E. Prada Llorente, J. Garzón Heydt, V. Casas Del Corral, and P. Cruz Sánchez, *Pastores: trashumancia y ganadería extensiva* (2016), Zamora.

Río, J. M. del, *Un viaje trashumante. Cervera, Mosqueruela, una cañada centenaria* (2004), Cuaderno 8. Benicarló: Centro de Estudios del Maestrazgo.

Robles, A. B., et al, 'Role of livestock grazing in sustainable use, naturalness promotion in naturalization of marginal ecosystems of southeastern Spain (Andalusia)', *Agroforestry in Europe: current status and future prospects* (2009), pp. 211–31, http://dx.doi.org/10.1007/978-1-4020-8272-6_10

Rodríguez Pascual, M., *La trashumancia: cultura, cañadas y viajes* (2001), León: Edilesa.

Ruiz, F., *Alternativas y resistencias desde lo rural-urbano: aproximación al estudio de las experiencias comunitarias agroecológicas* (2012), [Doctoral Thesis]. Córdoba: Universidad de Córdoba.

Saiz Moreno, L., 'Antiguas Vías de Circulación del ganado. La trashumancia del ganado merino en España y las epizootias', *Revista de Sanidad e Higiene Pública* (1983), n. 57, pp. 1229–53.

Sánchez Benito, J. M., 'Consolidación y práctica de la trashumancia en la Baja Edad Media castellana', in *Itinerarios medievales e identidad hispánica: XXVII Semana de Estudios Medievales, Estella 17 a 21 de julio de 2000* (2001), Pamplona: Gobierno de Navarra, Institución Príncipe de Viana, pp. 257–92.

Sánchez Gavito, L., *Vías pecuarias a través del tiempo* (1955), Madrid: Ministerio de Agricultura.

Sánchez Moreno, E., 'De ganado, movimientos y contactos. Revisando la cuestión trashumante en la protohistoria hispana: la meseta occidental', *Studia Histórica. Historia Antigua* (1998), n. 16, pp. 53–83.

Urquijo Torres, P. S., 'Los caminos de la trashumancia. Territorio, persistencia y representaciones de la ganadería pastoril en el altiplano potosino', *Revista de El Colegio de San Luis* (2017), vol. 7, n. 13, pp. 300–04, http://dx.doi.org/10.21696/rcsl7132017661

Vías, J., 'La cañada real de la Vera de la Sierra', in *Caminos naturales de España* (2011), Madrid: Ministerio de Medio Ambiente y Medio Rural y Marino, pp. 94–99.

Vidal González, P., 'Los estudios y la investigación sobre etnografía pastoril: estado de la cuestión', *Revista de Estudios sobre despoblación y desarrollo rural* (2009), n. 8, pp. 9–24.

Vidal González, P., Bajar al Reino. 'Antropología de un camino de ida y vuelta', in *Trashumancia de los pastores turolenses a la Sierra de Espadán, Castellón* (2006), F. J. Antón Burgos and P. Vidal González (eds.), Madrid: Universidad Católica de Valencia y Universidad Complutense, pp. 27–43.

Vidal González, P. and J. L. Castán Esteban, (eds.), *Trashumancia en el Mediterráneo* (2010), Huesca: Centro de Estudios sobre la Despoblación y Desarrollo de Áreas Rurales.

Vidal González, P., 'Sacred rituals and popular religiousness amongst transhumant shepherds of Teruel region, Spain', *Pastoralism: Research, Policy and Practice* (2013), vol. 3, n. 24, pp. 1–10, http://dx.doi.org/10.1186/2041-7136-3-24

Walker, K., 'The revival of a historic journey across Spain', *BBC Future Planet* (2021).

DVDs

Preparativos, hacer la vereda; la trashumancia. Grupo Lettera. Seville (2003).

Huellas trashumantes. Trashumancia en España. (10 episodes) (2006–2009).

Online Videos

'Trashumancia en Andalucía': https://www.adesalambrar.com/documentos/ Guia%20Transhumancia_ASOC.pdf

Tierra y Mar: La Trashumancia en Sevilla: https://www.youtube.com/watch?v=XN_X3cz1TNo *Interview with Jose Ortega, pastor.*

Trashumancia de Santiago de la Espada: https://www.ideal.es/jaen/jaen/inician-trashumancia-santiago-20191126135825-nt.html?ref=https:%2F%2Fwww.google.com%2F ; https://www.youtube.com/watch?v=rPbOWXrRMys

Diario de Jaén, 2020 documental de una hora sobra la trashumancia tradicional: https://www.diariojaen.es/canal/viaje-cultural/ documental-de-la-trashumancia-en-jaen-sin-cortes-ni-rodeos-KH759573

Index

Constantina, Sierra Norte de Sevilla 8,
18–19, 25, 43–45, 47–48, 52, 57–58,
61–63, 65–67, 145, 169
consumers, consumerism 3, 8–10,
22–23, 25, 35, 61, 65, 68, 70, 79, 85,
88–89, 152, 169, 171, 173, 180, 184,
193, 197–198, 201–202, 205, 209–210,
214, 217–219
Cooperativa del Cordero Segureño 103
Cordel del Herrador 47
Córdoba 3, 15, 20, 25, 49, 51, 53, 96, 115,
117, 119, 121, 123, 125, 163, 172, 181,
189, 192, 197
cork, cork trees 4, 27, 31, 47, 52, 59, 116,
139, 154, 157, 160–161, 166, 170
CorSevilla 135
countryside 13, 18, 39, 50, 52, 54, 56,
60, 65, 83, 107, 117, 120–121, 133,
146, 148, 150, 154, 162–163, 167, 169,
191, 211
COVID-19 16, 23, 46, 64–65, 91–92, 112,
123, 136, 149, 172, 205–206, 208–210,
214
CSIC-Granada (Pastos y Sistemas
Silvopastorales Mediterráneos) 8,
180–182, 188, 214
Cuéllar, Mamen 192
cultural geographies 196
cultural identities 6, 10, 133

de Asís Ruiz Morales, Francisco (Paco)
188
Dehesa la Rasa 113–114
Dehesa San Francisco 21, 151–154,
156–157, 159, 162–163
dehesas in the Iberian Peninsula 4, 9,
14–15, 18, 20–21, 27, 31–32, 37, 47,
52, 96–97, 107, 113, 115–116, 122–123,
127–130, 137–138, 140–142, 152–157,
159–162, 165–166, 170–172, 178–179,
187, 195, 197, 203, 206
Delgado Ferrer, Fidel 183
del Río, Isabel 97, 113–115, 117–120,
122–123
del Río, Rafael Enríquez 20, 96–97,
113–124, 128, 150, 218

democracy 9, 11–12, 51, 102, 150, 155
depopulation 6, 8–9, 13, 31, 39–40, 60,
62, 94, 120, 218
direct sales 70, 85, 88–89, 149, 161, 210
diversification 3, 38, 96, 113, 116,
119–120, 174, 187, 206, 215
dogs 2, 26, 34, 47, 54, 56, 71, 72, 73,
75, 81, 84, 98, 129, 133, 136, 154,
160, 165, 216. *See also* Australian
Shepherds; *See also* Border Collies;
See also mastiffs; *See also* Portuguese
water dog
Don Quijote 11, 13, 132, 194
droving roads. *See vías pecuarias*/droving
roads
"dry" farming 25

economic crisis 2008 24, 35, 39–40, 65–66,
77, 80, 86–87, 92, 111–112, 115, 117,
120, 167, 207, 210–211, 217
ecosystems 3, 21, 26, 30–33, 38, 71, 83–84,
92, 105, 110, 113, 115, 117, 119, 122,
125, 129, 136, 138, 150, 156, 161–162,
166, 169, 173, 175, 179, 181, 183, 198,
209, 218
Ecovalia 178
education and shepherding 14, 21, 40,
46, 51, 65, 76, 82–83, 86, 89, 109, 146,
154–157, 161, 165, 172, 175, 187, 191,
194, 196, 212, 217
El Gastor 72
El País 194
endangered species 12, 15, 19, 34, 71,
84, 94
Entrelobos (film) 121
entrepreneurship 10, 17–20, 46, 62, 71,
78, 80, 90, 92, 102, 120, 122, 153
Entretantos 176, 185, 197
Escuela de Pastores (Shepherd School)
6, 8, 22, 71, 81, 84, 94, 167, 180–182,
186–188, 190–194, 205, 210, 212–214
Espinosa Calero, Carmela 21, 142–150
European Forum on Nature
Conservation and Pastoralism
(EFNCP) 197

About the Team

Alessandra Tosi was the managing editor for this book.

Almudena Jimenez Virosta and Jennifer Moriarty proofread this manuscript. Jennifer indexed it.

The cover was designed by Jeevanjot Kaur Nagpal; it was produced in InDesign using the Fontin font.

Jeremy Bowman typeset the book in InDesign and produced the paperback, hardback and EPUB editions. The text font is Tex Gyre Pagella; the heading font is Californian FB.

Cameron Craig produced the PDF, HTML, and XML editions.

We thank Dr Anastasios Ragkos for peer-reviewing this manuscript, together with two anonymous referees.

This book need not end here...

Share

All our books — including the one you have just read — are free to access online so that students, researchers and members of the public who can't afford a printed edition will have access to the same ideas. This title will be accessed online by hundreds of readers each month across the globe: why not share the link so that someone you know is one of them?

This book and additional content is available at:
https://doi.org/10.11647/OBP.0387

Donate

Open Book Publishers is an award-winning, scholar-led, not-for-profit press making knowledge freely available one book at a time. We don't charge authors to publish with us: instead, our work is supported by our library members and by donations from people who believe that research shouldn't be locked behind paywalls.

Why not join them in freeing knowledge by supporting us:
https://www.openbookpublishers.com/support-us

Follow @OpenBookPublish

Read more at the Open Book Publishers **BLOG**

You may also be interested in:

Ecocene Politics
Mihnea Tănăsescu

https://doi.org/10.11647/obp.0274

Living Earth Community
Multiple Ways of Being and Knowing
Edited by Sam Mickey, Mary Evelyn Tucker & John Grim

https://doi.org/10.11647/obp.0186

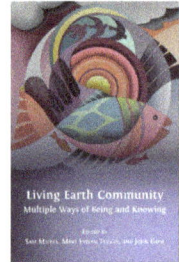

Reshaping Food Systems to improve Nutrition and Health in the Eastern Mediterranean Region
Ayoub Al-Jawaldeh & Alexa Meyer

https://doi.org/10.11647/obp.0322

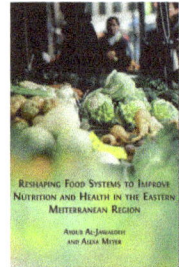

Forests and Food
Addressing Hunger and Nutrition Across Sustainable Landscapes
Edited by Bhaskar Vira, Christoph Wildburger & Stephanie Mansourian

https://doi.org/10.11647/obp.0085

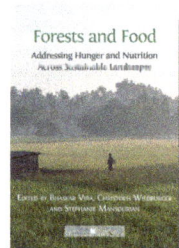

9 781805 112075